Stranglers & Serial Killers

John Denis

Published by Trellis Publishing, 2021.

STRANGLERS & SERIAL KILLERS

First edition. July 1, 2021.

ISBN: 979-8224619610

Written by John Denis.

STRANGLERS & SERIAL KILLERS

JOHN DENIS

JOHN REGINALD CHRISTIE

John Reginald Christie was a prolific serial killer active in England during the 1940s and 1950s. He murdered at least six women including his wife—and some believe this number is higher, as well as a baby—before being arrested, convicted, and hanged. He lured women to his flat under the guise of assisting them with some medical procedure such as abortion and strangled and raped them; oftentimes while they were unconscious or dead, thus giving rise to allegations that he was a necrophiliac. Christie also likely framed his neighbor Timothy Evans for the death of Evans' wife and infant daughter for which Evans was convicted and hanged.

Early Life

John Reginald Halliday Christie was born in Halifax, Yorkshire, England on 8 April 1899. His father was a strict disciplinarian who was often abusive and mother and sisters were domineering. Yet, he was his mother's favorite so while Christie's father despised his frailty his mother emasculated him with over protection. His four older sisters also reinforced his mother's protective nature but they also dominated him. One incident when he was ten disturbed him profoundly; that of seeing one of his sister's legs up to the knee which made him physically attracted to her. This likely contributed to Christie's development into a controlling, sexually-dysfunctional hypochondriac with an intense hatred and fear of women because he simultaneously desired those who tempted him but, consequently, knew he could not satisfy them.

Christie's maternal grandfather died when he was eight and when asked if he wanted to see the body during the wake, Christie said yes. He felt pleasure and a release of the tension he always felt when the man was alive because his grandfather was rather frightening and these feelings fascinated him. He started playing in the graveyard and liked to look inside the cracks of the broken vault where children's coffins were kept.

In school, Christie did rather well and got along even though he did not cultivate any long-term meaningful friendships. At age 11 he won a scholarship to Halifax Secondary School where he proved rather adept at mathematics and algebra, and also with high-detailed work. He had an IQ of 128, was a scout, and sang in his church's choir; however, he grew increasingly unpopular with his classmates and was often ridiculed for his ineptitude with girls being given the names "Can't Make it Christie" and "Reggie no Dick." By puberty Christie had associated sex with dominance, violent aggression, and death which rendered him impotent unless he was in complete control. At this time he would also feign illness—becoming a hysterical hypochondriac—to get attention.

Christie left school at age 15 and became an assistant movie projectionist. When World War I began Christie enlisted as a signalman. He allegedly was rendered unconscious and temporarily blind by a mustard gas attack and lost his voice for three years; however, physicians attributed his blindness and muteness as a hysterical reaction instead of a true physical ailment. Thus, Christie's fear led to his hypochondria and he would exaggerate illnesses to avoid unpleasant situations. More simply, he was a coward.

After his stint in the army, Christie became a clerk. On 10 May 1920 Christie married 22-year-old Ethel Waddington from Sheffield. She was a plump, homely, passive, and sentimental woman who many believed was afraid of her husband even though he was mostly mute during this time. The couple looked down upon others and, subsequently, maintained a high degree of privacy but also seemed quiet and rather pleasant, devoted to each other, and to their dog and cat. His ongoing impotence with his wife led to his frequent visits to prostitutes—which began when he was 19—when she was out of town.

After they married Christie became a postman. He once stole some postal orders and was, consequently, sent to prison for three months. Following his first period of incarceration Christie regained his voice during a temper tantrum with his father only to lose it again for six more months before being able to speak again. When he was 25, Christie was placed on probation with the post office after being charged with violence and accused of frequenting prostitutes. Christie subsequently left his wife and moved to London while she remained in Sheffield with her relatives.

Four years later, Christie was sentenced to prison for nine months on theft charges. Following this prison release he went through multiple jobs and lived with a prostitute who he physically assaulted with a cricket bat to the head and returned to prison for six more months. He was suspected of assaulting other women; however, the lack of evidence resulted in no arrests. A few years later he stole a car from a priest and was arrested again. After being released from prison this time he asked Ethel to move to London with him so they could be a married couple again.

Thus, in 1933 after a ten-year separation—and lonely at age 35—Ethel rejoined her husband, unaware of the type of man he really was or how her life would take a tragic turn.

Soon thereafter, Christie was hit by a car and required hospitalization which fueled his budding hypochondria. The literature suggests that over the course of 15 years Christie visited two physicians 173 times.

The Christies moved to the ground floor flat at three-story 10 Rillington Place in the Ladbroke Grove neighborhood of Notting Hill. At the time they moved here, Christie was a 40-year-old quiet inconspicuous man with reddish-ginger hair, light blue eyes, and an enormous forehead.

With World War II on the horizon, Christie signed up as a volunteer member of the War Reserve Police and became a Special Constable for Harrow Road Police Station for the next four years. Had his prior record been investigated—which it wasn't—there is no way that Christie would have received this appointment. Regardless, these four years were among Christie's happiest and he became almost fanatical about enforcing the law—so much so that he earned the nickname, "The Himmler of Rillington Place." Christie enjoyed wearing his uniform so much that the authority he had inflated his ego to the extent that he began to follow women and take notes of his endeavors. He also bored a peephole into his kitchen to watch his neighbors and ran down every single transgressor, no matter how minor the offense.

When his wife went to Sheffield to visit her relatives Christie developed a taste for peculiar sexual activities and found women who responded to his advances. One woman Christie met worked at the police station with him. She had a husband overseas in the war and Christie often spent time at her house with her. When her husband returned unexpectedly he filed for divorce and named Christie as a co-respondent after beating him up upon finding Christie in his house.

After this Christie began bringing women to his flat.

But first...

Timothy Evans

In the spring of 1948 Timothy and Beryl Evans moved into the third-floor flat. They were newlyweds and expecting their first baby. Timothy was 24 and Beryl was only 19; he drove a van for a living and was functionally illiterate. Known for his excessive drinking and often violent temper—likely due to his small stature of five-foot-five and 140 pounds—as well as his IQ of 70, propensity for lying, and proneness to self-aggrandizement, the Evans frequently quarreled. When the baby arrived—they named her Geraldine—Timothy's substandard income and Beryl's poor housekeeping and mothering skills caused them to fight even more, sometimes resulting in mutual physical violence. Beryl allegedly told Mrs. Christie that Tim had tried to strangle her and that she was pregnant again with an unwanted child. Beryl tried unsuccessfully to get rid of the baby.

It was around this time—the end of October 1948—that workers came to fix some floors and walls of 10 Rillington Place, as well as the community wash house.

In early November Beryl and Geraldine disappeared. There were conflicting accounts of their disappearance and subsequent murders; however, what is known is that that Christie offered to help Beryl with her pregnancy "problem" around noon one day. He is reported to have used rubber tubing to gas her for the procedure but she allegedly panicked so Christie began to hit her, and then strangle her, and then tried to have intercourse with her. When Evans came home that evening, Christie told him that the abortion hadn't worked and that if Evans went to the police it would only get them both in trouble and that police would not react well to reports that Evans and his wife fought often.

Christie proposed that he would dispose of Beryl's body and he hid her into the second-floor flat that belonged to Mr. Kitchener who was in the hospital at the time. Evans allegedly fed Geraldine and told Christie that he wanted to take his daughter to his mother's house but was dissuaded by Christie who told him that it would arouse too much suspicion. Christie told Evans that he knew a young couple who would take Geraldine and that Evans should tell people that Beryl and Geraldine were out of town on holiday.

Some speculate that Christie strangled the baby and put her with her mother in the second-floor flat and then blocked out what he had done.

Christie then told Evans to sell his furniture and leave town which Evans did.

Once the workmen were finished in the wash house Christie moved the bodies and hid them there. The following day he visited his doctor complaining of back pain. Despite Christie being a hypochondriac he had never had back problems. The doctor concluded that it was an injury sustained by unaccustomed exertion such as lifting a heavy weight.

Evans' mother Mrs. Probert did not buy her son's account that his wife and daughter were on holiday and discovered that her son staying with her sister, awaiting his wife. Mrs. Probert knew Evans was lying, that Beryl and Geraldine were missing, and that the furniture had been sold from their flat. After being confronted Evans stated that he disposed of his wife and put her body down the drain. He said that did not kill her and did not want to mention Christie because of the additional problems that would have caused. Evans said that he had met a man who gave him some medication to produce a spontaneous abortion but told Beryl not to use it. He said that when he returned from work he found her dead, took care of his daughter, and then pondered what to do next. Evans stated that he put his wife's body down the drain outside of the front door, stayed home from work, went in to give notice, and made arrangements for someone to take of Geraldine.

Police determined that Evans could not have disposed of Beryl the way he claimed to have done and he was arrested. During his interrogation and subsequent investigation Evans claimed that that he simply helped Christie put Beryl's body in the second-floor flat and that he had inquired of Christie about his daughter but was told that it was too soon to see her. Police searched the building and garden and in Evans' apartment near a pile of papers there were clippings from the newspaper about "a sensational torso murder, known as the Stanley Setty case" which was odd because Evans did not read, as well as a stolen briefcase.

During Evans' interrogation the Christies were also interviewed, she being coached by her husband.

Police went back to 10 Rillington Place and searched again. This time they found the decaying corpse of Beryl Evans, wrapped in a green tablecloth and tied with cord in the wash house, hidden behind some wood propped up against the sink. Underneath some wood behind the door was Geraldine's dead body with a man's tie still around her neck.

Dr. Donald Teare, the Home Office pathologist, performed the autopsy which showed that both had been dead about three weeks. Beryl had bruises on her lip and right eye consistent with being hit and that she had been strangled with some type of a cord. There was no evidence that she had ingested anything to try to abort her three-month fetus but her vagina had bruising. The pathologist did not take a swab to check for semen.

Additional interrogations yielded different stories by Evans. He first admitted that he did, in fact, kill them both and that he was relieved to confess. He said he killed his wife because she was running up debts and then killed his daughter a few days later after he quit his job. On the days Evans said he hid the bodies, the carpenters were still working on the wash house so this could not be true. Further, his confession contained words that were beyond Evans' intellectual capacity and that if he had sold all of his furniture like he claimed then the baby's pram and highchair would not have been in Christie's flat—an indication that Evans expected to see his daughter again. The next confession was even longer and contradicted the first one. After Evans' mother came to see him following his arraignment he insisted that "Christie done it."

Evan's trial began on 11 January 1950 at the Old Bailey for the murder of his daughter although evidence of his wife's murder was included in the testimony. Prosecutor Christmas Humphreys wanted to avoid any testimony such that Beryl may have provoked Evans which could possibly warrant a reduced charge of manslaughter with a lesser sentence which is why he only pursued Geraldine's murder; because it was without motive and clearly cold-blooded. Christie was Humphreys' chief witness in the proceedings.

Evans' defense was in the hands of Malcolm Morris from Freeborough, Slack, and Company; however, there was little investigation done to assist Evans, likely to save on time and money. They also failed to question the carpenters and friend Joan Vincent, and neglected to look into Christie's criminal record; all of which may have provided the jury with reasonable doubt.

During the trial witnesses such as the carpenters and Mrs. Christie changed their testimony from their original statements to "fit" Evans' confessions with respect to dates and times. The furniture dealer wasn't contacted either which would have demonstrated that Evans was only following Christie's direction and that Christie had, in fact, lied. Compounding Evans' troubles was that Christie's composed persona on the stand impressed jurors due to he was articulate, reflective and presented himself as the victim. His demeanor was diametrically opposite Evans' "apparent dazed and guilt-ridden presentation." When Morris brought up Christie's criminal past the court was impressed with the fact that he had been on the straight-and-narrow for the past 17 years. Little did the court know what Christie had really been doing during that time.

It took the jury only 40 minutes to reach a guilty verdict Evans was sentenced to death and was hanged on 9 March 1950. He would later be granted a posthumous pardon after Christie's trial when the truth was revealed even though some still believe that Evans did murder his family.

The Crimes

Mrs. Christie wanted to move since the only other tenants in the flat were Jamaicans against whom she was highly prejudiced. Further, after Evans' trial Christie went into a deep depression and lost a lot of weight, and also lost his post office job due to courtroom testimony about his past crimes. Ever the hypochondriac, Christie checked himself into a psychiatric hospital for three weeks and continued to visit his doctor for stress-related symptoms; 33 times in eight months.

He found work as a clerk with the British Road Service and things seemed to improve; however, Christie soon gave notice, citing that he had found a better job which was not true. His wife was not pleased with him being unemployed and around the house all the time. On 11 December Mrs. Christie watched television with a friend, on the 12th she took laundry to Maxwell Laundries, and then was never seen again. Nobody said she appeared to be distraught or that she said that she was going to take a trip.

Christie told her friends that she went to Sheffield and that he would follow shortly as he had a new job there. He told family members that his wife wasn't feeling well enough to write them.

At this same time Christie began to sprinkle his house and garden with disinfectant due to the increasingly putrid odor.

In January, Christie sold his furniture along with his wife's wedding band and watch. For more money he forged his wife's signature on a bank account she had and emptied it.

Shortly thereafter Christie met a Mrs. Reilly who was looking for a place to rent and he showed both her and her husband his flat. They paid him three months' rent in advance and kept his cat. Christie borrowed a suitcase, had his dog put down, and left. The Reillys ultimately left when the impending investigation commenced and they were told that Christie did not have the authority to sublet his flat.

Investigation

One of the upstairs tenants at 10 Rillington Place—Beresford Brown—noticed a hollow space behind a kitchen wall in Christie's old flat after the landlord gave him permission to use the kitchen since the flat was empty. Brown was looking for a place to mount a shelf for his radio and pulled away some of the wallpaper to try to open the door which he couldn't. When he shined a light through a crack he was horrified at what he found and called the police.

Chief Superintendent Peter Beveridge was on scene, as was Chief Inspector Percy Law of Scotland Yard, other officers, and the coroner. When the door was opened in the kitchen alcove they found a woman's corpse sitting in some rubble. Her back was to them and she was leaning forward. Behind her was something large wrapped in a blanket that was knotted to the victim's bra. Said bra was pulled up around her neck along with her black sweater and white jacket. Other than that she was nude save for a garter belt and stockings. She was taken from the cupboard and photographed and examined in the front room. She had been strangled with a ligature and her wrists were tied in front of her with a handkerchief tied into a reef knot.

Authorities focused on a second large object behind the woman and discovered it was another corpse. It had been propped on its head up against the wall. The blanket had been fastened with a sock tied in a reef knot around the ankles and the head was wrapped in a pillowcase that was also fastened by a stocking in a reef knot.

They noticed a third object. It was another body, also upside down, with her head beneath the second body. This one's ankles were tied with an electrical cord fashioned into a reef knot while a cloth covering her head was similarly knotted.

Investigators also took note of some loose floorboards in the rubble and found the wrapped body of Mrs. Christie amidst the rubble.

The first victim was a 20-something brunette who had been deceased for approximately one month. She had died from carbon monoxide poisoning and strangulation with a smooth type of cord. She had been sexually assaulted either at the time of her death or shortly thereafter. Scratches on her back indicated that she had been dragged across the floor. She was later identified as Hectorina McLennan, a 26-year-old prostitute.

The second victim was also a brunette and around 25 years of age. She, too, exhibited symptoms of carbon monoxide poisoning; particularly her pinkish skin color. She was also strangled and had had sexual intercourse around the time of her death. There was also evidence that she had been drinking heavily the day she died. She had poorly manicured hands and feet and was clad in a cotton cardigan and vest while another vest was fashioned into a diaper between her legs. It was estimated that she had died eight to 12 weeks earlier. She was later identified as 26-year-old Kathleen Maloney, also a prostitute.

The third victim was a mid-20s blonde, also poorly manicured, clad in a dress, petticoat, bra, cardigan, two vests, and another cloth fashioned into a diaper. She had also been poisoned with carbon monoxide and strangled. She, too, had been drinking before her death which was also eight to 12 weeks earlier and this victim was six months pregnant. She, again, a prostitute, was identified at Rita Nelson, 25.

The final victim—found under the floorboards—was a woman in her 50s, plump, and missing several teeth. She was rolled up in a flannel blanket with a pillowcase over her head. She was also wrapped in a flowered dress and silk nightgown and wore stockings. She had been dead approximately 12-15 weeks. She had been strangled by ligature but unlike the others there was no evidence of gas poisoning or sexual intercourse. She was identified as Ethel Christie.

Additional evidence found in the flat included potassium cyanide, a man's tie fashioned into a reef knot in the kitchen cupboard, a man's suit under floorboards of the common hallway, and a tobacco tin that contained four clumps of pubic hair; none of which belonged to any of the victims. From where Christie obtained the hair has never been resolved.

Police also found a human femur in the garden supporting a wooden trellis. Additional bones were uncovered in flowerbeds and beneath an orange blossom bush along with blackened skull bones with teeth, pieces of a dress, a newspaper fragment dated 19 July 1943, hair and teeth, and one skull. The coroner determined that there were two female corpses although only one skull had been found.

Forensic evidence enabled these last two victims to be identified as 21-year-old Ruth Margarete Fuerst who had arrived in England from Austria in 1939 and had disappeared 24 August 1943. She was around five feet seven inches with a tooth crown identified as being from Germany or Austria. When she disappeared she had been living in Notting Hill. The second victim was presumed to be Muriel Amelia Eady, 32, who had worked with Christie in a factory. The hair in Christie's garden matched hair from her former home. The black wool dress she was wearing when she disappeared matched remains in Christie's garden.

After Christie's failed affair with the woman whose husband was overseas, he didn't have any problems finding women who would, in fact, appreciate his attention. One day in a bar he met Fuerst. She worked in a factory and was also rumored to have been a prostitute. When Mrs. Christie was away she began to visit Christie at his home. One day in bed, Christie received a telegram telling him that his wife was on her way home with her brother. Christie alleged that Ruth had undressed voluntarily and asked him to have sex with her and then they could run away together. He stated that he refused and strangled her while they were having intercourse. He wrapped her in her coat and put her under the floorboards in the parlor until after his brother-in-law left and Mrs. Christie went to work. Christie then put Fuerst in the wash house and began to dig in the garden. That night he buried her in the garden. He found some of her clothing peeking up from the shallow grave and burned it.

It is hypothesized that Christie's lifelong hatred for women and repeated humiliations caused him to act the way he did. By strangling his victims he was able to exert some semblance of power and this was erotic for him as he was only able to achieve potency with women who were helpless: that being unconscious or dead. He admitted that after he killed Fuerst he experienced "a strange, peaceful thrill."

Christie met his second victim, Eady, in the company canteen as they both worked in the same factory. In October 1944 when his wife went to Sheffield to visit relatives Christie lured Eady into his house by telling her that he had a first-aid background from when he was with the War Reserve and could help her with the catarrh (mucous buildup in her nose and throat) from which she suffered. To avoid a struggle he was prepared with a contraption that resembled an inhaler with friar's balsam in a jar to mask the gas smell and a hose connected to the gas supply. Eady sat in a chair with a scarf over her head and as she inhaled, the carbon monoxide took effect; thus enabling Christie to strangle her with a stocking while simultaneously having intercourse as she was dying. He recounted experiencing the same peaceful thrill he had with Fuerst. Christie hid her body in the wash house and dug a shallow grave near the first. Later he found a broken femur bone while gardening and used it to prop up the trellis—something the police had not seen when they were investigating Timothy Evans for his wife's and daughter's murders.

Necrophilia is defined as having sexual relations with the unconscious or dead and keeping them close. There are three identified types. One is the violent variant wherein the perpetrator has an overwhelming urge to be near a corpse so they kill in order to satiate this urge. Often the individual visits the corpse where it is dumped and in some cases there is repeated sexual contact. Another type is the fantasy necrophiliac who makes death a central aspect of his or her erotic imagery. These types may ask a partner to play dead or take pictures of him or her looking dead so they can masturbate later. Christie is a textbook fantasy necrophiliac because, as mentioned, he was unable to perform absent the violence when he murdered his victims. He also had a violent necrophilia orientation in that he did, in fact, keep his victims nearby: in the alcove in his flat, under the floorboards, in his garden, and in the building's communal wash house.

Arrest

After Christie left his old flat he placed his borrowed suitcase in a locker and wandered around London. On 20 March 1953 he checked into a room at the King's Cross Rowton House with his real name and address. Despite booking seven nights he only stayed four. When a photograph of him emerged wearing his raincoat he purchased an overcoat from another man and gave him his raincoat instead. While he claimed at trial that he was in a daze, aimlessly wandering around London, his actions demonstrate that his contriving a disguise of sorts proved otherwise. He also claimed that despite news stories about corpses found at his house, he did not connect them with himself.

Out of money, Christie took to sleeping on benches and in movie theaters and was spotted by a police officer on 31 March near the Putney Embankment of the Thames River. After giving the officer a fake name and address, Christie was asked to remove his hat and was, subsequently, recognized and promptly arrested. On his being were his identification card, his Union card, an ambulance badge, a ration book, and an old newspaper clipping about the Timothy Evans trial with details about the murders.

Christie willingly gave his statement about four of his murders. He hinted that he couldn't remember something, essentially making the police "show their hand" by admitting that they did, in fact, find the two bodies in the garden. With respect to his wife Christie claimed that she had awakened him one night and she was choking; her face was blue. He tried to restore her breathing but she was suffering so badly that he got a stocking and strangled her to put her out of her misery. He then said that the bottle containing the phenobarbitone tablets he had been prescribed for insomnia was almost empty and he realized that his wife took the pills to kill herself. After leaving his dead wife in their bed for a couple of days he put her under the floorboards, admitting that he thought this was the best way to put her to rest and keep her close to him.

He managed to make the other three women's murders not his fault either. Since they were prostitutes he claimed that they were the aggressors, demanded money, and forced themselves into his flat. He claimed Nelson picked up a frying pan to hit him and they struggled and she fell into a chair "that happened to have a rope hanging from it." When Christie came to from his alleged blackout she was dead. He said he left her there overnight and in the morning—after he had a cup of tea—he wrapped her up, diapered her, and shoved her into the alcove cupboard.

With respect to Maloney, Christie said that he met her in a café and she went home with him and threatened violence and only remembers her being on the floor and that he put her into the cupboard. In reality, he gassed her, strangled her, had intercourse with her, and then diapered and wrapped her body.

Christie stated that McLennan and her boyfriend needed a place to stay so he invited them to live with him. He asked them to leave after "several uncomfortable days" and she had come back one night, struggled with Christie after he asked her leave; however, some of her clothing tore and got wrapped around her neck. He said he sat her in a chair but she appeared to be dead so he put her in the cupboard.

The numerous psychiatrists who evaluated Christie while he was in Brixton prison described him as "nauseating" and "sniveling" and he would whisper answers to questions he did not like; not unlike his demeanor during Evans' trial. He also allegedly dissociated when describing his actions, referring to himself in the third person; however, he boasted about his actions to other inmates saying that his "goal" was 12.

Trial, Conviction, and Execution

When faced with the myriad evidence against him, Christie quickly admitted to killing his first two victims but hesitated to take responsibility for Beryl Evans who he later admitted that he did, in fact, kill but not baby Geraldine. He said Beryl's was a mercy killing like his wife as a result of a botched suicide attempt on her part. Christie alleged that Beryl offered him sex to help her but he could not perform. None of the evidence corroborates Christie's account.

Christie's trial for murdering his wife commenced on 22 June 1953 at the Old Bailey. He pled not guilty by reason of insanity. His own attorney, Derek Curtis-Bennett, even called Christie a maniac and madman which was supported by Dr. Jack Abbott Hobson, a defense psychiatrist. The prosecutor's psychiatrists said that while Christie had a hysterical personality it was neurosis not a defect of reason and, therefore, Christie was not insane.

After a mere four-day trial and an 80-minute jury deliberation Christie was found guilty and sentenced to death. He did not appeal and was hanged at Pentonville Prison on 15 July 1953.

GIRL STRANGLER :
THE TRUE STORY OF SERIAL KILLER

DANA SUE GRAY

ERIN PIERCE

Dana Sue Gray was born on December 6th, 1957 in Pasadena, California. Her mother, Beverly Arnett, was a former beauty queen who worked as a professional model. Her father, Russell Armbrust, worked as a hairdresser and was married three times prior to marrying Beverly. The couple had several miscarriages before Dana was born.

Her mother was born for the camera and loved attention. She liked being pampered, getting her make-up done and wearing flashy outfits. Beverly modeled for Bullock's, did print ads for Hamilton watches and was once a Rose Princess at the Tournament of Roses Parade.

LIKE MOTHER LIKE DAUGHTER

Russell divorced Beverly, however, when he witnessed his wife attack an older woman that had angered her. Beverly had also maxed out his credit cards, putting him financial peril. Dana was only two years old at the time of the divorce and rarely saw her father.

"Some kind of estrangement had taken place," forensic psychologist Lora Dixon said. "After her parents divorced she had turned down invitations in her teen years to visit her father on all of the holidays and birthday get-togethers."

"There is also something to think about here in terms of Beverly's own temper. Dana clearly witnessed violence and bullying from her mother at an early age. She inherited those characteristics from her mother with tragic results."

Dana had discipline problems early on as she sought attention from her narcissistic mother. Her mother would discipline her but Dana would retaliate by stealing money to buy candy. Her mother had two other children from a previous marriage. Dana would go into the rooms of her step brothers and urinate in their beds.

Her mother would continue to try and discipline her to no avail as Dana would lash back with violence. This facet of her personality was never placed under her control.

"Mommy and daughter didn't get along," Dixon said. "But obviously that isn't unusual nor does mean she was destined to become a serial killer. There was some deep seated issues festering here though. This is evident when Dana gave her mother a snake for Christmas. 'A snake for a snake' the card must have read."

Nonetheless, it did not appear on the surface that Dana had to endure the brutal childhood that gave birth to so many other serial killers. Cedric Ward, one of her step brothers, did admit that Dana did not have the best of childhoods. "It was not happy growing up," he recalled.

SCHOOL AND SEX

Dana did not get along with other students and achieved low grades in all of her classes. She was a chronic truancy case and often forged notes to get out of class. Dara was sexually active at a very early age as she would lose her virginity at the age of twelve. She would ultimately go from one relationship to the next, using sex to lure men into her web of narcissism.

"Dana has a problem," said Richard Singer, a boyfriend of her mother. "She does not want to be told no. She has her own thing, and nobody could tell her any different. You could not tell Dana what to do."

"Her mother would pretty much try to control her, but Dana would go off on you. You could not tell her what to do. Dana is very hyperactive and opinionated."

During her adolescent years, she loved horror movies and read Grimm's Fairy Tales numerous times. As a teenager, she and a neighbor built a catapult. They would tie tiny parachutes on the cat's backs and then hurl them into the air, with the parachute carrying them down into neighborhood swimming pools.

A MOTHER'S DEATH

Beverly contracted breast cancer when Dana was fourteen. Dana decided to become a nurse after witnessing the way the nurses at the hospital treated her mother. Her mother died and Dana was forced back to live with her father.

"The temptation here is to say that Dana was inspired to become a nurse by witnessing the compassion the nurses shown her mother during her illness," Dixon said. "But I would posit a different psychological scenario. Dana saw that the nurses had power over her mother. That for once, her mother was weak and had to defer to other people for the first time in her life. Dana wanted power. Control. What better way to get that then to become a nurse?"

Dana went into a depression after her mother died and would reveal her sentimentality in letters she would write to her then boyfriend, Don Lane, in jail.

"Tomorrow, Good Friday, 4-1-94, is also April Fool's and also my real mom's 76th B-day. It's been 22 years since her death, and I still celebrate her B-day for her. I celebrate it for her 'cause she died when I was 14 and we never got to get past the 'grow years' to become friends like my dad and I are. She was wild-but made my younger years a total adventure: camping, clamming @ Pismo, best Halloween parties and the best Xmases a poor family could have. She could make a fun time out of just anything."

"Again, you see in her letters a sense of victimhood," Dixon said. "She makes no mention of her mother ignoring her birthdays. And she describes her family as 'poor.' They lived in relatively affluent area, becoming strapped for cash primarily because of Beverly's spending."

GROWING UP

Dana's father Russell had remarried, living with his new wife Yvonne who had a daughter named Cathy. Dana would move in with the couple, sharing a room with Cathy. The reunion between her and her father would be a short-lived one, however, as Yvonne would find marijuana in Dana's room.

Russell's wife then kicked Dana out of the home.

On her own at the age of fifteen, Dana would move-in with her sky-diving instructor, Rob Beaudry. The union would produce two pregnancies but Rob talked Dana in to getting abortions both times. These were decisions that she would later come to resent.

At five-foot-two and weighing a stocky 135 lbs, Dana would nonetheless inherit her mother's penchant for fancy clothes and desire to be pampered with manicures and pedicures. Despite her taste in high-end living, associates would describe her appearance and demeanor as "hard."

She would graduate from Newport High School in 1976 and enter nursing school at Saddleback College in Mission Viejo, California. Dana paid her way through nursing school while working as waitress. She also taught herself screen printing techniques and sold screen printed items for extra cash.

"Dana inherited her mother's psychology when it came to money and relationships," Dixon said. "She operated from a 'lack mindset', in that she always saw herself as poor. She was industrious but felt sorry for herself that she had to work so hard, paying her way through school and working for a living. The shopping sprees were a relief to her perceived burden."

ESTRANGED FROM FAMILY

Dana became estranged from her half-brothers, her older siblings from Beverly's previous marriage. The reasons were always financial as she become embroiled in a dispute over the proceedings from their aunt's estate.

She had run-ins with her half-brother Rick in particular.

Dana reacted with anger after he told her to sell belongings to pay her mounting bills. Rick wrote back telling her that she had no consideration for others.

"Nuts," is how her sister-in-law described her. "Not even normally greedy. Crazy. Gray is missing a conscience. I do not think it is there. When you talk to her, she has no concept of other human beings."

"The half-brothers clearly knew she was trouble," Dixon said. "They did the right thing in distancing themselves.

NURSING CAREER.

Immediately upon graduating from Saddleback, Dana landed a nursing job at Corona Community Hospital. She used that as a springboard to a high paying position as an operating room nurse at Inland Valley Regional Medical Center (some reports have her identified as a labor and delivery nurse). She was described by one nursing supervisor as "very caring."

During this time, she had found another boyfriend, a windsurfer whom she would accompany on trips to Hawaii where they would pursue various outdoor activities. This relationship would be an on-again, off-again type deal until Dana would marry Tom Gray. The couple would tie the knot at a winery in the affluent Temecula area.

Tom was an active sportsman and had a crush on Dana since high school.

"She was a hard core athlete," Tom recalled. "A sky diver, wind surfer, mountain bike enthusiast and snorkeler, and she was skilled in each sport."

Dana took pride in her physical strength and would often roll up her sleeve to reveal her bicep muscle. 'She how strong I am?' she would ask.

Living in the gated community of the affluent Canyon Lake suited Dana as it would have been something that would have pleased her mother. Her and Tom started numerous businesses where they used the name "Graymatter."

Tom could not stop Dana's spending habits, however. The couple took out a loan for $47,000 and another for $20,000 within the first nine months of their marriage.

"She was replicating the marriage of her mother and father," Dixon said. "She liked the empowerment that came from having a lot of money. Having money, or rather the act of spending money is what fed her ego. Only in Dana's case she took it way beyond her mother. She was willing to kill for that feeling."

The marriage quickly soured when Dana's spending habits sent the couple into overwhelming consumer debt. Her alcoholism also worsened, particularly after she suffered a miscarriage. Dana indulged in three or four glasses of wine while cooking dinner and then having more with the dinner itself. Her days off from the hospital were adventures in bourbon whiskey, 7-Up and Tequila shooters. Later, she would admit to using marijuana and cocaine.

When Gray unexpectedly received a $7500 inheritance, Dana took the money and blew it on a trip to Europe, leaving her husband behind at home. When she returned , she began an affair with Don Lane, a musician in her husband's band. When Lane agreed to support her, she moved out of the Canyon Lake house and spent $11,000 in five months.

In March of 1992, however, Dana began seeing a psychiatrist. He prescribed Paxil for her, probably to stave off depression among other things.

Lane had a five year old son at the time and would later tell authorities of Dana's "mood changes" and her propensity to break out into "hysterical tears" with little provocation.

She filed for divorce from Tom but this would not be finalized until much later. In September of 1993, Tom and Dana were forced to file for bankruptcy to prevent foreclosure on their Canyon Lake residence.

Despite the value of the home increasing, the amount they owed on the house was more than its worth. They owed $177,500 on a house valued at $125,000 because of double mortgages.

She suffered a miscarriage, exacerbating more depression as well as alcohol and drug abuse.

FIRED FROM THE HOSPITAL

The trouble continued for Dana as two months later she would be fired from the hospital for stealing Demerol and other opiate pain killers.

"What Dana was trying to do was medicate herself," Dixon said. "The new marriage, the exotic vacations, the fancy house and cars. It was never enough to quell the demons that spoke in her head. A control freak out of control. So she struggled to constantly fill the void with booze and drugs. Then this spirals into an affair with a friend of her husband. Again, this life trajectory happens to a lot of people. In Dana's case, however, she needed that extra thrill. Something more than the rush of sky-diving, cheating on her husband, and getting high. She needed the ultimate adrenaline rush. The power to take someone's life."

TIME TO KILL

In later reports, hospital authorities would reveal their own problems with Gray.

"She is sarcastic," Darlena Addison, the former nursing supervisor who fired Gray for stealing drugs. "She does get her point across if she's crossed or doesn't get her way."

"The problem was a condescending attitude, as Dana believed that she was smarter than everyone and had a need to dominate."

The hospital would later report that they did not have any "unusual" deaths during Gray's tenure.

"Of course that is what you would expect them to say," Dixon said. "If they admit to any 'unusual' deaths then it certainly opens them up to a lawsuit. The opportunity would certainly be there for Dana to steal credit cards from elderly patients and rack up bills. It appears, however, that she did not put her murderous impulses into action until after her dismissal. Dana fell in love with the struggle. The fight of her victim as long as she would emerge on he winning end. Poisoning her victims to death in the way it would have been possible for her as a nurse would not have given her that adrenaline rush."

After the loss of her job, Dana would amp up her indulgences in alcohol, drinking straight Vodka, loving the Smirnoff brand in particular.

On Valentine's Day in 1994, Dana contacted Tom's parents (after their separation he had kept his phone number and address a secret). She informed Tom's parents that she wanted to meet with him.

Tom agreed at first but later did not show up.

Tom would find out that Dana had taken out an insurance policy on him without his knowledge. The policy payout would have been enough to pay down the Canyon Lake home the couple used to share.

Later that day, Dana murdered Norma Davis.

THE FIRST VICTIM

Norma Davis was 86 years old at the time. She was the mother-in-law of the woman (Jeri Davis Armbrust) who married Dana's father in 1988. Jeri's first husband, Bill Davis, was Norma's son. Bill died in the early 1980s, and his widow married a newly divorced Russell.

But Jeri continued to care for her elderly mother-in-law, even after she remarried. Dana would also come to know Norma very well.

On February 16th, 1994, however, the body of Norma Davis would be found by a neighbor named Alice Williams. She had been dead for two days as someone had stabbed her in the neck with a wood-handled utility knife. The blade had been inserted so deep that it nearly severed Norma's head.

She also had a filet knife sticking out of her chest.

Police would discover no forced entry into the home. Norma always kept the doors locked unless she was expecting a visitor. Her neighbor, Alice, stated that she could not remember if Norma had mentioned she was expecting company.

"We didn't have a lot of information," Detective Joe Greco said. "The only piece of evidence that we had was the entry way of the condominium. There was a faint shoe print on the condominium and it was a 6 ½ size shoe."

Detectives would find the Nike shoe print and Davis' Social Security check in plain view. Additionally, on the first floor of the condo, they found a smear of blood on an armchair and a torn phone cord.

A modus operandi had been established. Dana would manually strangle her victims with a phone cord, then use an object to smash or stab.

The coroner concluded that Norma Davis was strangled first then stabbed. She was stabbed eleven times with Dana leaving the knives stuck in her body.

Police described the scene as one of the most brutal they had ever encountered.

"It was a shock because it was only my second homicide case as a detective," Greco said. "It was overwhelming. It crossed my mind that I had a serial killer on my hands."

SHE DEVIL ON A RAMPAGE

"The community was very affluent," Greco said. "They don't have a lot of homicides."

On February 28th, 1994, 66-year old June Roberts was found murdered. She had lived in the gated community of Canyon Lake along with Dana.

Dana had known Roberts and visited her that day saying that she wanted to borrow a book about either overcoming alcohol addiction or vitamins, the reports vary. Dana had her boyfriend's five year old son waiting out in front in her Cadillac.

Ignorant of Dana's true motives, Roberts allowed Dana into her home. She went to retrieve the book Dana inquired about while her would-be killer ripped out the cords to June's phone

Dana would later describe their interaction taking a turn when she became "really annoyed" that June came back with the wrong book. She also told a psychologist that she became infuriated that June allegedly said that she "didn't do enough" to save her marriage with Tom.

When asked what made Dana believe that Roberts and her other victims were looking down on her, Dana responded that she did not like their body language.

"The arching of the eyebrow," Dana said. "That is what happened. All three."

Dana then used the phone cord to strangle Roberts to death.

"I was right behind her," Dana recalled. "I choked her with the phone cord. She was holding on, trying to get the cord off. I pulled her down. She was on her back. I hit her in the head with a bottle. I lost it. I was so consumed. I don't know the time span in there-must have been very quick. She must have stopped moving, and I left. As I walked out, she had a little wallet thing. I grabbed it."

"We went out and proceeded to shop up a storm. "

In talking to psychologists,.Dana appeared unaware of the concept of remorse.

"It was very brutal," Greco said. "The victim had been strangled with her own telephone cord and actually tied to a chair. And she was struck so hard (by the wine bottle) she fractured her skull."

Her autopsy noted a "moderately deep ligature furrow" and a "6 x 3 purple contusion." The cranium contusion was caused by a heavy glass wine bottle striking her with tremendous force. The volume of blood in and near the bathroom door, the walls and pooling under the body made it impossible to gauge the age of the victim.

"This is when the profile of Dana Sue becomes highly unusual," Dixon said. "With female serial killers, you usually see poison or the use of a gun as the weapon of choice. Dana Sue, however, approached her victims with a high level of physical violence that rivaled a male serial killer. There was nothing lady-like about her approach. She was a cold blooded, hands on killer."

TIME TO SHOP

Dana did not hesitate after murdering Roberts, she had to get her shopping fix met.

She would go to Bally's Wine Country Cafe in Temecula, eat crab cake and scampi while charging the meal to Robert's credit card. She could not finish the entire meal, however, and had the waitress pack the rest.

She then got an eyebrow wax and a perm then treated her boyfriend's son to a stylish haircut.

"The fact that she had the little boy accompany her on both the murders and the shopping trips deserves mention," Dixon said. "Dana remained childless throughout life. She was regretted getting two abortions and suffered a miscarriage during her marriage with Tom. Going out and about with her boyfriend's son made her feel like a Mommy. She could be the Mommy that she never had, treating the young child to things she always wanted."

Dana signed "June Roberts" on the $164.76 charge at the salon. She then went to the mall and spent $511 on a black suede jacket, several pairs of cowboy boots, and then $161 on a pair of diamond earrings all charged to Roberts. Her addiction still not satiated, she went to a drug store, picking up dog treats, two bottles of Smirnoff and a toy police helicopter for the boy.

The day after, Dana loaded up on suntan lotion, got a massage at Murrieta Hot Springs resort and then went on another power shopping spree.

"She had absolutely no remorse," Dixon said. "There was no hiding out and laying low like some other wimpy male serial killer. Dana Sue was different. She killed and then she had to do the one thing that gratified her. She had to get to the mall. She had to get the high from buying stuff. She had to enjoy the power while it still lasted."

Ironically, none of her victims had anything stolen aside from their credit cards.

"Dana didn't take any rings from her victims," Greco said. "Or some valuables from the home that were obvious. So I don't think any of the crimes were motivated by money."

Ten days after the Roberts' murder, Dana would enter an antique store, the Main Street Trading Post in Lake Elsinore. Dana stated to the cashier, Dorinda Hawkins, that she wanted to buy a picture frame for a photo of her deceased mother.

"Dana came in asking about picture frames," Greco said. "During their interaction, Dana felt that Dorinda was being condescending to her.

"I felt sick to my stomach," Dana said. "I wanted to vomit. I wanted her to die."

Dana asked if Hawkins was working alone and then she attacked her, strangling her with the store's telephone cord.

"Dorinda is begging for her life when Dana is strangling her," Greco said. "And Dorinda told her 'you can have anything you want. Take the cash, I have eight kids, just let me live.' And Dana told her 'I'm not doing this for the money.' She said that twice. And that really gives you an insight on what Dana is thinking while she's committing these crimes."

Dorinda, however, continued to fight, resisting Dana all the way.

"Relax," Dana said, trying to coax Hawkins into dying. "Just relax."

Hawkins grabbed a broom and poked Dana with it to no avail.

Dana then shoved Hawkins to the ground and stepped on her head as a brace to better choke her.

"Her eyes were flat," Hawkins recalled. "I could tell she had killed before."

Believing her victim dead, Dana stole five dollars from Hawkins' purse and twenty dollars from the cash register.

An hour later, she began another shopping spree, still using Roberts' credit cards.

Hawkins, however, would survive the attack and provide the police the required description of Dana.

THE ATTACKS CONTINUE

Nearly a month after her first killing, on March 16th, 1994, Dana would kill the 87-year old Dora Beebe.

Moments after Beebe arrived home from a doctor's appointment, Dana pulled up in front of her house. She knocked on the door and asked Beebe for directions.

"Here we see Dana getting bolder," Dixon said. "With Norma Davis and June Roberts, she knew the victims beforehand. And the attempted murder in the antique store seemed to be a spur of the moment thing. But the Beebe murder is the first occasion where Dana has picked out a stranger. Elderly women were her preferred target, specifically those who were alone, and tragically Beebe emerged in her cross-hairs."

Living in the same neighborhood for several years, it was improbable for Dana to become lost. But she used that as an excuse when she came knocking on Beebe's door asking for directions.

Dana became angry when Beebe said "I don't have time for this." She was able to hide her anger as Beebe capitulated and allowed Dana insider her home to look at a map. Once inside the home, however, Dana assaulted the elderly woman.

'She turned her back on me," Dana said. "I choked her with the phone cord. I hit her in the head with an iron. As I remember it, it wasn't much of a fight."

Using a stainless steel Black and Decker iron that Dana found in the home, Dana bashed Beebe in the head so hard that it dented the appliance.

Less then an hour later, Dana would be at the mall with Beebe's credit cards in hand.

"She enjoyed doing things that were risky," Greco said. "She was a thrill seeker. I think that she really enjoyed what she was doing. She got a thrill out of it."

PANIC IN THE STREETS

The residents in the gated community of Canyon Lake went into panic mode. Some of the elderly citizens moved in with family until the killer was caught. A group of elderly widows organized themselves to sleep together at designated houses, not wanting to be alone.

There were some who thought the killings where the product of a cult engaging in the ritual sacrifice of the elderly.

"Rumors circulated around the entire community," Dixon said. "A terrifying time for everyone, the elderly in particular. This was a relatively well-to-do neighborhood. People were unused to killings, let alone a serial killer. Numerous people bought guns and kept it by their bedside while others banded together in the belief that there were safety in numbers."

FALSE SUSPECT

Police detectives were at a loss early on in finding a suspect. Prospects were so bleak that a supervisor in charge had seriously thought about using a psychic. Dana was not anywhere near the police's list of possible killers. Instead, the police initially suspected that her mother-in-law, Jeri Armbrust, might be the killer.

The police determined that Armbrust used to be married to Davis' son and continued to care for her former mother-in-law.

Detectives grew suspicious because it was unusual that Jeri would continue to take care of someone who was not a blood relative. Norma Davis herself was on death's door, recovering from a triple bypass surgery.

Police determined that Jeri had been in Davis' house the Sunday before the murder and that she wore a pair of Nike shoes.

Jeri stated that she did come to Davis' house but only came to drop off groceries. She heard the TV on upstairs but did not go up to say hello. She left the groceries on the counter and went home.

Police questioned why she didn't say hello but after weeks of questioning police determined that Jeri was not a suspect. She instead became an ally to the investigation.

CAPTURE

Descriptions obtained from the various merchants at the shopping center were eventually used to catch Dana. She had been buying so much stuff that the credit card company called June Roberts' family to inquire about the excessive spending.

Police detectives went to all of the stores where Roberts' credit card had been used, interviewing the cashiers. They obtained a physical description of Dana, surmising that the killer had dyed her hair recently and was accompanied by a little boy.

Detective Greco relayed this information to Jeri Armbrust.

Jeri surmised that the killer was in fact, her step-daughter Dana. She said that Dana recently dyed her hair red and had a boyfriend who had a young son.

Greco then obtained a search warrant and called for the aid of ARCNET (Allied Riverside County Narcotics Enforcement Team) to stake out Gray's home in Lake Elsinore.

Unfortunately, Dana was murdering Dora Beebe just hours before they determined her to be the killer. They followed Dana to a bank where she used Beebe's credit card and then went out for another shopping spree.

"We were able to follow the paper trail created by the use of these credit cards," Greco said. "With the merchants we were able to get a general description of the suspect."

Later that day, Greco arrested Dana while she was cooking dinner. Assisting officers took her boyfriend and his son in for questioning.

HOUSE OF STOLEN GOODS

Police did a thorough search of Dana's home after her arrest.

"They found jewelry, food, liquor, a ski mask, a purse with nearly $2,000 stuck in the washing machine, and many items of clothing," one report stated. "The police obtained a wealth of evidence: Gray's use of credit cards, clerks who had seen her directly after each murder, handwriting experts who identified her signatures on various items."

Dana was interrogated for hours.

"In the interview," Greco recalled. "Dana talked about finding a purse. And that purse belonged to a woman by the name of Dora Beebe. I knew that I had the right suspect in this case. But I didn't not know that on the same day we were serving her search warrant she was killing her last victim."

Dana stated that she never took the credit cards but after police revealed that they had evidence of her using them, Dana claimed that she found both Roberts' and Beebe's cards.

She maintained this story throughout the questioning. When asked why she kept the cards she said that she "had an overwhelming need to shop."

NO REMORSE, NO SYMPATHY

Dana displayed no sympathy for the victims. One psychologist noted that some of Dana's answers were like a robot answering in a manner they believed a normal human should.

After a hearing, Deputy District Attorney Richard Bentley wanted the death penalty. Dana pleaded insanity for all charges. But a witness came forward and stated that she saw Dana at Roberts' house on the day of her death, Dana quickly changed her plea to guilty and robbing and murdering two women as well as the attempted murder at the antique shop.

"At the end of the day," Dixon said. "Dana didn't want to die. When a witness came forward and said she saw Dana at the Roberts' house perhaps she knew that she was done for and would have been executed. Maybe she did not have enough confidence in her ability to pull off the insanity defense. So she struck a deal. She would plead guilty and avoid the death penalty."

Nonetheless, prosecutors were still unable to determine how Dana left the bloody crime scenes without a speck of blood on her or any sign of a struggle. All the clerks and waitresses spotted nothing out of the usual.

LIFE WITHOUT PAROLE

On October 16th, 1998, Dana Sue Gray was sentenced to life without parole.

"It's hard to find words to describe the atrocity in this case," Judge Patrick Magers said during Dana's sentencing. "The crimes were horrendous, callous and despicable."

Dana is currently jailed at the California Women's Prison in Chowchilla.

"She enjoyed the power," Dixon said. "She got addicted to the power she obtained while she killed people who were helpless to fight back. She liked watching them struggle. Liked having control over them before they died."

Jail has not seemed to bother Dana as she referred to her incarceration as her "county condo." She continues to pester her jailers to replicate her high-maintenance civilian lifestyle. She insists on a vegetarian diet and wants the use of a chiropractor. She has requested a mirror and has lobbied consistently for the return of her belongings.

Dana has drawn chilling clown faces, cobbling her paints together from M&M's candy coating, cherry drink mix, lipstick and and baby powder.

Her family came to visit her and brought her a pair of cheap Nike's. She refused them, wanting the high-end models.

Dana continues to thumb her nose at authorities as she sometimes sends collectibles to "murderablia" websites. She has sold her panties at $250, where she autographs them and writes in her prison identification number. She sells her hand tracing for $65 and a 'prison worn shirt', decorated with a drawing of a blue butterfly perched on a skeleton's hand.

"We can look back and say that she was simply psychotic," Dixon said. "And it is really easy to dismiss her killings as someone who was simply crazy violent and not read into it anymore than that. But in looking at the ages and gender of the victim, we can see the connection. All of her victims were old enough to be her mother. So perhaps in Dana's mind she saw her victims as substitutes for her late mother with whom had a lot of anger toward. And I mean violent, aggressive anger. So when she subdued her victims with the phone cord, she would unleash a torrent of rage, smashing them with irons, stabbing them with utility knives,bashing them over the head with wine bottles. She would attack them and have flashbacks of her battles with her Mom, doing things to the victim that she was powerless to do to her mother as a little girl."

"She was doing it all for Mommy."

THE HILLSIDE STRANGLERS

NAOMI ROBERTS

Cousins Kenneth Bianchi and Angelo Buono, Jr. are collectively known by their media epithet "The Hillside Strangler". These two men were responsible for the murders of at least nine females, ages 12 to 28, during the late 1970s in Los Angeles, California, and Bianchi killed two more in Washington. After their first three victims did not gain much attention because they were prostitutes, Bianchi and Buono decided to abduct and murder middle-class "nice" girls. Five victims were found on hillsides in the Glendale-Highland Park area during Thanksgiving weekend in 1977 and the resulting panic led to the coining of the moniker "Hillside Strangler".

Lead Los Angeles Police Department homicide investigator Detective Sergeant Bob Grogan, along with his partner Dudley Varney as well as Los Angeles Sheriff's Department's Detective Frank Salerno, believed that the murders were the work of more than one killer but figured the less the murderers knew about what police knew the better.

Bianchi later moved to Washington where he murdered two more women before being caught.

Both Bianchi and Buono were convicted of multiple counts of first-degree murder and sentenced to life. Buono dies of a heart attack on 21 September 2002 while serving his time in Calipatria State Prison in Calipatria, California. Bianchi continues to serve his sentence at Washington State Penitentiary in Walla Walla.

Early Lives

Kenneth Bianchi

Kenneth Alessio Bianchi was born on 22 May 1951 in Rochester, New York, to a 17-year-old alcoholic prostitute who gave him up for adoption two weeks after he was born. He was adopted by Nicholas Bianchi and Frances Sciolono and despite a stable upbringing, Bianchi became a pathological liar at a very early age. Further, as a result of petit mal seizures he suffered at the age of five, Bianchi often daydreamt as if he were in a trance.

Bianchi suffered from insomnia and frequently wet the bed as a child (one of the triad symptoms of serial killers). Frances took him to the doctor on multiple occasions for his urination problem and being examined by the doctor caused Bianchi much embarrassment and humiliation. He also had a bad temper and was diagnosed with passive-aggressive personality disorder which is characterized by an individual who may appear to be enthusiastic about and actively comply with others' desires and needs while simultaneously resisting them, thus resulting in increased anger and hostility. At the core of this disorder is that the sufferer resents responsibility and instead of openly expressing his or her feelings, demonstrates said resentment through actions such as procrastination, forgetfulness, and inefficiency. Despite having a rather high IQ of 116, Bianchi was a chronic underachiever in school. When Frances took him to a psychologist, it was determined that Bianchi was overly dependent upon his mother.

On 2 January 1957, Bianchi fell off of a jungle gym and landed on his face. His mother then sent him to a private Catholic elementary school where he excelled in creative writing. In July 1963, Bianchi pulled down a six-year-old girl's pants after "spontaneously decid[ing] that he liked doing so".

His adoptive father died in 1964, thus leaving an unemotional Bianchi having to attend public high school where he joined a motorcycle club and dated frequently. His adoptive mother was forced to work and she was known for keeping Bianchi home from school for extended periods of time.

While in high school, Bianchi set high standards for his many girlfriends such as complete fidelity and outwardly absolute devotion; however, these standard did not apply to him.

He graduated in 1971 from Gates-Chili High School in Rochester and, soon after, married his high school sweetheart, Brenda Beck; however, the couple divorced after only eight months. Rumor has it that Brenda left without a word.

Bianchi enrolled at Monroe Community College to study police science and psychology after deciding that he wanted to become a police officer; however, after only one term he dropped out and then was rejected for several positions both in Rochester and, later, Los Angeles. Consequently, Bianchi worked a series of menial odd jobs, eventually becoming a jewelry store security guard for which he was fired for stealing and giving his girlfriends the stolen jewelry. He would steal from other employers over the years.

He then left Rochester and moved to Los Angeles in late 1975 at the age of 26.

Angelo Buono, Jr.

Angelo Anthony Buono, Jr. was born on 5 October 1934, also in Rochester, New York, to first-generation Italian-American immigrants originally from San Buono, Italy. His parents divorced when he was young and a five-year-old Buono moved to Glendale, California, with his mother Jenny and his sister Cecilia, where his mother supported the family by doing piecework in a shoe factory. Raised Catholic, this had no effect on Buono's development as a decent human being.

Buono displayed a very high interest in sex from a young age and when he was a teenager claimed that he had raped and sodomized number of girls. Buono idealized serial rapist Caryl Chessman, also known as "The Red Light Bandit", calling Chessman his hero but added that Chessman should have murdered his victims. He developed a deep loathing of women and desire to injure and humiliate them, including his mother who he would verbally abuse; however, he was emotionally tied to her until her death in 1978.

Buono began stealing cars and was sent to the Paso Robles School for Boys.

In 1955, Buono married his high-school sweetheart, Geraldine Vinal, who was 17 years old at the time, who he had impregnated; however, less than a week later he left her. She would later give birth to a son, Michael Lee Buono, on 10 January 1956. Buono filed for divorce and refused to pay child support or let his son call him "Dad". He was back in jail for car theft when his first son was born.

Later, he impregnated Mary Castillo who gave birth to his second son, Angelo Anthony Buono III, at the end of 1956 and then married her in 1957. The couple would have four more children: Peter in 1957, Danny in 1958, Louis in 1960, and Grace in 1962. In 1964, Buono was believed to have sexually assaulted his two-year-old daughter Grace; however, there is insufficient literature to know fully the circumstances of the allegation. Buono's second marriage to Castillo also ended in divorce that same year after she purported that he had been physically, emotionally, and sexually abusive toward her. In a last-ditch effort to reconcile with him, Castillo was "rewarded" with his handcuffing her and threatening to kill her at gunpoint. Castillo would later recount a night during the first year they were together where Buono tied her spread-eagled to the bedposts and "raped her so violently she was afraid that he was going to kill her" and "her pain seemed to him his greatest pleasure" and, thus, he had no qualms of hurting her and didn't seem to care that the children witnessed the abuse. He avoided paying child support again.

Buono married a third time in 1965 to a 25-year-old single mother named Nannette Campino and the couple had two children of their own: Tony in 1967 and Sam in 1969. Despite being treated as poorly as Mary Castillo had been, Campino feared for her life on a daily basis but stayed until he began to sexually abuse her 14-year-old daughter. Buono allegedly bragged that he raped his stepdaughter because "[s]he needs breaking in" and then turned her over to his sons for their pleasure. Campino finally took her children, filed for divorce, and fled the state in 1971.

Buono, again, was arrested for auto theft and was sentenced to one year in prison; however, due to his large family his sentence was suspended so he could work to support them.

Buono married yet again, on a whim, to a woman named Deborah Taylor; however, the couple did not live together, nor did they ever divorce.

In 1975, he became a car upholsterer and purchased his own place at 703 E. Colorado Street to live and work. Despite his abuse, cockiness, overbearing nature, and lack of good looks, Buono was considered very attractive by women, particularly younger ones who were usually naïve about sex so it was easy to convince them that his outrageous demands and proclivities were normal. Thus, he frequently forced women to engage in sex acts with him and began a relationship with a teenage girl whom he twice impregnated.

He was ugly inside and out; very coarse, vulgar, ignorant, selfish, and sadistic.

Bianchi and Buono Together

At the age of 41, Buono came into contact with his cousin Kenneth Bianchi, the latter who, in 1975, moved to California and in with his cousin. Bianchi found his older cousin with "dyed black hair, gold chains around his neck, a large gaudy turquoise ring on his finger, red silk underwear and a virtual harem of jailbait girls". Buono taught Bianchi how to use fake police badges in order to coerce free sex from prostitutes. When they needed money the two also became pimps for a short time until the two girls who worked for them—Sabra Hannan and Becky Spears—escaped after enduring relentless abuse by Buono. Bianchi, still desiring to become a police officer, applied for jobs at the Los Angeles Sheriff's and Glendale Police Departments but neither were hiring. He then procured employment with a title company and used his first paycheck on an apartment and a Cadillac, moving in with coworker Kelli Boyd. Boyd rejected his marriage proposal as she considered Bianchi to be very jealous, immature, and a liar; however, in May 1977 she told him she was expecting their first child together. The couple moved to an apartment at 1950 Tamarind Avenue in Hollywood.

Bianchi also rented some office space and set himself up as a psychologist with a fake degree and credentials. He did not have many clients and when Boyd found out she was outraged. During the "Hillside Strangler" investigation, Bianchi told Boyd he had lung cancer and was undergoing chemotherapy and radiation to explain for his work absences; however, this was a lie. One day, detectives came to his apartment to ask questions but were "favorably impressed" and did not consider him a suspect at that time.

The Murders

In October 1977, the two men committed their first murder together. Their M.O. was to cruise around Los Angeles and use fake badges to convince women that they were undercover police officers. After persuading them into Buono's car that the men said was an unmarked police car, the two would take their victims to Buono's house where they would rape, torture, and strangle them with their "signature" weapon—a garrote (a handheld ligature such as a chain, rope, or strap)—although some of their victims were reportedly killed by lethal injection, electric shock, and gas asphyxiation. Their bodies were thus disposed of outside, frequently in hilly areas.

Yolanda Washington, 19

19-year-old tall, leggy, African-American prostitute Yolanda Washington disappeared on 17 October 1977 from Cathedral City, California. She was found the next day dumped just outside Forest Lawn Cemetery, beaten, raped, and strangled with a piece of cloth. Her corpse was cleaned and there were faint marks around her wrists, ankles, and neck. Her body was posed in a grotesque sexual position.

Judith Lynn Miller, 15

On 31 October, 15-year-old Judith Lynn Miller, a runaway, was found in a La Crescenta-Montrose neighborhood, face up on a parkway in a residential area. The homeowner covered her with a tarp so that neighborhood children wouldn't see her. After the incident, that same homeowner relocated his family to another state.

The victim was small and thin, perhaps 90 pounds, with medium length reddish-brown hair. She had bruising around her neck. She had also been raped and sodomized and her body had been posed with her legs in a diamond-like position.

Los Angeles Sheriff's Department Sergeant Frank Salerno was called to the site. He noticed insect activity upon her skin and on her eyelid was "a small piece of light-colored fluff" that he saved for forensic experts. He surmised that she had been killed elsewhere and her body had been deliberately placed where it would quickly be found.

At her autopsy, the coroner determined that she had been killed around midnight and was raped and sodomized.

There was no missing person's report matching this latest victim so after a couple of days, Salerno had the newspapers run a small story on her with a request to contact the police if anyone could identify her. Still nothing. Salerno then took her picture to Hollywood Boulevard and showed it to hundreds of runaways, addicts, homeless people, and prostitutes. The name Judy Miller kept coming up as a young destitute prostitute. One man named Markust Camden—a self-proclaimed bounty hunter—told Salerno that he saw Judy Miller leave the local fish and chips restaurant at 9:00 p.m. the night before she was found dead. In fact, he would pick Buono out of a police photo lineup, but failed to recognize Bianchi.

Eventually, Salerno was able to track down the Miller family and got a positive identification. They had nothing useful to contribute to the investigation.

Elissa "Lissa" Teresa Kastin, 21

Lissa Kastin, 21, was working as a waitress at the Healthfaire Restaurant to pay for ballet lessons as she was an avid dancer. She also worked part time for her father's real estate and construction business. She was last seen leaving work the night of 5 November. She was found the next day near the Chevy Chase Country Club in Glendale on 6 November; which was also near to where Buono lived. She had been beaten, raped, and strangled to death.

Salerno compared notes with the Glendale Police Department and noticed similarities between his latest victim and this new one. Both bodies had the same five-point ligature marks—ankles, wrists, and neck—and had been dumped within six miles of each other. This latest victim had been raped but there was no evidence of sodomy.

When Salerno looked at the dump site he was confident that at least two men were involved due to the large guardrail between the street and where the body was found and the near impossibility that one man could have gotten her body over it alone.

Dolores Cepeda, 12 and Sonja Johnson, 14

After their early murders failed to attract much publicity, Bianchi and Buono decided to find some younger victims.

12-year-old Dolores Cepeda and 14-year-old Sonja Johnson were abducted in Highland Park, California, on 13 November.

They had last been seen getting off a school bus heading home from St. Ignatius School and approaching a large two-tone sedan that, reportedly, had two men inside.

Both young girls were found on 20 November in the hills between Glendale and Eagle Rock, near Dodger Stadium by a young nine-year-old boy who was treasure hunting in the trash on the hillside.

Los Angeles Police Department Homicide Detective Dudley Varney had been called to this site.

Kristina Weckler, 20

That same day, 20-year-old Kristina Weckler was found on the other side of the same hillside where Cepeda and Johnson were found.

Weckler was a quiet, loving, and serious honors student at the Pasadena Art Center of Design and lived in Glendale.

She was found nude, raped, tortured, and strangled to death as evidenced by ligature marks on her neck, as well as around her wrists and ankles. She had blood oozing from her rectum and bruises on her breasts. Weckler was the first victim to show additional overt signs of torture; having been injected with Windex glass cleaner she had oozing injection marks on her arms.

Los Angeles Police Department Homicide Detective Sergeant Bob Grogan—Varney's partner—was called to this site. He noticed that there was no indication of any disturbance of the foliage in the area or evidence that the body had been dragged there. Grogan made a mental note that she likely had been killed elsewhere and then carried and dumped in this location by one or maybe two men.

At this point, police were entertaining the idea that there was more than one killer and that they were becoming increasingly more sadistic.

Jane Evelyn King, 28

28-year-old actress Jane King disappeared in Los Angeles around 10 November 1977, and was found near the Los Feliz off ramp of the Golden State Freeway on 23 November. She had been sodomized and strangled and her body was badly decomposed. After King was found, Los Angeles Police Department officials—in addition to Glendale Police Department and Los Angeles County Sheriff's Department officers—created a task force to catch the "Hillside Strangler".

Lauren Rae Wagner, 18

18-year-old student Lauren Wagner lived with her parents in the San Fernando Valley. Her parents had gone to bed on 28 November, expecting their daughter to return home before midnight. The next morning, they found her car parked across the street with the door ajar.

Wagner was found later that day in a wooded area near Glendale's Mount Washington area. She was lying partially in the street, nude, with ligature marks on her ankles, wrists, and neck. Wagner, too, had been tortured as the palms of her hands contained several burn marks.

At the dump site was also a "shiny track of some sticky liquid, which had attracted a convoy of ants". Police considered that if the substance was saliva or semen from the killer then, perhaps, his blood type could be determined, as tests on semen found inside the earlier victims revealed nothing. It was later found that Bianchi was not a secretor, in that his blood type could not be determined by other bodily fluids. DNA testing had not come into popularity at this time.

When Wagner's father questioned the neighbors, it turned out that the woman who lived in the house where his daughter's car was parked, Beulah Stofer, saw Wagner's abduction. Stofer said that Wagner had pulled over to the curb at around 9:00 p.m. and two men had parked their car beside hers. After some type of disagreement, Wagner "ended up in the car with the two men".

When Grogan went to talk to the neighbor, she told him that she had just had a phone call from a man with a New York accent who told her to "keep her mouth shut about what she had witnessed or he would kill her". Stofer also told Grogan that the car was a large dark sedan with a white top and that one of the men dragged Wagner from her car into his while Wagner protested, "You won't get away with this!" Stofer described one man as tall and young with acne scars while the other was older and shorter, Latin-looking, and with bushy hair. She said she was positive that she would identify them again. This statement rang true when she picked both Bianchi and Buono out of a photo lineup shown to her by Grogan.

Kimberly Diane Martin, 17

Tall, blonde prostitute Kimberly Martin, 17, disappeared from Echo Park, California, and was found strangled to death on 13 December 1977 on a steep hillside on Alvarado Street. Martin had worked for the Climax "modeling agency".

Police believed they had two reasonably good leads in this case. First, Martin's last "client" called her to 1950 Tamarind, apartment 114; however, this turned out to be a vacant apartment. Secondly, the murderer called from a payphone in the lobby of the Hollywood Public Library on Ivar Street. Unfortunately, nothing came from these leads.

Cindy Lee Hudspeth, 20

On 16 February 1978, 20-year-old Bible school teacher and secretary at an Echo Park church Cindy Hudspeth was found in the trunk of her bright orange 1977 Datsun B210 that had been pushed over a cliff on Angeles Crest in Los Angeles National Forest near La Canada. She had been raped and strangled, with the strangulation marks similar to those associated with the "Hillside Strangler".

Hudspeth was also a neighbor of Weckler even though the two women did not know each other. Interestingly, Bianchi also lived in the same apartment complex; however, this lead was never pursued even though both Grogan and Salerno believed that there was a good chance that at least one of the murderers lived in the Glendale area.

After this case, the lack of additional victims resulted in the disbanding of the "Hillside Strangler" Task Force.

Jill Barcomb, 18 (originally believed to be a Hillside Strangler victim)

18-year-old prostitute Jill Barcomb was abducted in Beverly Hills and found near the famous Hollywood sign on 9 November. Whereas it was originally believed that she was a victim of the "Hillside Strangler" because she had been raped, beaten, and strangled, in 2005, her death was conclusively proven through DNA analysis to have been committed by Rodney Alcala, the "Dating Game Killer".

Also, sometime in 1977, the two men gave Catharine Lorre a ride with the intent of killing her; however, when they learned that she was the daughter of famous actor Peter Lorre who played a child murderer in Fritz Lang's 1931 masterpiece film M, they let her go. She had no idea who the men were until they were arrested.

The two stopped killing after their ninth victim, Hudspeth (although at this time it was presumed they had ten victims with Barcomb), likely due to the birth of Bianchi's son and, as some surmise, that he had made some acquaintances within the Los Angeles Police Department who would take him on ride-alongs around the city, ironically, looking for the killers, and Bianchi could talk about nothing else while in police presence. On the night they had tried to abduct another victim, the two men got into a heated argument when Bianchi told his cousin that he had been questioned in the "Hillside Strangler" case. After Bianchi's confession about being questioned by police, Buono, furious, threatened to kill his cousin.

Bianchi's Washington Murders

Bianchi's girlfriend, Kelli Boyd gave birth to their son, Sean, in February 1978, and in March Boyd decided to return to her parents in Bellingham, Washington, as she was tired of both Los Angeles and Bianchi's lifestyle. After three months of pleading to be reunited, Boyd relented and Bianchi moved to Washington in May. Bianchi's role as boyfriend and father was relatively successful and he even took a job as a security guard, ultimately earning the trust of his supervisors. However, this way of life did little to alleviate Bianchi's murderous urges. Within six months he was actively looking for new victims.

On 11 January 1978, Bianchi lured two Western Washington University students—roommates Karen Mandic, 22, and Diane Wilder, 27—to a house he allegedly "guarded" under the pretense of housesitting. Once there, he raped, tortured, and murdered them.

On 12 January, police were informed that two female students were missing after Mandic's boss became worried that she didn't arrive at work that day. He did remember that she had told him she had accepted a housesitting job in a wealthy Bayside neighborhood from a security guard friend of hers. When former-priest-turned-Bellingham-Police-Chief Terry Mangan went to the girls' home he found a hungry cat, as well as the address of the home where they were to housesit. The name of one security guard kept coming up, as well as a record that Bianchi had used a company truck that same night, supposedly to take into the shop for repairs. This never happened. Mangan began to consider the fact that the women had met with foul play.

Police then went to the Bayside house and found a wet footprint. They also interviewed a neighbor who told them that a security guard asked her to check on the house except for the night the women disappeared because "there was special work being done to the alarm system and he didn't want her to be taken as an intruder".

After a press conference, a woman called police to report that a car had been abandoned near her home in a heavily-wooded area. In the car were the bodies of Mandic and Wilder. Both had bruising and had been strangled to death.

Mangan had the security guard picked up. He gave them no trouble. His name was Kenneth Bianchi.

There was ample forensic evidence in this case; most notably foreign pubic hairs on the girls and fibers from the house's carpet matching fibers on the dead girls' clothing and shoes. Additionally, when police searched Bianchi's home they found several items stolen from job sites where he worked.

Remembering back to the "Hillside Strangler" cases in Los Angeles—and knowing Bianchi had lived there—Mangan called the police departments in California who had worked on the task force. He spoke to Detective Frank Salerno to whom everything finally made sense. Detectives tirelessly worked to link Bianchi to the strangler cases and were confident that he was one of the murderers.

Investigation and Arrest

Bianchi was not as careful this time, having left significant clues, most notably his car with California license plates was seen and subsequently connected to the addresses of two Hillside Strangler victims. Without mastermind Buono, Bianchi didn't have the wherewithal to cover his tracks.

Bianchi was arrested the following day, on 12 January 1979.

Buono was arrested on 22 October 1979, after Bianchi told police about his cousin's complicity in the murders.

Trial and Conviction

Prior to his 1981 trial, Bianchi decided to plead not guilty by reason of insanity and claimed to have a separate personality named "Steve Walker" who had committed the murders. After several interviews by experts specializing in multiple personality disorder and hypnosis, it was determined that he was faking. Immediately after Dr. Martin Orne mentioned to Bianchi that in genuine cases of multiple personality disorder there are typically at least three personalities, Bianchi created another alter ego named "Billy", shortly followed by two more. It was later determined that the name "Steven Walker" came from a student whose identity Bianchi had previously tried to steal to enable him to fraudulently practice psychology. Further, in Bianchi's apartment investigators found several psychology books which laid credence to Bianchi's ability to fake the disorder. He was eventually diagnosed with antisocial personality disorder with sexual sadism.

During trial, there was significant physical trace evidence against the two men; including fibers from Buono's upholstery from his home and workshop on two of the victims; an imprint of a fake police badge on his wallet; and hairs from rabbits he had raised on another victim.

Bianchi agreed to plead guilty and testify against his cousin in order to get leniency, albeit uncooperatively (evidence of his passive-aggressive personality disorder).

Judge Ronald M. George—who would later become California Supreme Court Chief Justice—said during Buono's sentencing hearing, "I would not have the slightest reluctance to impose the death penalty in this case were it within my power to do so. Ironically, although these two defendants utilized almost every form of legalized execution against their victims, the defendants have escaped any form of capital punishment." On an interesting side note, George's roommate at the time was author Darcy O'Brien who, four years after the trial, wrote a book about the case.

Both men were sentenced to life in prison.

While incarcerated, Buono married mother-of-three Christine Kizuka in 1986 while she was visiting her husband—and father of her children—who was in the cell next door to Buono at the Los Angeles County Jail, serving 18 months for assault with a deadly weapon. She worked as a supervisor at the California State Employment Development Department.

Whereas the 64-year-old Bianchi continues to serve his life sentence at the Washington State Penitentiary in Walla Walla, Buono died of a heart attack on 21 September 2002 while serving life at Calipatria State Prison in Calipatria, California. Denied for parole on 18 August 2010, Bianchi will next be eligible for parole in 2025.

Aftermath

Bianchi is also a suspect in the "Alphabet Murders"—also known as the "Double Initial Murders"—which occurred in the early 1970s in his hometown of Rochester wherein three young girls were raped, strangled to death, and dumped in the wilderness. At the time he worked as an ice cream vendor situated near two of the murder sites. On 16 November 1971, ten-year-old Carmen Colon disappeared and was found two days later in Churchville, New York, 12 miles from where she was last seen. 11-year-old Wanda Walkowicz disappeared on 2 April 1973 and was found the next day in Webster, New York, off State Route 104, seven miles from Rochester. Finally, on 26 November 1973, Michelle Maenza, 11, disappeared and was found two days later in Macedon, New York, a mere 15 miles from Rochester. They were called the "Alphabet Murders" because not only did the young victims have the same initial for their first and last name but they were also found in cities which began with the same letter.

Whereas Bianchi has repeatedly tried to get his name cleared from these murders he remains a suspect because his vehicle was seen near two of the murder sites.

Another series of murders with similar circumstances occurred in California in the late 1970s and investigators have hypothesized that they are connected to the Rochester "Alphabet Murders". In 1977, Roxene Roggasch, Paula Parsons, and Carmen Colon (like one of the original "Alphabet Murder" victims) were found raped and dead. Whereas Bianchi was tried for six murders, DNA exonerated him of the California "Alphabet Murders".

A 2008 movie entitled The Alphabet Killer was very loosely based upon the murders, and in 2010 a book written by Cheri Farnsworth called Alphabet Killer: The True Story of the Double Initial Murders was released.

In 1980, Bianchi started a relationship with a Veronica Lynn Compton, who was a defense witness during his trial. Compton, a cocaine addict who was fascinated by serial killers, was working as a scriptwriter in Hollywood. On one of her numerous visits with Bianchi while he was incarcerated, she gave him a copy of her screenplay entitled The Mutilated Cutter, about a female serial killer, and asked for this input. Compton grew increasingly fixated and allegedly fell in love with Bianchi. Later, she was convicted and incarcerated for attempting to strangle a cocktail waitress who she had lured to a hotel in a ploy to have the world—and authorities—believe that the real "Hillside Strangler" was still on the loose and that the wrong man was incarcerated. To make it look like an authentic "Hillside Strangler" murder, Bianchi manipulated and used Compton as a means to get out of prison by giving her semen of his smuggled out of the facility in a rubber glove to plant on the body. Despite that DNA forensics had not been utilized at that time, semen could still be analyzed to demonstrate the killer's blood type; however, Bianchi was not a secretor. The intended victim managed to get away and Compton was tried and convicted of first-degree attempted murder and sentenced to life. Compton was paroled from prison in 2003.

In 1992, Bianchi sued Catherine Yronwode for $8.5 million for putting an image of his face on a trading card. He claimed his face was his trademark. The case was dismissed with the judge saying that if Bianchi's face was, indeed, his trademark during the murders then he would not have tried to hide it from police.

In 2007, Buono's grandson, Christopher Buono, shot his grandmother—Mary Castillo who was married to Buono at one time—and then committed suicide. Christopher was unaware of his grandfather's true identity until 2005.

Bianchi and Buono are immortalized in film. The 1989 film The Case of the Hillside Stranglers—based on O'Brien's book—starred Dennis Farina as Buono and Billy Zane as Bianchi. In the 2004 film The Hillside Strangler, Buono was portrayed by actor Nicholas Turturro and Bianchi was portrayed by C. Thomas Howell.

The 2006 movie Rampage: The Hillside Strangler Murders starred Tomas Arana as Buono and Clifton Collins, Jr. as Bianchi.

In 2001 the Discovery Channel aired an episode of The New Detectives that revisited the murders.

Bianchi and Buono have also been mentioned several times on the television show Criminal Minds as an example of killer teams with psychopathic predatory sexual sadist personalities who murdered their victims together.

ROADSIDE STRANGLER

JASMINE GREY

When one envisions a serial killer, they think of a cold, calculating, heartless monster. As humans, some of us have developed ways to recognize other humans that are looking to cause us harm. If we look at a mug shot of famous another serial killer, like Charles Manson or Jeffery Dahmer, one could say that these men "look" like serial killers. Maybe it's because of their wild eyes, the way that they hold themselves, or the "creepy" feeling one receives from their presence. These factors are enough to make a person stay as far away from the killer as possible, but sadly, not all predators come with a warning sign. Michael Bruce Ross, later to be known as the Roadside Strangler, was a ruthless predator that slipped under the radars of the multiple women that he attacked, raped, and murdered. Detective Malchik, Ross' arresting officer, described this serial killer as, "There was nothing threatening about him, there was no signal to any of these people that there was a dark side or something that they should be afraid of. He was able to conceal that until it became time for him to attack these innocent, young women." Ross seemed to be an average-looking man of completely average-strength and abilities, but underneath his calm and normal exterior beat the heart of a man who struggled with his sadistic, sexual compulsions. When someone spoke to Michael Ross, they would say that he put off a very friendly and articulate demeanor seemed very well educated and kind, but it was merely a costume that he had created over a lifetime. The creepy part about Michael Ross, despite how honest and upfront he is about his murders, is the mystery behind his words. Is he being genuine or is this merely an act? Is he being honest or are we being deceived? His state of mind drifts from monotone claims to not possess any remorse for his monstrosities to genuine pleas for a chemical castration to reduce his perverse sexual desires. Michael Bruce Ross' case was a strange one, to say the least, and his mental condition will forever be remembered as a very dark part in Connecticut history.

The Childhood

Michael Bruce Ross was born on July 26, 1959. Among three other children, Michael Bruce Ross was born into the life of a middle-class chicken farmer. His mother Pat was impregnated in high school and forced into a shotgun marriage with Michael's father, Dan Ross. Needless to say, they did not go on to lead a very happy marriage. Pat Ross was a very mentally unstable woman, who underwent two abortions and was institutionalized twice. She abandoned her children and family once to run off with another man, but she soon returned to a depressing and emotionally unhealthy life on the farm. Pat Ross seemed to resent Michael more than the other children. His sister claimed that Michael received the brunt of their mother's aggression. Michael Ross claimed that he didn't remember his dark childhood or his emotional abuse-ridden family; he only had fond memories of working on his father's farm. The joyous memories of working on the farm centered on his peculiar job; Michael's job was to ring the necks of sick and malnourished chickens.

He recalled that he began to experience sexual fantasies around this time, like most boys his age, but they weren't anything like the hellish compulsions he faced in his adulthood. He explained his boyish daydreams as non-violent, although they might've been considered peculiar by most. In an interview, Michael describes his early, innocent fantasies of women, "I would kidnap women and take them to my safe place, and then they would fall in love with me, and never want to leave." It has been said that Michael was molested as a child by his mentally ill uncle while babysitting. As an adult, Michael Ross claimed that he did not remember this incident or his uncle at all; Michael was only six years old when the suspected uncle committed suicide. Whether Michael was too young to recall the incident or if he merely repressed the memory, the irreparable damage that comes along with molestation could be a very influential part of Michael's slip into sexual sadism. Despite his strange desires, his dysfunctional family, and his history of abuse, Michael was considered to be a pretty average child. As a teenager, he excelled in school, graduating as number sixteen in his high school class, and he eventually moved to Cornell University to study Agriculture and Life Sciences.

College Years

He continued to excel academically throughout his years at university. He studied Economics, Agriculture, and Life Sciences, and excelled in all of his academic endeavors. He joined the FFA (Future Farmers of America) and the Alpha Zeta fraternity. Ross' sophomore year roommate and Alpha Zeta brother, described Ross in 1977, "He kind of followed his own drum and went his own way." Michael never made any real connections in his fraternity, nor did he really make connections to anyone besides the long string of girls that he dated. In his college year, Michael Ross was rarely without a girlfriend, and he was rarely thinking about anything but. "There was always a certain obsession on his part regarding women," said his Alpha Zeta roommate, "That seemed to be such a big issue, a constant topic—needing a woman, needing to have a girlfriend. He would be obsessed about the relationship."

Ross claims that he did not experience truly violent sexual fantasies until his years at Cornell University. He especially did not begin to fantasize about raping women until his sophomore year in college. Michael Ross said that somewhere in his undergraduate years, he began to embrace the desires that brewed within him. He started his downward spiral with a very small step. He began to stalk his fellow students on campus. He would follow close by, making it known that he was behind her. "I would get a thrill by them knowing that I was following them. That they would be scared and that gave me a thrill," Michael explained his early experimentation with his predatory nature. When simply stalking the women wasn't enough, Michael eventually turned to towards rape. He hid in the bushes of Beebe Lake and raped a visiting student. Later, he attempted to rape another girl outside of the school observatory but failed. These assaults were only stepping stones to the full-fledged horror that Michael Ross was destined to cause. During his senior year at Cornell University, Michael Ross met Dzung Ngoc Tu, a Vietnamese student, and his very first murder victim.

The case of Dzung Ngoc Tu perplexed officials everywhere. She was found on May 17, 1981, in the Fall Creek Gorge. She died from a skull fracture and her body laid there for five days until she was discovered. It appeared to be a suicide, as if she had jumped from the bridge overhead and hit her head upon the fall, but there was no suicide note left at the scene. Close friends and family of Dzung Ngoc Tu claimed that there absolutely no signs of suicidal tendencies when she was alive and investigators found absolutely no reason for killing herself. Her body showed no signs of sexual abuse, there were no suspects, and the police had no idea that the culprit was actually Michael Ross, a man who was only connected to her by their similar majors. The case went cold when the police couldn't find a suspect. It wasn't until Michael Ross was already in prison for the murders and rapes of four other women when he confessed to murdering and raping a Vietnamese girl that went to his school in New York.

The Attacks and Murders of The Roadside Strangler

Michael Ross chose his victims merely off of chance and circumstance. If he encountered a woman that was in a vulnerable position, he felt this undeniable compulsion to attack. "There's nothing they could've said or done. It was me, it wasn't them," Michael Ross admitted with a solemn tone of voice, years after his final attack, "They were dead as soon as I saw them, I think."

Michael claimed that he only attacked women to relieve pressure that built up from his personal relationships with the women in his life. When he was working in North Carolina, shortly after he graduated from college, Michael recalled that he had a very difficult visit from his fiancé, which caused him to attack a random woman shortly after he dropped his fiancé off at the airport. He noticed a woman walking on the sidewalk with a baby stroller, so Michael pulled the car over and attacked her, using her own child as a weapon. "I told her that if she didn't do what I wanted, I would smash the baby's head against the wall of the house," Michael described in an interview, he seemed as if he were on the verge of tears, "I've always said that I never understood why these women never really resisted me. I'm not a big, strong guy, but nobody ever seemed to fight. I've always just contributed it as I must say something like that, or similar to it, to the other victims." He raped and strangled the woman, then left her for dead in her driveway.

On June 15, 1982, a 23-year-old woman named Debra Smith Taylor was attacked by Michael Ross in a park. He pulled her over where no one could see them, raped her, and forced her to roll over on her stomach; he then strangled her from behind. The young girl's body was discovered much later in a dried up river bed, only a few miles away from the location of another of Ross' victims, Tammy L. Williams. "Each time I killed, I made myself believe that I wasn't going to kill again," Michael Ross explained in an interview. It wasn't very long before he killed again.

His next attack occurred on a cold Thanksgiving Day in 1983. Michael Ross encountered Robin Stavinsky outside of Norwich State Hospital. He saw the woman in a vulnerable position and he took advantage of the situation. He forced the 19-year-old girl into a wooded area and demanded her to remove her clothing. Ross forced himself on the young girl then told her to roll over on her stomach. He strangled her from behind until the innocent Robin

Stavinksky died in his hands. "Serial killers like to strangle their victims and that is, I guess, the most common form of killing because there's more of a connection there. It's more real and it's not as quick," Michael Ross explained why he enjoyed strangling so much. After he was finished with her, he covered her body with leaves and left her for dead.

The Roadside Strangler struck again on Easter Sunday, 1984. April Brunias and Leslie Shelly were hitchhiking on the side of the road when Michael Ross happened to drive their way. He pulled over and offered the young girls a ride. The girls did not find Ross threatening so they got into his car and asked him to drop them off at the next gas station. When Michael passed the gas station, one of the girls drew a kitchen knife and threatened to stab him. In an interview Michael Ross explained what happened next, "I almost drove off of the road, I was so surprised. I don't know what I said, but I said something and she gave the knife to me. It obviously scared her." He parked the car at Beach Pond and used a cloth to bound both of the girls by their hands and feet. He put Leslie Shelly in the trunk of his car, then dragged the girl named April a few feet away from the car. He raped the young girl, flipped her over onto her stomach, and strangled her until she died. He then took Leslie out of the trunk and did the same thing to her. "The smallest one, Leslie Shelly, has always bothered me more than the others. I think it was because she was so small, I think it was because she was so cooperative, and I think it was because the way she was killed was so close to the fantasy. That was the one that was... it was like it was fantasy," Michael explained. The girls were only fourteen years old when they were murdered.

It was a summer afternoon, around three o'clock on June 13, 1984, when the Roadside Strangler committed the murder that would finally get him caught. He was driving home from work when he passed Wendy Baribeault, who was walking down the side of busy Route 12 in Libson, only a few miles away from his home. Michael Ross pulled the car over and began to speak to this 17-year-old girl; he repeatedly invited her to his company picnic. After a little bit of conversation, Michael forced the beautiful, young girl over a stone wall and into the woods. "When I attacked her, I don't believe that I was in control. I don't think I would've been able to stop," Michael Ross explained his mental state during this attack, "I didn't really feel anything. I knew what was going on and I saw what was going on, but it was more like watching an old film..." Michael then raped the innocent girl and strangled her, just like the others, then entombed her in the stone wall that lined the busy road. The road was so busy, in fact, that there were several eyewitnesses to the attack.

The Investigation of the Roadside Strangler

The police had absolutely no leads on the murderer (a.k.a. The Roadside Strangler) that had taken Connecticut by storm. That was until Wendy Baribeault's body was found. There were dozens of eye witnesses to her attack and composite drawings were created that matched the facial features of local Michael Bruce Ross. Witnesses also noted that the attacker was driving a blue Toyota. Michael Malchik, the investigator assigned to the case, compiled a list of several thousand blue Toyotas. This tiny bit of evidence eventually led investigators directly to Ross' house, which was only three miles away from the location of the crime scene. Michael allegedly dropped hints that he was the murderer upon speaking to the police. "It all had to end," Michael Ross explained. It wasn't long before Michael was called into an interview with police in 1984. After a few hours of grueling interrogation, Michael Bruce Ross confessed to all crimes that he'd committed in Connecticut, but left out the murders in New York. "It's a mystery to me to this day, but it's typical of him," stated Detective Malchik, "Here he is, confessing to six murders, and he thought enough ahead not to tell us about the New York ones. Looking back at it, it's obvious he was thinking of something. He was always thinking two steps ahead. He's got his own agenda, but I couldn't for the life of me tell you what it is."

When Michael confessed to the murders, he seemed very sorrowful and remorseful, but he claimed not to feel a blink of remorse, "I don't want to say that I don't have any remorse, it's just like they weren't real..." Michael explains his feelings towards hid victims in a later interview, "I can't see them as I was killing them, so when I say I don't have any remorse, that doesn't mean that I don't have any regrets, or wish that didn't happen, or there was something that I could do to bring them back or anything – I don't have any feelings towards them. I feel like I should be tormented by them - by what they look like when I was killing them – or tormented by what was happening immediately before I killed them – but none of that's there. None of that's there at all."

"The only time he said he was sorry, was that he was sorry for getting caught," Michael's arresting officer explained, "He (Michael Ross) told me matter-of-factly, he said, 'If you hadn't caught me, I would've just kept on killing, again.'" This eerie statement by itself was enough to put the Roadside Strangler to death immediately, but his strange nature kept investigators questioning his motives behind being so upfront and honest about his heinous crimes. Did he secretly want to get caught? Was this all part of some big plot to instill his insanity?

Anne Cournoyer, Michael's correction counselor, described his mannerisms as he spoke of the horrible crimes that he committed, "One minute he's very, you know, looks like he on the verge of crying, and the next minute he's sort of giggling nervously - or sadistically – you just really don't know. You think that maybe, it's out of nervousness, but he could be getting pleasure out of talking about it."

A full-scale investigation of Michael Bruce Ross' life led to the realization of his wavering mental stability. Michael Ross explained that he could never recall the faces of his victims, even directly after the murders, "You'd think that if you killed someone, you would have the face imprinted in your mind and that you wouldn't be able to get it out of your mind – I don't have that. I never had that," He explained, "The only faces I could see was what was in the newspapers a few days later when they were missing. You know, the high school pictures and 'anybody know where this girl is?' type of thing. When I think of them, that's the picture that I see. I don't see them as they were when I killed them. If you had stopped me right after and gave me a composite drawing of like twelve pictures - you know - some blondes, brunettes, whatever – I wouldn't have been able to pick them out. Even immediately after I killed them."

The names of all eight women were: Dzung Ngoc Tu (25), Paula Perrera (16), Tammy Williams (17), Debra Smith Taylor (23), Robin Stavinksy (19), April Brunias (14), Leslie Shelley (14), and Wendy Baribeault (17). He was only charged with the murders of the four Connecticut women because the murders of Dzung Ngoc Tu and Paula Perrera took place in New York. He was sentenced to death on July 6, 1987, but remained on death row for eighteen years after his sanity was called into question.

The Curious Case of Michael Bruce Ross

Michael spent the next eighteen years of his life caught in a battle of the Connecticut justice system. In court, a team of psychiatrists flocked to the defense of Mr. Michael Ross. After a parade of psychiatric evaluation, Michael was deemed mentally unwell, due to his dark childhood and his undeniable compulsions. Dr. Fred Berlin, the well-known co-founder of the Johns Hopkins Sexual Disorder Clinic, testified that Ross was struggling with a mental disorder called sexual sadism. Meaning that he gained sexual excitement from the pain and suffering of others. This discovery alone was not enough to save Ross' life, but Michael's claim to lose all self-control during the murders was enough to set back his execution date. Connecticut's state psychiatrist reluctantly agreed that Ross was not mentally capable enough to be responsible for his own actions, and therefore, it was not right to put him to death. Dr. Robert Miller wrote in a private letter, "I can't see how I could testify against psychopathology playing a sufficient role in defendant's behavior." Although this letter was never presented in court, Michael Ross' death sentence was overturned in 1994 and a new sentencing hearing was scheduled in 2000.

Michael Bruce Ross spent most of his time on death row writing about the mental disorder that took hold of his entire life. Michael claimed to have no control over his actions due to his compulsions. He described his sexual sadism as "a mental illness that drove me to rape and kill" and "made me physically unable to control my actions." During his time in prison, Michael still fell victim to his compulsions. It was impossible for him to control his sexual desires, so he spent the first few months of his incarceration reliving the murders. He claimed that he would fantasize these murders over and over again, hurting himself and causing sores from compulsive masturbation. It wasn't very long before he begged for some type of relief from his sexual desires, which came in the form of chemical castration. Ross was given medication that was designed to lower his testosterone levels and it finally relieved him from his sadistic compulsions. Thanks to this medication, Michael Bruce Ross was finally able to think clearly and he was able to see the true nature of his crimes.

The team of prosecutors naturally disagreed with the defense's attempts to lessen his blame. Prosecutors claimed that if he were unable to control his desires, he would've made less calculated attacks. It was reasonable to assume that Ross experienced these sexual desires constantly, which means that he probably experienced these feelings while in public places, or places where his actions could've been seen and reprimanded. Instead, Ross chose his victims very carefully, only acting when the girls were vulnerable and alone. Disproving the defenses' claims more so was the fact that Ross' hid their bodies after the attack, which further strengthened his blame and the case that he knew precisely what he was doing when he was doing it. "I'm not saying I wasn't there or it was multi-personality or any of that type of crap," Michael Ross later explained the strange fog he experienced while he murdered these innocent women, "I was there and I did it, but I wasn't one hundred percent there." To set light upon Mr. Michael Ross' guilt, Prosecutors relied on the "Policeman at the Elbow" test: would

Ross have committed the crime even if a policeman had been standing next to him?

The defense team immediately disagreed with the statement that all of Ross' attacks were calculated and well thought out, considering the murder of Ms. Wendy B. who was murdered next to a busy road with several eyewitnesses, "When I attacked her, I don't believe I was in control. I don't think I could've stopped." Michael spoke about the murder that eventually resulted in his incarnation. "Could he control himself? Well, two juries rejected that," Detective Malchik recalls, "As the state's attorney said at the trial if Ross was so out of control, why didn't he just rape the girl in between the yellow lines of Route 12? He made it simple for the juries to understand."

John Blume, a professor at the Law school and co-founder of the Cornell Death Penalty Project, noted the how the jury in Ross' case did not take the opinions of the psychological experts seriously. "The thing that's disturbing," Professor Blume stated, "is that even when the experts all say your client is insane, juries will still reject it." Despite the team of psychologists on Ross' side, claiming that he was completely unable to stop himself from committing these monstrosities, the jury chose not to believe them.

Somewhere in the eighteen years of Michael Ross' incarceration, he decided that he did not deserve to live anymore. Shortly after Michael wrote a story called "It's Time for Me to Die", he reconnected with a woman named Kathy Jaeger, who served as his pastoral advocate that converted Ross to Catholicism. Ross wrote in a newsletter that Jaeger, "was able to breach my defenses and was able to touch my soul as no one else ever has." He later called Ms. Kathy Jaeger "the most important woman in my life" and claimed that "If I were a free man, I would ask her to marry me." Although Kathy rejects his claims to romance, she continued to support Michael Ross throughout his decisions.

After she entered Michael's life, there was a great shift in the nature of his case. Michael was done fighting for his life and the mental condition that wreaked havoc on his entire existence. After his original death sentence was overturned in 1994, the court ordered a new penalty hearing, but instead of going through the hearing with his public defenders, Ross acted as his own attorney. He worked with prosecutor C. Robert Satti to created what was deemed as "death pact" that allowed the imposition of the death penalty without a penalty hearing. "Please allow me to go into the courtroom . . . to accept the death penalty as punishment for my actions," Ross wrote in a letter to Satti. "I'm not asking you to do this for me, but for the families involved, who do not deserve to suffer further and who, in some small way, might gain a sense of peace of mind by these actions and my execution." The "death pact" was rejected by the judge as a "short cut" involving a human life, so Michael Ross flip-flopped back into his old ways. Ross returned to his defense team and reverted back into fighting for his life, claiming that his crimes were merely a product of his mental illness. He was resentenced to death soon after.

Jaeger said that Ross's sudden acceptance of death was a sincere attempt to provide closure for the families of his victims, "He told me, 'You know I don't want to do this. But I have to.' He just really felt anguish over what he had done. Really, really harsh anguish and self-loathing. Contrary to media reports, he doesn't want to die. He wishes that the justice system got it right years ago and gave him life sentences because he does have a mental illness. And the sad thing is, if they had done that, the families of his victims wouldn't have been re-victimized [by the ongoing appeals]. Michael is trying, in essence, to save them from any more of that."

Whether his acceptance of the death sentence was sincere, or not, Michael Bruce Ross was sentenced to death by lethal injection on May 13, 2005. He chose not to speak any last words before his death and died peacefully in the execution chair. Some family members believed that his death was too peaceful. Debbie Dupuis, Robin Stavinsky's sister, stated that she thought she would "feel closure" but instead just "felt anger" as she watched Ross simply lay there, go to sleep and die.

The state of Connecticut finally decided to end the life of the Roadside Strangler and put an end to the anguish that the families had to endure. After a very tragic and dark lifetime, Michael Bruce Ross and his sadistic compulsions were finally laid to rest.

Conclusion

Michael Bruce Ross is the type of cold, calculating, manipulative killer that we only read about in horror novels. His crimes almost seem too heartless and brutal to be true, but the victims of the Roadside Strangler would tell you that he is nothing but a cruel reality. In only a few years, Michael assaulted a countless number of women and murdered eight. Although he was only charged with four murders, Ross was forced to withstand eighteen long years of debate over his life sentence. In prison, he transitioned from a vicious killer who was truly non-remorseful for his brutal crimes to a man who seemed to genuinely regret his life choices and the pain that he subjected. Towards the end of his life, Ross begged for removal from his troubled existence, not only for himself but to end the long and grueling process of the legal system. Despite his transition into humanity, Michael Bruce Ross never took full blame for his actions. He flip-flopped between blaming his childhood, his compulsions, and his interpersonal relationships for these terrible crimes. He claimed to never feel any guilt or remorse for his actions, simply because he wasn't completely there while they were taking place. During these attacks, Michael claims that he was under some type of spell, some type of fog that completely disconnected him from his actions. He was completely able to murder and rape these innocent women without feeling guilt or remorse, or even being able to recall the very faces of his victims', only moments after their attack. Michael Ross was an extremely troubled man who suffered from a very extreme case of sexual sadism. Michael explained his cruel, heartless, attacks with vivid details and an undetached tone of voice. The scariest part about his calm demeanor is the monotone way that he described the way he stole the lives of these young, innocent women. He speaks as if he were not responsible for killing these beautiful and young women, although he willingly confesses to the murders. He claimed that he was merely a victim of his sexual compulsions since his college years and the women he attacked were merely in the wrong place at the wrong time. Whether his desires were really uncontrollable or if it was merely an excuse, Michael Bruce Ross' case remains to be one of the most perplexing cases in American history. His mere mental condition was enough to perplex the entire state of Connecticut – how could this well-spoken, articulate man with such a great personality, commit these terrible crimes? Why didn't anyone notice his decline and stop it? What was it that made this seemingly normal man snap into the Roadside Strangler? Although the answers to these questions are uncertain, they definitely are unnerving. Michael Ross was created by circumstances, by his dark upbringing, and a lifetime of people letting him slip through the cracks. Everyone saw him as an average, everyday college student, so no one thought to ask. The woman that he murdered were sadly only stepping stones into the downward spiral into his sickness and they were eventually caused the end of his vicious, murderous cycle.

STOCKWELL STRANGLER : The True Story of Kenneth Erskine

NATALIE MARSHALL

Kenneth Erskine, known as "The Stockwell Strangler" due to the geographic proximities of his murders, was a deeply troubled young man who had demonstrated worrisome signs of violence and schizophrenia from a young age. He was a gerontophile in that he had an unnatural sexual attraction to the elderly. Gerontophilia, essentially, is the opposite of pedophilia. Erskine would break into elderly men's and women's London flats and strangle them while they were in bed; after which he would rape and/or sodomize most of them. To demonstrate his own warped sense of love for his victims he would cross their arms across their chest, close their eyes, and tuck them into bed. Also, perhaps to hide his shame, he would turn his victims' family photographs face down. There was much speculation among mental health professionals that Erskine also suffered from schizophrenia from a very young age.

He was eventually convicted of seven murders and one attempted murder and sentenced to life in prison in 1988 at the age of 25. However, in July 2009, following an appeal his murder convictions were reduced to manslaughter on the grounds of diminished capacity and he received a hospital order to serve his life sentences at Broadmoor Hospital. While he has the potential to be granted parole in 2028, the trial judge's original order was that Erskine should spend at least 40 years behind bars, thus making him at least 65 years of age before potential eligibility for release.

Early Life

Kenneth Erskine was born in Hammersmith, London in July 1963. His mother Margaret was British and his father Charles was from Antigua. He was one of four boys, had an average IQ when tested at eight years old, and was remembered by neighbors to be a "chubby, Bible reading soul"; however, he became increasingly violent and difficult to control. For example, as a child, Erskine had tried to hang his younger brother, John, twice.

Erskine was then sent to a series of schools for maladjusted and troubled children where he received his formal education. He frequently and violently attacked his teachers and classmates and was identified as inhabiting a fantasy world with murderous impulses. In his own private fantasy world he would take on the role of Lawrence of Arabia, attacking and tying up smaller and weaker children—a theme that would resurface when he targeted the weaker elderly during his murder spree. During a school-sponsored swimming outing he had attempted to drown several classmates by holding their heads under the water until teachers were forced to intervene. He set fires at school and once pushed a classmate off of a moving bus. On another occasion he stabbed a teacher in the hand with a pair of scissors. In another event, a psychiatric nurse who tried to examine Erskine was taken hostage by him as he held a pair of scissors to her throat. He strangled the classroom guinea pig. Whenever any female staff tried to be empathetic and show him any type of affection he would expose his genitals or rub up against them.

There was frequent talk that Erskine demonstrated clear signs and symptoms of schizophrenia as a teenager but nothing ever came out of it. He never had therapy or medication or any real psychiatric evaluation.

By the time Erskine was 16 years of age he had turned to drugs and particularly enjoyed inhalants. This latest display of misbehavior was too much for his mother who eventually kicked him out of the house, forcing him to survive on his own. When Erskine tried to give his younger brother marijuana she finally disowned him. He never saw any of his family members ever again and was forced to spend the next seven years of his life "drifting through the twilight world of London's homeless and rootless" living in squats and hostels in Brixton and Stockwell and getting involved with petty crime which primarily took the shape of failed burglaries on primarily the elderly.

Erskine's violent tendencies continued to worsen.

When he was 18 he stabbed a young male with whom he was having a homosexual relationship at the time. Erskine had burst into his boyfriend's bedroom and stabbed and slashed at his body while he lay in bed. Whereas this may have been the first attack of someone in bed it was a glaring omen of the terror he would wreak in six years.

Erskine was described my many who knew him as a persistent loner who drifted through life and due to no direction of any type of social support system started a life of crime. Erskine was also a Rastafarian due to his Caribbean heritage but was shunned by fellow Rastafarians due to his habit of theft.

An unsuccessful burglar, he was jailed on many occasions.

Among Erskine's favorite "drugs" were solvents—such as glue—which he would inhale. Among the most oft-cited short term effects of huffing glue are hallucinations, delusions, and hostility. Long-term effects include depression, irritability, memory impairment, diminished intelligence, and serious and sometimes irreversible brain damage. There continues to be speculation as to whether Erskine was born with his psychopathic tendencies (nature) or whether his upbringing and environmental stimuli were to blame for his problems (nurture). The consensus is that a combination of factors worked together to create Erskine's sick and murderous persona.

Erskine subsequently spent considerable time in Borstals—youth detention centers—due to being apprehended following his many failed burglaries. While in one for burglary in 1982 Erskine would paint and draw pictures of elderly people in bed with gags in their mouths, with daggers in them, or burned to death. Additional pieces of "artwork" included headless figures with blood spurting out from their necks, people holding human hearts in their hands, disemboweled people, screaming faces, and copious pools of blood. Again, this was a chilling omen of what was to come. In one documentary about Kenneth Erskine and his crimes, one of his cellmates at Borstal, named James, described how horrific Erskine's paintings were and how he would frequently smile and laugh while painting them. As Erskine's only "friend" James became his confidant as well. The two would play chess to pass the time and then there were Erskine's disturbing paintings. James stated in an interview that Erskine always spoke very quietly—rarely above a whisper—and was very weird.

Borstal doctors were concerned enough to the point of asking the authorities not to ever free Erskine because they were seriously worried that he might try to replicate his paintings; however, he was, in fact, released and four years later he would begin his killing spree.

The Crimes

At some point Erskine decided to act out his fantasies and began to murder. He is classified as a geographically-stable serial killer who confined his murders to a specific area. As Erskine had no vehicle and roamed around the Stockwell area frequently confining his murders to this area was likely due to simple necessity.

The Stockwell section of South London is a favored place for the elderly to retire. In the summer of 1986, however, a serial killer conducted a reign of terror throughout the community that resulted in seven known deaths—and possibly another four—attributable to The Stockwell Strangler.

Eileen Nancy Emms, 78

Emms was a 78-year-old retired schoolteacher who lived in an "unkempt basement flat" on West Hill Road in Wandsworth. She was sexually assaulted and strangled by Erskine on 6 April 1986.

Emms' body was found on 9 April 1987 by her home help who, upon knocking on her bedroom door and receiving no response one morning, let herself in to find Emms in bed with the covers pulled up to her chin, seemingly asleep. There were no obvious marks upon her body. Initially, the cause of death was attributed to natural causes. The doctor called to the scene estimated that she died approximately three days earlier and signed a death certificate that stated natural causes.

Once the victim's home help noticed that her small portable television was missing, the police were called.

During her autopsy, the medical examiner revealed that Emms had been strangled by bare hands. There was heavy bruising to her chest which strongly suggested that her assailant had kneeled atop her while strangling her. Further examination revealed that she had been sodomized as the assailant had left semen around her anus.

A short Afro-Caribbean head hair was found on her sheet.

Janet Crockett, 67

Janet Crockett was Erskine's first July 1987 victim. She was chairwoman of her local tenant's association. Her body was found on 9 June in her flat in the Overton Estate in Stockwell. She had been strangled but, unlike Erskine's first victim—and subsequent ones—she was not sexually assaulted.

Police were able to immediately conclude that she had been murdered as she had considerable bruising on her chest due to sustaining two broken ribs as a result of someone kneeling on her while she was strangled to death. Additionally, her nightgown had been ripped from her body and folded neatly and placed upon a bedside chair.

Police also noticed that framed family photographs on the bedroom mantel had been placed face down or turned around. This action would be repeated at several of his crime scenes and speculation abounds as to what Erskine's underlying motive for doing this was. Some psychological experts have surmised that his anger at his own parents' rejection without a healthy outlet for his emotions led to an insane jealousy of normal family ties. Another hypothesis was that he felt ashamed at his actions and didn't want any "witnesses."

Police were able to find a smudged thumbprint on a displaced planter and a palm print on the bathroom window.

Pathologist Dr. Iain West conducted Crockett's autopsy and compared it to Emms. He concluded that their methods of strangulation were similar. He stated that with weaker elderly victims unconsciousness would occur within 30 second and death after approximately three minutes. While Crockett's and Emms' murders were similar—and that they were both elderly—police had nothing else to link the two victims.

Frederick Prentice, 73

In the early hours of 27 June, 73-year-old retired engineer Frederick Prentice was asleep in his council-run elderly people's home on Cedars Road in Clapham when he was awakened by the sounds of someone entering his bedroom. He saw a young man enter and Prentice turned on his bedside lamp and ordered the intruder to leave. Erskine then pounced atop the old man, placed his index finger to his own mouth as a threat for Prentice to be quiet, and then sat upon his chest where he alternated squeezing his windpipe powerfully, then relaxing his grip, and repeated this multiple times. Prentice told police that his assailant had whispered only one word over and over: "Kill." Prentice was able to push the alarm button near his bed which caused his assailant to leave.

After talking to Prentice the police were fairly confident that all of the victims thus far were, in fact, linked. A shoeprint found at the scene would also serve to connect this attack with some of the other murders.

Prentice would later identify Erskine in a lineup.

Valentine Gleim, 84, and Zbigniew Stabrawa, 94

The next day Erskine murdered 84-year-old World War II veteran Valentine Gleim and 94-year-old Polish immigrant Zbigniew Stabrawa in their adjoining rooms at Somerville Hastings House, an old folks' home on Stockwell Park Crescent. Both men had been manually strangled and sodomized.

The intruder had been seen by alert night duty staff but had vanished before the police arrived. Point of entry was, again, determined to be an open window. Staff were also able to see Erskine fleeing the scene and estimated his height at approximately five-feet-eight-inches with a slim frame so at least now investigators had a clue about their suspect.

Of particular concern in these two cases was the discovery of a used flannel towel and electric shaver which suggested that the murderer had calmly washed up and shaved after killing two people.

Approximately one hour prior to the double homicide an elderly woman in a Stockwell old folks' home was attacked while she was in bed by a man grabbing her arm. She fought off her assailant so vehemently that he had to run off. Her description of Erskine matched Prentice's.

William Carmen, 82

Two weeks after his previous double homicide, Erskine struck again by strangling and sexually assaulting 82-year-old widower William Carmen on 8 July. This time he threw a monkey wrench at detectives by murdering on the other side of the Thames river, in Islington, North London. Carmen was discovered dead in his bed in his flat on the Marques Estate by his daughter. As was the case with Erskine's other victims, Carmen was in bed with the covers pulled up neatly to his chin and had been sodomized.

This time there was clear evidence of ransacking and theft as approximately £400 of Carmen's savings was missing. Family photos were also placed face down or turned around.

William Downes, 74

On 20 July the body of 74-year-old William Downes was found by his son in his Holles House on Overton Road flat in Brixton; the same location where Erskine's second victim, Crockett, lived. He was naked and in bed with the covers pulled up to his chin, his eyes closed, and his arms folded across his chest—classic Erskine signature. Downes' son had reminded him to keep his windows locked firmly at night a few days ago so as not to fall victim to the Strangler but he failed to heed these instructions and point of entry was, again, determined to be through an unlocked window.

Downes had been strangled and sexually assaulted like the majority of Erskine's other victims. There were semen stains on the sheets.

Investigators lifted a palm print from the kitchen wall and another from the garden gate which were eventually matched to the prints found at Crockett's home. Finding the owner of these prints, however, was not as easy as the process is today. In 1986, while fingerprints were on file on computer discs at Scotland Yard, palm prints were not. Investigators had a stack of four million files; however, by concentrating on London-based burglars and petty thieves, they were able to compile a more workable load. They were subsequently able to match the prints to those Erskine, a small-time crook with an extensive rap sheet for burglary.

Unfortunately, the police did not know where to find Erskine and while they were looking he struck again, killing his final victim.

Florence Tisdall, 80

80-year-old partially blind and deaf Florence Tisdall was found in her apartment at Ranelagh Gardens near Putney Bridge on 24 July. The caretaker of the apartments noticed her walker in the communal corridor and knew something was wrong as Tisdall was unable to get around without it. He found her strangled, sexually assaulted, and with broken ribs as a result of her killer sitting atop her chest. She had spent the previous day watching the televised wedding of the Duke and Duchess of York—Prince Andrew and Sarah Ferguson—even having her own hair done especially for the big event. Tisdall had lived in an almost empty block of flats where she had resided for the past 60 years. A cat lady, she had left her windows open so the cats could come and go as they pleased and this is how Erskine got into her flat.

It was at this scene where Erskine made, perhaps, his biggest mistake. Detectives knew immediately that Tisdall had been murdered because she was found in her nightgown, tucked into bed with the covers up by her chin. In reality, however, Tisdall's neighbors who frequently checked on her because of her disabilities stated that she always slept atop the covers in the clothing she had been wearing that day. When Erskine undressed Tisdall to rape her, he attempted to cover up his misdeeds by making it look as though she went to bed as usual and died of natural causes. Family photos were also placed face down or turned around as was the case at the Crockett crime scene.

One of Tisdall's neighbors stated that she saw Erskine near the victim's flat shortly after the murder had occurred "looking disgusted with himself." Thinking this to be odd she promptly notified the police.

All of Erskine's victims were pensioners and in all but one case there was evidence of sexual assault that took the form of sodomy; however, investigators and forensic specialists cannot say whether it occurred before or after the victims' death.

Investigation and Arrest

After the Crockett murder, Scotland Yard's Serious Crimes Squad Detective Chief Superintendent Ken Thompson—a Scotsman with 26 years' experience—was put in charge of the case and given over 200 detectives to devote to the search for The Stockwell Strangler. Interestingly, Erskine was originally nicknamed "The Heatwave Killer" because the murders occurred during the summer; however, when the majority of his murders occurred in and around Stockwell this nickname was changed. Further, plainclothes officers would stand guard throughout the night wherever the elderly lived.

At the height of the investigation, as many as 350 law enforcement officers were on the Strangler case which included 150 detectives and senior officers from the C1 Murder Squad who worked out of five separate incident rooms throughout London which were linked to a special Home Office computer. This network was called HOLMUS and was used to prevent wasting time by cross checking paperwork which proved to be detrimental to the investigation for Peter Sutcliff, The Yorkshire Ripper. Other police officers set up fixed observation points in neighborhoods with a high population of elderly residents and instituted extra patrols.

A psychologist was enlisted to create a profile of the Strangler and to provide potential insight into his signature to determine whether he was attempting to cover his tracks or was fulfilling some bizarre fantasy. The suspect was determined to be suffering from gerontophilia; or a sexual attraction to the elderly and the complete opposite of its better known opposite, pedophilia. Speculation abounded as to whether the killer's sexual paraphilia was a result of some relationship problems with his grandparents. Additionally, as his victims were all selected at random, authorities could not link the victims together with the hopes of finding some commonality between them that would enable them to identify and apprehend the man responsible.

The suspect was classified as a process-focused serial killer. The majority of serial killers are of this type; the other being act-focused wherein their own psychological gratification from the kill itself is the underlying cause. Instead, process-focused killers achieve a hedonistic psychological "reward." These types frequently "get off" on the method of their kill and they enjoy the perverse sexual thrill that accompanies the act of killing. The literature identifies four types of process-focused serial killers: gain in which the killer kills for profit or personal gain; thrill in which the act of killing gives the killer a rush or a high; power in which the killer enjoys dominating and manipulating victims and while sex is usually involved it is primarily tertiary to the kill itself; and lust wherein murder is associated with sexual pleasure and this type of killer will commonly have sex while in the process or killing or may engage in necrophilia after death. As far as Erskine is concerned, he can be classified in multiple subtypes. First, since he did rob his victims and steal money he demonstrates some elements of the gain process-focused serial killer. Secondly, he did obtain a rush or high from killing his victims and, therefore, does demonstrate some elements of a thrill killer. This element is particularly salient when he was seen by a witness—who would later testify against him—getting sick on the sidewalk after his final kill near where his last victim was found. The act of his getting sick appears to be directly attributed to the thrill her received from killing and having sex with his victim. Finally, since Erskine likely sodomized his victims after he killed them his sexual fantasies were of a higher priority than is typically the case for power killers. Thus, he demonstrates elements more aligned with a lust killer.

Coupled with the fact that Erskine targeted the same type of people and that he engaged in specific rituals which were part of his signature makes Erskine a classic serial killer. His smaller size likely contributed to his choice of the elderly as his victims because in their weakened conditions he wouldn't have much trouble overpowering them.

The palm prints were the most damning evidence investigators had at that point; however, they only placed Erskine at two of the murder scenes. Despite similarities among all of the victims' crime scenes, the fact that Erskine wasn't cooperating with police required detectives to find other evidence. Investigators from Scotland Yard took the unusual step of distributing his Erskine's picture to the media to try to find more witnesses and potential leads by hopefully jog people's memories as to whether anyone may remember seeing him. Thompson also did something very uncommon; he appeared on television, appealing to Erskine to turn himself in.

After Tisdall's death the search for Erskine intensified even more than was already the case; however, being that he was a drifter with no permanent address or any real belongings to speak of they had to search through the hundreds of hostels and squats in South London. His life was so devoid of meaning and friends to help detectives find him.

Investigators got their big break when they realized that since the suspect was likely unemployed that he would be receiving social security and unemployment benefits. Upon further investigation they discovered that Erskine picked up his benefits on alternating Mondays from a Department of Health and Social Security office in Southwark, South London, and that he was due to collect his next check on 28 July. The building was placed under surveillance and when Erskine turned up, right on time, he was arrested and handcuffed without any struggle.

Whereas items and cash from the victims' homes were, in fact, missing, police did not believe that robbery was the driving motive in the homicides. There were neither signs of struggle nor any signs of forced entry. Police surmised that Erskine entered the flats through unsecured windows.

Forensic evidence linking the cases relied upon the fact that the victims were all murdered in similar ways: by the assailant kneeling on the victims' chests and then placing his left hand over their mouths and strangling them with his right hand. The semen collected at nearly all crime scenes suggested the same genetic fingerprint in that the same suspect was responsible for all of the sexual assaults. Additionally, there was a single hair found in Emms' flat, as well as matching shoeprints from three of the scenes.

A hairdresser informed investigators that Erskine had approached her wanting his head and pubic hair bleached. While she agreed to the former she refused the latter. Apparently, while he was sitting in the shop waiting for the bleach to take effect he self-applied the bleach to his pubic region and eyebrows, the latter resulting in his getting chemicals in his eyes and requiring assistance in washing it out.

When questioned by Detective Inspector Brian Jackson and other detectives, Erskine's responses indicated that the detectives' jobs were to be much more difficult than they thought. Erskine spent the majority of the interrogation giggling, staring out of the window or into the sky, or masturbating. After he was arrested, psychologists placed Erskine's mental age at 11 even though he was 24 at the time. He had first denied that he was, indeed, The Stockwell Strangler claiming instead to be a petty burglar who had no motive to kill anyone. After vehemently denying his culpability and blameworthiness in the string of murders and seeing that he wasn't getting anywhere, Erskine then changed his tune and said, "I don't remember killing anyone. I could have done it without knowing it. I am not sure if I did it." He also tried to blame the murders on a whispering female voice in his head. He once stated,

"It tries to think for me. It says it will kill me if it gets me," and, "It blanks things from my mind."

He was clearly disturbed but not a fool in any sense. In fact, when searched, detectives found ten bank and building society accounts that Erskine had opened to hide the proceeds of his crimes. During the three-month span of murders, he had deposited over £3,000; quite a large sum of money for someone who was unemployed. This included a £350 deposit into one of his accounts on the morning after the Carmen murder. It was evident at this point that Erskine was amassing profits from his burglaries while simultaneously collecting unemployment benefits. This demonstrated that whereas Erskine did suffer from some degree of mental retardation and likely some psychosexual paraphilia he was not stupid by any means. In fact, he told detectives that his motive was to achieve notoriety. He said, "I wanted to be famous ... I thought I would never get caught."

During a lineup—or identity parade as it is called in England—surviving victim Frederick Prentice was able to definitively identify Erskine. Another woman who had witnessed Erskine vomiting on the sidewalk near Putney Bridge a mere 200 yards from the scene of the final murder on the night in question also picked Erskine out of a lineup.

Trial and Conviction

Erskine's trial commenced at the Old Bailey on 12 January 1988. He pled not guilty to the charges of seven murders and the attempted murder of Prentice. During his trial he would stare out the window or down at his feet as was the case when he was interrogated. When details of the murders were brought up, Erskine would masturbate.

The jury heard him confess to the burglaries of the deceased victims; however, he claimed that someone else must have followed him and killed the individuals after he had left. Nobody was buying this story.

After an 18-day trial, the jury unanimously found him guilty on all eight counts and he was sentenced to seven life terms plus 12 years for attempted murder with a recommended minimum of 40 years; one of the heaviest penalties ever handed out in British legal history. However, diagnosis of schizophrenia and other mental illnesses pursuant to the Mental Health Act of 1983 led to a successful appeal of Erskine's murder charges which were eventually reduced to manslaughter. He is currently serving his time at the Broadmoor Hospital.

In addition to his seven known victims, the police suspected Erskine of four other murders for which he has never been charged due to insufficient evidence to prove that he was, in fact, the murderer.

John Jordan, 57

On 4 February 1986, 57-year-old John Jordan was found in his Josephine Avenue flat in Brixton strangled beside his bed.

Charles Quarrell, 73

73-year-old Charles Quarrell was found suffocated in his bed on King James Street in Suffolk on 6 May. He had two handkerchiefs stuffed into the back of his throat, effectively blocking his windpipe.

Wilfred Parkes, 70

70-year-old Wilfred Parkes was found on 28 May in his Stockwell flat, suffocated and in bed. A nearby pillow was presumed to have been the murder weapon.

Trevor Thomas, 75

On 12 July 75-year-old Trevor Thomas was found dead in the bath at his home on Barton Court, Clapham. As Thomas had been dead for quite a while there was inadequate forensic evidence for investigators to link his murder to the others; thus resulting in Erskine not being charged with his death even though Thomas was almost certainly one of his victims.

As mentioned, Erskine has never been charged with these additional deaths; however, police were so confident that Erskine murdered them that they effectively closed the book on all of these cases. There is also much speculation that he likely killed prior to his first known victim—such as was the case with Mr. Jordan—and that because of his choice of victims their deaths may have simply been attributed to natural causes.

Aftermath

There is not much more information on Erskine due to a lack of any detailed studies of him as is commonly the case with other serial killers where the literature is rife with speculation as to what influences led to the individual turning to serial murder. His only possessions were meager clothes and some books from the building society. Other than a post-arrest diagnosis of schizophrenia, the mind of Kenneth Erskine remains mostly shrouded in mystery. In fact, his mentally-disturbed state has worsened to the point where he has been told that he will never be released from Broadmoor Hospital.

Psychiatrists have never been able to fully penetrate his mind and discover what makes him tick. He clearly has a problem differentiating fantasy from reality and appears to be locked in his own childlike world. However, there is one incident that clearly demonstrates his understanding between right and wrong. On 23 February 1996, Erskine prevented the possible murder of Peter Sutcliffe, known as the "Yorkshire Ripper" by alerting guards while another inmate, Paul Wilson, attempted to strangle Sutcliffe with the flexible cord from a pair of stereo headphones. Erskine was able to restrain Wilson from inflicting further injury upon Sutcliffe until guards arrived.

Erskine found himself on the receiving end of an assault. On Christmas Eve in 1997 he was attacked by fellow inmate, 34-year-old Keith Hanger. Hanger was serving time for the 1992 shooting of his friend after having escaped from prison. He walked up to Erskine and squirted liquid from an aerosol can into his face before lighting it with a lighter. Erskine was taken to Frimley Park Hospital in Surrey, in agonizing pain and worried that he would lose his eyesight; however, his temporary blindness was just that—temporary.

Psychiatrists continue to attempt to probe Erskine's mind trying to uncover more and more of his psyche toward, perhaps, finding what makes him tick. Currently, he is unable to answer for his crimes, as demonstrated by the reduced sentence due to diminished capacity.

THE BOSTON STRANGLER

94

NATALIE MORTON

Albert DeSalvo, the infamous "Boston Strangler" is considered to be "America's first 'serial killer' of the modern era". He is responsible for as many as 13 women's murders in the Boston area between 14 June 1962 and 4 January 1964. Victims were as young as 19 and as old as 85. Whereas police did not believe that all of the murders were committed by the same person, the public was convinced that one person, dubbed "The Boston Strangler", was the sole suspect.

During the hunt for the Boston Strangler, police were also investigating two separate strings of rapes committed by the "Measuring Man" and, later, the "Green Man"; both of whom were, in fact, DeSalvo. He was arrested on 27 October 1964. At the time DeSalvo was not connected to the murders; however, likely due to his insatiable thirst for infamy and attention, he confessed that he was. He was sentenced to life in prison in January 1967, and was stabbed to death while in prison in November 1973.

There continue to be doubts as to whether DeSalvo was truly the Boston Strangler. In 2001, DNA evidence proved that the semen left in his last victim's body was not DeSalvo's. Thus, the cases of the Boston Strangler—as well as why DeSalvo was murdered and who committed it—continue to remain open.

Early Life

Albert Henry DeSalvo was born on 3 September 1931—the third of six children—in the poor town of Chelsea, Massachusetts, to Frank and Charlotte DeSalvo. The DeSalvo children, particularly Albert, had miserable childhoods. Frank was a violent alcoholic who would bring prostitutes home and have sex with them in front of his wife and children. On one occasion Frank broke his wife's fingers, one by one, by bending them backward and knocked out all of her teeth. Frank was also physically abusive with his children and allegedly once sold young Albert and two of his sisters as slaves to a farmer who paid $9.00 for all three of them.

The details of the following six months are unclear as DeSalvo never talked about it.

Not having any healthy relationship upon which to use as a model, DeSalvo desperately sought the love of women. He claims that he and his siblings experimented with sex acts as young as five years old and that he started having sex at age eight with girls and women, in addition to prostituting himself to homosexuals. During his adolescence, DeSalvo was exposed to graphic sexuality; from his father's activities with prostitutes to his neighbors who were very promiscuous and who DeSalvo watched whenever he could and this likely had a huge impact on his sexual development and resulting paraphilia.

DeSalvo started school at age six and due to several childhood illnesses missed much school which resulted in his failing second grade and being placed into special education classes when he was in fifth grade. He graduated junior high school at age 16 and that was the end of his formal education.

As a child, DeSalvo tortured animals—one of the triad factors common to serial killers and present in 36% of serial murderers in an FBI study—and as a young adolescent he committed shoplifting and thefts, common to 81% of serial killers in the same study. As a result, DeSalvo had many run-ins with the law.

He began working at the age of 12; performing odd jobs such as delivering flowers and shining shoes in an effort to make life easier for his siblings who he loved very much. In fact, despite the violence and brutality for which he would be later known, he was very docile with his family members; even when provoked.

At age 16 he worked in a Cape Cod motel as a dishwasher and, in his free time, would watch couples making out through windows. His first sexual aberration was as a voyeur.

At this time, on 12 November 1943, DeSalvo was arrested for the first time; for battery and robbery of a newspaper boy—over

$2.85. He did receive a suspended sentence from incarceration but was sent to the Lyman School for Boys the following month. His IQ was tested while there and was 93; low-average. He commented after his arrest that one "can learn about every form of sexual perversion" in reform school. After his parole in October 1944, he obtained employment as a delivery boy; however, in August 1946 he was returned to the Lyman School for stealing a car.

When he was released the second time, at the age of 17 and with nothing more than a junior high school diploma, DeSalvo joined the Army and worked as a military police officer. During his time in the military he had a reputation for being obsessively clean and a self-proclaimed ladies' man who bragged about his many affairs with officers' wives. While he was getting the sex he craved, he said he didn't have the love he also wanted. In Germany DeSalvo met and fell in love with a young woman named Irmgard and they married in 1949.

Irmgard often complained that her husband's libido was too high and she did not want to have sex with him as often as he wanted it. She was also distressed by DeSalvo's common practice of masturbating frequently, sometimes even after they had just had intimate relations. His sexual problems would increase when he, Irmgard, and their infant daughter—Judy, born in 1955—returned to the United States after DeSalvo was honorably discharged from the Army in 1956. Judy had been born with a congenital pelvic disorder that caused a deformity in her legs which kept them in a permanent frog-like position so she required special braces. DeSalvo would massage her little legs and would tie bows around her braces.

The family settled in Fort Dix, New Jersey, where, less than one year later, on 5 January 1955, he was accused of molesting a nine-year-old girl while her mother ran out for a quick grocery trip. DeSalvo was apprehended and charged with carnal abuse of a child and released on $1,000 bail; however all charges were dropped when the mother did not want to subject her young daughter to having to testify in court.

The family moved to Boston to get a fresh start. DeSalvo took whatever jobs he could find; at a shoe factory, a shipyard, and then settled into construction work.

In 1959, the DeSalvos had a son, Michael.

DeSalvo was very restless working odd jobs but his lack of experience or education precluded him from finding anything he would consider to be better. DeSalvo always had a lust for infamy and he was already headed down that pathway.

The "Measuring Man" and "Green Man" Rapes

DeSalvo's "career" as a sexual predator began in 1961 when he pretended to be a representative of a black-and-white modeling agency and approached young women telling them that he had to take their measurements to see if they would fit the clothing. He would tell them that he was authorized to give them each $10 for taking measurements; $15 for doing so with the women clad only in a bra and panties, and $25 if they were nude, which would facilitate his sweet-talking himself into their beds for sex. However, some women complained to the police of his unwelcomed and inappropriate touching.

At this time, DeSalvo was also perfecting his breaking and entering techniques and was arrested for burglary; however, much like his earlier crimes, he managed to receive suspended sentences. However, DeSalvo made a serious misstep when, on 16 March 1961, he was arrested for burglary and, in an effort to self-aggrandize himself, told the police about his measuring "scheme". As would be expected, DeSalvo was promptly arrested for breaking and entering, assault and battery, and lewdness and was faced—for the first time in his life—with a prison sentence. In exchange for a guilty plea to the first two charges, the prosecutor agreed to drop the lewdness charges.

DeSalvo served 11 months in prison and was released in April, 1962. When asked why he perpetrated his "pathetic charade" DeSalvo said that he was neither good-looking nor educated but "was able to put something over on high-class people" and that he was able to outsmart college kids.

The first Boston Strangler murder would occur a mere two months later.

In May 1964, after the Strangler struck for the last time, there was another string of rapes in Boston, courtesy of DeSalvo. In this, his latest scheme, he was dubbed the "Green Man" because he would wear a workman's green overalls in order to gain access into single women's apartments under the guise that he was there to fix a leak or check something allegedly broken or whatever. Once inside, he would bind and sometimes rape the women. Occasionally he would ejaculate prematurely after he bound them and would then apologize and loosen their bindings. On some occasions he would also apologize to his victims when tying them up, telling them he had to fulfill "the urge." He never killed anyone during this time. Four victims went to the police and, as luck would have it, one police officer remembered DeSalvo from his "Measuring Man" assaults.

When the murders surfaced, the city of Boston's residents were terrified not simply because there was a serial killer on the loose but that the victims were not prostitutes or vagrants or some other type of "unsavory" character but respectable, middle-aged or elderly women who were attacked in their own homes. Things worsened when the murderer began targeting young women too.

The Murders

Initially, the Boston Strangler targeted elderly or middle-aged women; however, by December 1962, he had turned his attention to younger women with two victims being in their 20s.

While the manhunt for the Strangler was going on, Boston women were gripped by tremendous fear. Dogs were adopted from shelters in record numbers and hardware stores quickly sold out of deadbolt locks. Because there was never any indication of forced entry, police could tell women to be extra aware; however, the killings continued.

Anna Siesers, 55

In the evening of 14 June 1962, 55-year-old Latvian seamstress Anna Siesers was preparing a quick after-dinner bath before getting ready for her son, Juris, to pick her up for a church memorial service. The petite divorcee looked younger than her age would indicate and had left Latvia over a decade earlier with her son and daughter, relocating to the Black Bay area of Boston on 77 Gainsborough Street.

There was a knock at her door.

When her son arrived an hour later and could not get his mother to answer the door, he forced the door open and found her lying dead on the bathroom floor with the belt from her housecoat tied around her neck.

Boston Police officers James Mellon and John Driscoll found Siesers in a "shockingly exposed position": outstretched, on her back, her blue taffeta housecoat completely open, in a grotesque position with her legs spread apart. Her head was a few feet from the open bathroom door and the cord from her housecoat knotted tightly around her neck with the ends tied into a bow. This bow would become a signature of the Boston Strangler and some speculate that it had something to do with the bows DeSalvo would tie on his daughter's leg braces. There were also signs that Siesers was sexually assaulted with some unknown object.

The murderer made it look as though he ransacked her apartment; however, nothing of value was taken.

At first, police believed that the crime likely began as a burglary and when he saw the victim in her housecoat he couldn't control himself, sexually assaulted her, and then killed her so he couldn't be identified.

This first murder was highly organized and proficient. DeSalvo confessed that he parked his car blocks away, wore gloves, disposed of his bloodied clothing quickly, and engaged in conversation with someone on the street as an alibi.

Mary Mullen, 85

On 28 June 1962, DeSalvo knocked on 85-year-old Mary Mullen's door under the guise that he was there to do some repairs on her apartment. Of particular interest was that most of his victims' apartments were of lower-rent and always in need of some type of repair so the residents had little reason to disbelieve anything that he told them.

`DeSalvo said that when she turned her back to him he put his arm around her neck and that she must have died quickly from a heart attack. He left her body on the sofa and investigators ruled her death as from natural causes until DeSalvo confessed to having a role in it years later.

Nina Nichols, 68

Just two days later on 30 June, at 1940 Commonwealth Avenue in Brighton, retired physiotherapist and widow Nina Nichols, 68, met her unfortunate fate at the hands of the Strangler. She was talking on the telephone to her sister when her door buzzer rang. Nichols told her sister—who also heard the buzzer—she would call her back soon but never did.

Like Siesers, Nichols' apartment had been ransacked but nothing was taken. She was found with her housecoat and slip pulled up to her waist and her legs were spread. Two of her own nylon stockings were tied tightly around her neck with the ends culminating in a bow. She had been sexually assaulted with a wine bottle and there was seminal fluid on her thighs.

Time of death was determined to be around 5:00 p.m.

Helen Blake, 65

That same day, 15 miles north of Boston in Lynn, Massachusetts, 65-year-old Helen Blake was strangled with one of her nylons and her bra had also been tied around her neck and fashioned into a bow.

She was discovered face-down on her bed, naked, with vaginal and anal lacerations but no sign of seminal fluid.

Nichols' apartment had been ransacked and nothing was taken except for the two diamond rings she had been wearing. The murderer had also unsuccessfully tried to open a metal strongbox and footlocker.

Ida Irga, 75

The next time the Strangler struck was nearly two months later on 21 August, with 75-year-old "shy and retiring widow" Ida Irga his latest victim. She was found dead two days later at her apartment at 7 Grove Avenue in Boston's West End. Up until-and including this time—there were no signs of forced entry, indicating that she had likely voluntarily let the murderer in.

Sergeant James McDonald described how he found Irga: on her back on the living room floor, clad in a light brown nightdress that was torn, thus exposing her body. A white pillowcase was knotted tightly around her neck and her legs were spread open with her feet propped upon individual chairs, facing the door so her displayed body was the first thing anyone saw when they entered her apartment. A bed pillow was placed under her buttocks. There was evidence of sexual assault but no spermatozoa were present.

The pillowcase had been tied so tightly that she had dried blood inside of her ears and around her mouth. This would be common with most of the Strangler's victims.

Jane Sullivan, 67

On 30 August, nurse Jane Sullivan, 67, was found, murdered, in her apartment at 435 Columbia Road in Dorchester. She had been dead approximately ten days before she was discovered.

Police found Sullivan "on her knees in her bathtub with her feet up over the back of the tub and head underneath the faucet." Her face was in about six inches of water and her bare buttocks were exposed. Her underwear was around her ankles and it was determined that she was killed in another room and then posed. She may have been sexually assaulted as there was a broom with bloodstains on its handle; however, her body was too badly decomposed that it could not be definitively determined whether she had been.

Again, there was neither sign of forcible entry nor was the apartment ransacked; however, Sullivan's purse was found open.

The city of Boston was gripped with fear and the Strangler wouldn't strike for three more months; thus, giving police the opportunity to investigate possible suspects.

Investigators claimed that the posing of the victims, the selection of apartments, and the use of household items with which to strangle the victims demonstrates a disorganized-personality serial killer; however, DeSalvo's ability to talk himself into his victims' apartments and his attention to not leave fingerprints by wearing gloves is characteristic of an organized-personality serial killer. Thus, DeSalvo was classified as the rare mixed-personality type of killer—one that was both organized and disorganized at the same time and a very difficult challenge for investigators. DeSalvo was about to make it even more perplexing for detectives.

Sophie Clark, 20

The next murder occurred on 5 December—DeSalvo's wedding anniversary—and it sent detectives reeling. After having strangled six women to death in two months, the Strangler stopped for four months. Some believe that his anniversary may have triggered him returning to action. Also troubling was that instead of being an older white woman, 20-year-old Sophie Clark—a popular student at the Carnegie Institute of Medical Technology—was a young, pretty black woman. Most sexual murderers do not cross racial lines, nor do they typically have victims of such diverse ages. This led to much speculation that there were two murderers at large in Boston at that time.

Clark was found by her two roommates with whom she shared an apartment at 315 Huntington Avenue; a few blocks from Anna Siesers' apartment. Clark had been writing a letter to her boyfriend when the Strangler struck.

Like the other victims, Clark was lying on the living room floor, nude with her legs spread wide apart, and three of her own nylon stockings knotted and tied tightly around her neck, along with her slip. Again, there was evidence of sexual assault; however, this time semen was found. There were signs that Clark struggled with her attacker and he had rummaged through her magazines and record collection.

In his confession, DeSalvo said he talked his way into her apartment with his usual repairman ruse and then told her that he was scouting for models and he would give her $20-30 per hour. When he asked her to turn around, he grabbed her from behind.

Clark's neighbor, Marcella Lulka told investigators that at approximately 2:20 p.m. that afternoon a man knocked on her door telling her that the super had sent him to talk to her about painting her apartment. After telling her that he would have to fix her bathroom ceiling, Lulka said that the man asked her if she had ever considered modeling because she had a nice figure. She put her finger to her lips and said that he became angry, almost as though he changed completely. When she informed him that her husband was asleep in the next room, she said that he said he had the wrong apartment and ran out.

She described him as between 25 and 30 years of age, of average height with honey-colored hair, and wearing a dark jacket and dark green pants. The super stated that he had not sent anyone to any of the units and this was approximately the time Clark was murdered.

Patricia Bissette, 23

The last of the Strangler's victims for the year was 23-year-old secretary Patricia Bissette who was murdered on New Year's Eve, three weeks after Sophie Clark. Bissette's boss went to her apartment that morning to pick her up for work but she did not answer her door. After he got to work and saw that she had never arrived, he went back to her place at 515 Park Drive in the Black Bay area; very close to where Anna Siesers and Sophie Clark lived. With the assistance of the building custodian, her boss climbed through a window.

Bissette was found face-up in bed with the covers pulled up to her chin. Underneath the covers, however, she had several stockings knotted and entwined with a blouse that was also knotted around her neck and tied in the signature Boston Strangler bow. There was evidence of recent sexual intercourse and some damage to her rectum. Of particular interest to investigators was that Bissette's legs were together and she had been covered which usually indicates guilt on the part of the perpetrator.

DeSalvo, in his confession, said, "She was so different. I didn't want to see her like that, naked and ... She talked to me like a man, she treated me like a man." He said that he knocked on her door pretending to be looking for one of her upstairs neighbors whose name he had gotten from the downstairs mailboxes and she invited him inside to wait. She made coffee and they talked. He said that he didn't want to hurt her.

Bissette was in the early stages of pregnancy when she was killed.

Mary Brown, 69

On 9 March 1963, in Lawrence, Massachusetts—25 miles north of Boston—69-year-old Mary Brown was found beaten, raped, stabbed, and strangled to death after letting the murderer in believing he was there to fix her stove.

This time the murderer brought along a lead pipe which he used to bludgeon Brown about her head. He also stabbed a fork into her breast several times, leaving it embedded in her flesh. And also rather disturbingly, the assailant raped the victim after she was dead.

Beverly Samans, 23

On 6 May, pretty 23-year-old graduate student Beverly Samans missed choir practice at the Second Unitarian Church in Back Bay. A friend went to her apartment and unlocked her door with the spare key she had given him. The first thing he noticed was Samans lying on a sofa bed, her legs spread apart. Her hands were bound behind her back with one of her scarves and a stocking and two handkerchiefs were knotted together and tied around her neck. A cloth was places over her mouth that covered another cloth that had been stuffed into her mouth.

At first glance she appeared to have been strangled to death; however, the real cause of death was the four stab wounds to her throat. She had sustained an additional 18 stab wounds arranged in a bullseye pattern around her left breast. The ligature around her neck was not tied tightly enough to kill her. She had also been repeatedly raped. The bloody knife was found in her kitchen sink.

Her time of death was estimated at approximately 48 to 72 hours previously.

Because Samans was studying to be an opera singer there was speculation that her throat muscles were too developed and caused problems for the murder when he attempted to strangle her, thus resulting in his stabbing her to death.

Evelyn Corbin, 58

On 8 September, pretty 58-year-old divorcee Evelyn Corbin was found murdered in her apartment. She was lying face-up across the bed, nude, with her underwear stuffed into her mouth as a makeshift gag. It was determined that Corbin had been manually strangled and the killer left his trademark bow tied by a nylon around her ankle. There were several lipstick-marked tissues which contained trace amounts of seminal fluid. Spermatozoa were found in her mouth only.

Her apartment had been searched but nothing had been taken. Of particular interest was a lone, fresh doughnut outside her window on the fire escape that had not been put there by anyone in the building.

Joann Graff, 23

On 23 November 1963—the day after John F. Kennedy was assassinated and the entire nation was mourning his death—23-year-old conservative and religious industrial designer Joann Graff was raped and murdered in her ransacked Lawrence apartment by the Strangler. She had been strangled with two of her own nylon stockings which were tied tightly and in an elaborate bow around her neck. She had teeth marks on her breast and the outside of her vagina was lacerated and bloody.

The neighbor in an apartment in the building said he saw a young man in his mid- to late-20s with "pomaded hair" and dressed in dark green pants with a dark shirt and jacket knocking on the door of the unit across the corridor. The neighbor said that the stranger asked him if "Joan Graff" (mispronouncing her name) lived there. The neighbor told the man that she lived in the apartment below and then said that he heard the door below being opened and shut.

Ten minutes later, a friend tried to call Graff but there was no answer.

Mary Sullivan, 19

Sullivan would be the Strangler's last victim and also his most brutal murder. On 4 January 1964, she was found by her roommates atop her bed, naked, and propped against her headboard with her legs wide open, knees bent, and a broomstick handle inserted into her vagina. There was seminal fluid dripping from her mouth onto her breast and also seminal stains on the blanket. She had been manually strangled and a stocking and two print silk scarves were tied around her neck into a large bow. A cheery Happy New Year card was left by her body.

After this last Boston Strangler murder was committed, DeSalvo began another string of rapes; the "Green Man" ones.

Investigation and Arrest

Almost immediately after Sullivan's murder, Massachusetts Attorney General Edward Brooke took over the investigation and on 17 January 1964 he announced that the Boston Strangler cases was his top priority. Brooke created the Strangler Bureau that was headed by Assistant Attorney General John S. Bottomly; this choice much to the chagrin of Boston Police Commissioner Edmund McNamara. The team was comprised of Boston Police Detective Phillip Di Natale and Special Officer James Mellon, Metropolitan Police Officer Stephen Delaney, and State Police Detective Lieutenant Andrew Tuney.

A medical-psychiatric advisory committee was also created and headed by Dr. Donald Kenefick. The latter's first priority was to develop a criminal profile. They decided that the Strangler was at least 30 years old; neat, orderly, and punctual; works with his hands or has a hobby involving handiwork; probably single or divorced; would not come across as crazy to the casual observer; and has no close friends of either sex.

Several so-called experts had and continue to have conflicted opinions as to whether DeSalvo was, in fact, the Boston Strangler.

DeSalvo was arrested on 3 November 1964 after a "Green Man" victim identified him—the police remembered DeSalvo from his "Measuring Man" cases—and he was taken to the Bridgewater Mental Hospital.

Strangely, his wife was not surprised as she knew her husband was obsessed with sex and that one woman would never be enough for him. In fact, the "Green Man" assaulted four women in one day in different cities in Connecticut. He admitted to breaking into roughly 400 apartments and assaulting some 300 women; however, DeSalvo's propensity for exaggeration left investigators doubting as to whether this was an accurate number.

DeSalvo confessed to 13 murders as the Boston Strangler—two more than the police thought.

At Bridgewater, DeSalvo struck up a friendship with convicted murderer George Nassar who would play a pivotal role in this case. DeSalvo allegedly confessed to Nassar who is also among the suspects in the Strangler case. Nassar has been serving a life sentence for the 1967 shooting death of a gas station attendant in Andover, Massachusetts. His multiple attempts for appeal have been denied by the Massachusetts Supreme Court in 2008 and 2009, as well as his 2011 request for a writ of certiorari by the United States Supreme Court.

Former prison psychologist Dr. Ames Robey, who examined both DeSalvo and Nassar, called Nassar a "misogynistic, psychopathic killer and a far more likely suspect than DeSalvo" as the Boston Strangler, and he is not the only one with this opinion.

Some speculate that since DeSalvo was going to serve life in prison for his role in the "Green Man" attacks, the two colluded so Nassar could collect the reward money that the two men would split. Further, some speculate that DeSalvo's tremendous need for notoriety made him believe that his confession would make him world-famous and that he might get book and movie deals from his "story".

During a 1999 interview, however, Nassar denied his involvements in the Strangler murders and that the speculation had "killed his chances for parole".

It was Nassar, in fact, who brought F. Lee Bailey and DeSalvo together as Bailey was also Nassar's attorney.

At one point in his confession, DeSalvo admitted, "I would go home and watch what I had done on TV. Then I would cry like a baby."

There was no physical evidence tying DeSalvo to the murders; however, he did know a lot of specific details. Something that disturbed the police was that DeSalvo's misinformation grossly matched the misinformation in the newspapers as well. Even family members of the Boston Strangler's victims believe DeSalvo was not the Strangler. They point to his taped confession and asserted that even though police said he had to be the killer because he knew things that only the killer would know, in fact, he confessed to certain events that simply did not happen. Therefore, many still believe—to this day—that DeSalvo got his information from the real Boston Strangler while in prison. Even DeSalvo's brother, Richard, believes that his brother confessed to being the Boston Strangler because he knew he was going to prison for life and wanted to "cash in" on book and movie deals while fulfilling his desire for fame, even if that fame was infamy.

Trial and Conviction

In an attempt to prove DeSalvo insane in his rape cases F. Lee Bailey tried to get his client's confession admitted into evidence; however, a restraining order and the appointment of a legal guardian for DeSalvo led to his confession being recorded but not used as evidence in his trial. Consequently, after an eight-day trial, the jury—after only four hours—found DeSalvo not insane and guilty of the "Green Man" assaults.

DeSalvo was sentenced to life in prison on 9 January 1967.

Escape and Death

In January 1967, DeSalvo and two other inmates escaped from Bridgewater Hospital. DeSalvo had left a note on his bunk addressed to the superintendent stating that he had escaped to force attention upon the hospital's conditions and to protest his being sentenced to a prison instead of a mental hospital. With the Boston Strangler loose again, the city was once again sent into panic.

Police offered a $5,000 reward leading to information on the whereabouts of DeSalvo and his own attorney, Bailey, offered to double that reward if his client was caught unharmed.

The first thing DeSalvo did was go see his brother Richard who gave him clothes and a gun. He then went to Lynn, Massachusetts, where the police department was already on alert. Dressed in an old Navy uniform, DeSalvo went into a shoe store and told an employee he needed to use their telephone because he "had to call F. Lee" who then called the police. One employee asked DeSalvo if he was the Boston Strangler, to which he replied, "I honestly don't know. I know I did some of them."

DeSalvo was rearrested in Lynn, Massachusetts, and was transferred to the maximum-security prison in Walpole where he later recanted his confessions.

On 25 November 1973, at the age of 42, Albert DeSalvo was stabbed to death in the Walpole Prison's infirmary.

Of particular interest was that DeSalvo called Dr. Robey a mere 12 hours before his death saying that he wanted to "tell the real story" of the Boston Strangler.

DeSalvo wrote a poem while incarcerated, a couple of years before he was killed. It ends:

Today he sits in a prison cell,

Deep inside only a secret he can tell.

People everywhere are still in doubt,

Is the Strangler in prison or roaming about?

Both DeSalvo's murder case and that of the Boston Strangler remain open; the latter due to doubts that DeSalvo was, in fact, the real killer.

Aftermath

In 2001, George Washington University Professor of Forensic Evidence James Starrs asserted that DNA evidence found on Mary Sullivan's body did not match DeSalvo's DNA. The team of forensic scientists revealed that their tests discovered DNA from two individuals other than Sullivan and that DeSalvo was not one of them.

Sullivan's nephew Casey Sherman, a television producer who penned a book in 2003 entitled A Rose for Mary, has spent the past dozen or so years trying to prove that DeSalvo did not murder his aunt based upon the fact that DeSalvo "was convicted solely on the basis of a confession, which was riddled with inaccuracies." Sherman, like others, believes that DeSalvo, being faced with many years in prison, made up his confession with the hopes of procuring a book and movie deal so he could support his wife and children. Further, Sherman believes that DeSalvo was killed in prison because he was preparing to tell the real story, that his death was a "hit", and that prison officials were complicit. Sherman alleges that in order to get to DeSalvo, his murderer "had to go through six checkpoints, stab him 28 times, and then go back through those six checkpoints covered in blood."

DeSalvo's life was the subject of the 1968 film The Boston Strangler that starred Tony Curtis as DeSalvo, Henry Fonda and George Kennedy as the officers who apprehended him; however, the film was highly fictionalized, assuming that DeSalvo was, in fact, guilty and suffered from multiple personality disorder. Additionally, the Rolling Stones' 1969 song, "Midnight Rambler" has lyrics based upon DeSalvo.

TIMOTHY WILSON SPENCER

JEFF THOMAS

Timothy Wilson Spencer has the distinction of being the first American serial killer to be convicted on the basis of DNA evidence—evidence that also exonerated a man who had been in prison after being wrongly convicted of committing one of Spencer's murders. A troubled adolescent from Arlington, Virginia, with a deep hatred of women, Spencer utilized his cat-burglar skills, strength, and agility to gain entry into his victims' homes, lay wait, and then bind, rape, torture, and murder them. In total, Spencer had been linked to five murders and at least nine rapes in both Richmond and Arlington, Virginia. He was convicted of the murders of four of his victims and sentenced to death. Spencer was ultimately executed in the electric chair on 27 April 1994.

Early Life

Timothy Wilson Spencer was born on 17 March 1962 in Arlington, Virginia, and raised in the Green Valley section of town which was known as a lower-income, tough, predominately Black neighborhood. His parents were hard workers and had attended college but had divorced when he and his younger brother Travis were young. Travis commented that their mom was the best mother ever who worked hard to support them and spent time with them.

As an adolescent he had become increasing rebellious, first getting into trouble at the age of nine and again at 12 for urinating and defecating in the school yard. He was a poor student but intelligent. In the professional literature Spencer would be classified as a life-course-persistent offender who began deviant behavior at a young age which continued throughout his life with escalating degrees of crime. He had been implicated and/or convicted of six prior burglaries (three as a juvenile) and three counts of trespassing before being arrested for burglary in 1984 for which he served three years in prison before being released to a halfway house in the Southside area that was a transitional residence for nonviolent offenders. Because Spencer's conviction was for burglary he was considered to be nonviolent even though the evidence would ultimately show that he was a deliberately violent rapist and murderer. While in the halfway house Spencer was a loner who ate at the end of the table away from others and even watched television away from the rest of the residents. He did speak to one woman who worked at the halfway house and worked on her car so that he could borrow it. Whereas among the house rules were that residents sign in and out every time they come and go and had to follow a curfew, this procedure was poorly supervised and enforced.

In an interview, Spencer's younger brother Travis reiterated his utter disbelief that his brother was capable of what he did. Burglaries and other property crimes he said he could accept but someone who displayed such anger toward and hatred of women and who wanted to control them as badly as Spencer did by the systematic torture and strangulation of his victims was too much for him to believe. He even mentioned one time in his childhood where he and a friend stole some candy from a local store and were brought home in a police car that his older brother told him to never become like him.

A big question that has remained since Spencer's execution was whether someone like him was the product of nature or nurture. Some forensic psychologists say that deviant sexual preferences are hard-wired and that when combined with certain other factors can lead to deviant and aggressive behavior. The literature suggests that predatory psychopaths suffer from atrophy of the parts of the brain responsible for moral decision-making and aggression control and whereas this may be genetically influenced, the right combination of such traits coupled with environmental influences can make someone commit heinous acts. Spencer exhibited some of the "classic" signs of the serial killer typology—bedwetting, cruelty to animals, and a propensity for setting fires—which facilitated the escalation of his actions from breaking and entering to arson to burglary to rape to murder.

The Crimes

Debbie Davis

Spencer's first reported victim was 35-year old Debbie Dudley Davis. On 18 September 1987 he entered her home through a kitchen window with a rocking chair below it and bound, raped, tortured, and murdered her. Detective Ray Williams—who was dispatched to this and each subsequent murder scene in Richmond and stated that he had never seen such disturbing crime scenes in his entire career—remarked that the intruder had to have been exceptionally strong and agile.

The assailant utilized materials found on the premises to fashion his homemade ratchet strangulation contraption and this would be a commonality at all his subsequent crime scenes. In this case, he utilized socks, shoelaces, and a 16-inch vacuum cleaner extension hose.

There was very little forensic evidence at the scene—no hair or fibers—and no witnesses which suggested that the assailant was very meticulous. Except for the semen.

Autopsy results on Davis suggested that she was murdered between 9:00 p.m. on Saturday, 18 September and 9:30 a.m. on Sunday, 19 September. At the time of her murder, Spencer lived 2.7 miles from her apartment which would be approximately a 37-minute walk. The halfway house log showed that he left at 7:30 p.m. on Friday and returned at 12:30 a.m. Saturday. Davis had spoken to her parents on the phone from 8:30 p.m. to 9:00 p.m. that Saturday evening.

She had been strangled with a sock and vacuum cleaner hose that the Virginia court said had been "fashioned into a ligature and ratchet-type device." According to the medical examiner, the contraption had been twisted two or three times, ultimately causing Davis' death. The pressure of the ligature was so strong, in fact, that her neck muscles, larynx, and voice box were cut; blood was congested within her head; one of her eyes suffered a hemorrhage; and her nose and mouth were bruised. Her hands were bound by shoelaces and were attached to the neck ligature. It was posited that the more the victim struggled, the tighter the ligature became and that the suspect did this repeated times before finally killing her.

There were copious amounts of seminal fluid at the scene on Davis' nightgown and sheets, and vaginal and anal swabs demonstrated the presence of spermatozoa. The amount of semen suggested that the perpetrator repeatedly masturbated while alternatingly tightening and releasing the pressure of the ligature on Davis' neck. Two foreign hairs were found in the victim's pubic hair that were later identified through forensic analysis as being Negroid and, subsequently, consistent with Spencer's underarm hair. With respect to the semen, investigators discovered that the suspect was a secretor, defined as someone whose blood characteristics are found in other bodily fluids such as seminal fluid.

Analysis of Spencer's blood revealed him to be a Type O, enzyme grouping PGM type 1, PGM subtype 1+, peptidase A type 1. This particular configuration is shared by 13 percent of the population; however, specific characteristics of the analyzed DNA demonstrated that the sample would match only one in 705 million Black individuals. There are only approximately ten million adult Black males in the United States.

Dr. Susan Hellams

Two weeks' after Davis' death, on 2 October Spencer struck again when he beat, raped, tortured, and killed Dr. Susan Hellams. Hellams' husband discovered his wife's beaten partially-naked body on the floor of their closet. Point of access was discovered to be a second-story window that had a large portion of screen cut from it. Detective Williams commented that this was one of the most brutal murders he had ever seen.

The medical examiner identified the cause of death as ligature strangulation from two belts around her neck. Hellams also sustained a fractured nose, blunt force injury to her lower lip, a number of bruises and scrapes, and an injury consistent with a shoe on the back of her leg. Petechiae in her eyes suggested that she had been strangled and revived for at least 20 minutes before she was killed which suggested that the assailant was likely aroused by having complete control over his victim, not unlike the Davis case. Evidence of rape and sodomy included seminal fluid on her back and in the gluteal fold; small mucosal tears of the anus; and the presence of spermatozoa on vaginal, rectal, and perianal swabs. Additionally, an ample amount of seminal fluid was found on the victim's skirt and slip. Subsequent forensic and serologic examination determined that the seminal fluid and spermatozoa were consistent with Spencer's secretion type and could not have belonged to Hellams' husband. DNA analysis ultimately proved that the fluids were Spencer's.

After Hellams' murder, the unknown perpetrator was dubbed the "Southside Strangler" and the area went into panic mode over the term "serial killer." Panic ensued in Richmond; residents of the area left their lights on all the time, every deadbolt lock was purchased from stores, and even dogs from local animal shelters were adopted in record amounts. Police had told single women to nail their windows shut. A preliminary profile suggested that he was a white adult male, approximately 35 years old, a loner, intelligent, not a criminal beginner, and likely had considerable success as a cat burglar of sorts due to his agility and ability to enter residences without making a sound.

The police sought to find a connection between the victims to help identify a suspect. Nearby Cloverfield Mall in Chesterfield County proved to be that link. Davis had worked in a bookstore and Hellams had purchased books from her.

Diane Cho

Not long after, on 22 November, 15-year old high school student Diane Cho was bound, raped, and strangled to death. Cho lived less than a mile from the Cloverfield Mall and wanted to go to medical school. She was studying in her bedroom when Spencer entered through her bedroom window and overtook her so quickly that her parents and brother who were in the next room didn't hear a thing the entire time Spencer was assaulting and murdering her.

Spencer had carved the infinity symbol on Cho which, according to experts, signified his taking, keeping, and sealing the victim for himself since she was a virgin.

Cho lived very close to the Cloverfield Mall.

Susan Tucker

While on furlough from the halfway house in Arlington visiting his family for Thanksgiving, Spencer attacked Susan Tucker, 44, in the same fashion as his other victims on or about 27 November (her body wasn't discovered until 1 December). She was home alone at the time as her husband was away on a business trip. Spencer entered through a basement window and Davis was hog-tied with a rope, raped, and subsequently died from ligature strangulation. When her body was found she had been dead for a few days and those on the scene remarked that it was extremely disturbing and unsettling.

During her autopsy four-to-eight intact non-motile sperm were collected from vaginal swabs and DNA from semen stains were determined to have been left by a secretor. As mentioned, Spencer was that secretor.

Carol Hamm

Back on 25 January 1984, 32-year-old attorney Carolyn Hamm was raped, bound, and hanged in the door between her garage and house. Her body was found naked, face down, and her robe was on the living room floor alongside a piece of cord cut from a Venetian blind and a knife.

At the time, a McDonald's janitor, David Vasquez, was arrested and convicted of Hamm's murder after two witnesses placed him on her street that day. Despite police having doubt that Vasquez was guilty because of his less-than-70 IQ, he did confess and was, subsequently, serving a 35-year prison sentence. Authorities wondered if he had a partner who might still be at large.

Absent any leads at the time, Detective Horgas visited Vasquez at the Buckingham Correctional Center near the Blue Ridge Mountains on 7 December 1988. Vasquez seemed confused; he retracted his confession insisting that he couldn't have killed Hamm because he didn't drive and had no way to get to her house after work. He also denied having an accomplice. After the interview Horgas told the warden that he believed Vasquez to be innocent.

Other Crimes

Prior to Hamm's murder, there was a string of rapes between June 1983 and January 1984 in Arlington. Nine women had been attacked by a masked Black male in his 20s who carried a knife and broke into their homes via a window and who was dubbed the "black masked rapist." The last rape, in fact, occurred on the day Hamm's body was discovered. Detective Horgas wondered whether these rapes and Hamm's murder were connected. When he heard about the first two murders in Richmond, Horgas called Detective Williams to discuss the similarities between Horgas' rapes and the Hamm murder in Arlington and the two (at that time) murders in Richmond. Williams also mentioned a recent attack in Davis' and Hellams' neighborhood wherein a Black masked man had entered a woman's apartment through a window and was in the process of tying her up when neighbors came over to investigate noises and scared him away. Whereas Horgas was virtually convinced that the crimes in both Arlington and Richmond had been committed by the same person, Williams was skeptical due to the distance between the two cities and the fact that FBI profilers asserted that serial killers are almost always White.

Williams did tell Horgas that the Richmond police were trying DNA testing which, he said, identified an individual's unique genetic material that is found in every cell of a person's body and that they had already sent samples from the Davis and Hellams murders to Lifecodes, a New York State private laboratory that analyzed DNA for paternity tests. Prior to this, nobody in the United States had ever used DNA testing in a homicide investigation.

The Investigation

All of the murders shared overwhelmingly similar characteristics which demonstrated that the deceased were the victim of a serial killer with a particular signature that was unique to him. All of the victims were bound—wrists to neck—with handmade tourniquets fashioned from materials the killer found at the house through which he could repeatedly tighten and loosen the ligatures so that he could suffocate and revive the victims multiple times. There was substantial semen left at the crime scene near the body which suggested that the suspect likely masturbated while torturing his victims. None of the victims had defensive injuries which demonstrated that they were overcome quickly. All of the victims were White or Asian with a "stocky" build. All of the murders occurred on the weekend. Additionally, in every case the victims' bodies were laid crosswise on their beds (except for Hellams who was in her closet) representing submissiveness and in each case the victims' were "covered": Davis was redressed in shorts, a sheet was placed over Cho's buttocks, a blanket was placed over Tucker's buttocks, and Hellams' closet door was closed. Some experts have suggested that posing the bodies enabled the perpetrator to extend the crime scenes to make him feel even more powerful than he already did and that his covering them was like putting a lid on a trash can. The point of entry in every case was through a window in which glass was either broken or a screen was cut.

Detective Horgas was the first to overcome what is known as "linkage blindness" in which clues exist to link particular crimes but the Richmond investigators wore blinders as to how certain cases were, in fact, linked. One of the most glaring examples of this was that Richmond police were so intent on looking for a White suspect based upon their preliminary profile and, therefore, were initially against considering the possibility that the killer was, in fact, Black.

Horgas also reinterviewed the burglary and rape victims from Arlington prior to Hamm's murder. He discovered glaring similarities and a pattern of escalation that ultimately culminated with the perpetrator "graduating" to murder. Similarities included the fact that the point of entry was always through a window; lengths of Venetian blind cords had been cut and found near the crime scenes in multiple cases; and victims had been tied up, raped, and tortured. In some cases the victims' mouths were covered with duct tape (Cho's mouth was also taped). The fifth victim was locked in a car that was lit on fire but she was able to kick her way out and escape. Perhaps most damning was that the three-year break in between Hamm's death and the other four women's deaths correlated to the time that Spencer was in prison and that for every recent murder he had signed out of the halfway house; even seeking approval for a furlough to return to Arlington for the Thanksgiving holiday.

And then there was the DNA evidence. In addition to the samples from Richmond, Horgas hand-delivered samples from the Hamm and Tucker murders as well as some of the rapes to Lifecodes on 28 December 1988.

While waiting for the results, on 29 December FBI agents Stephen Mardigan and Judson Ray from the Behavioral Science Unit at Quantico went to Arlington to examine Horgas' evidence and ultimately agreed with his theory that the crimes in both cities had been committed by the same person. The profilers said that the key to all of the crimes was to reexamine the first rape in Arlington and that the perpetrator likely lived nearby because he would have wanted to commit his first assault where he felt comfortable such as in his own neighborhood. The agents also iterated that based upon their profile, this type of person would only stop if he were incarcerated of died. This spurred Horgas to look for a suspect who was arrested and incarcerated shortly after Hamm's murder in January 1984 and released just prior to the first Richmond murder in September 1987.

Spencer demonstrated classic signatures of an anger-retaliatory rapist-murderer who utilized sexualized violence against women who are perceived to have threatened or otherwise harmed the killer's self-image. Most of these perpetrators targeted victims usually in the same age range or older than the killer; however, in the case of Cho, despite being only 15 she looked older. Since he cannot kill the actual target of his anger he finds surrogate targets who he stalks prior to the assault. Spencer punished his victims for some wrongdoing by systematically degrading, humiliating, and incapacitating them.

The next day Horgas drove to South Oxford Street where the first victim was assaulted in a nearby wooded lot after being abducted from a phone booth at South Glebe Road and Second Street in June 1983. He racked his brain trying to remember who he may have arrested nearby during that time. He and his partner Mike Hill then went through over 300 files trying to recall. Four days later the name Timmy popped into his head. Horgas remembered investigating Timmy for burglary and arson of either a house or car. On 6 January 1988 Horgas remembered Timmy's last name: Spencer. Horgas conducted a driver's license check for Timothy Spencer and found that he resided in Richmond and that he had been arrested on 29 January 1984 for a burglary in Alexandria, Virginia, just four days after police discovered Hamm's body. After serving time in prison, Spencer was released to a halfway house in the Southside area on 4 September 1987—a mere two weeks before Davis was killed. Further, Spencer's mother lived less than a mile from both murder sites in Arlington and a mere 200 yards from the Oxford Street crime scene. Horgas said that it was like a puzzle wherein all the pieces fit together perfectly. On an interesting side note, had it not been for Horgas' memory he would never have found Spencer's name in any of the parole files through which he looked so diligently as convicts released to halfway houses were not technically considered paroled.

Spencer was placed under surveillance by the Richmond Police Department; however, after a week without him doing anything suspicious the surveillance was called off. This was much to the dismay of Arlington prosecutor Helen Fahey who—not unlike Tucker—was a single woman who lived alone in a rented townhouse far too similar to Tucker's home. She contacted Horgas and the two brainstormed ideas of how to get Spencer off the street before he struck again. Fahey suggested asking for a grand jury indictment which was considerably more difficult to challenge in court that an arrest warrant.

Arrest

On 20 January 1988 at 5:50 p.m. with his grand jury indictment in hand Horgas arrested Spencer at his Richmond halfway house on suspicion of burglary.

During the drive back to Arlington, Spencer was very tight-lipped, not volunteering any statements. Horgas knew that he needed either a confession or Spencer's consent to volunteer a blood sample. Horgas asked Spencer to submit to a blood test under the guise that it was necessary to compare to some blood found on a broken window in a burglary. Unaware of the advent of DNA analysis and that a blood test could be utilized to match a semen sample, Spencer agreed, to the delight and astonishment of Horgas.

On 16 March Horgas was notified that Spencer's DNA matched fluids left at the murders of Davis, Hellams, and Tucker, as well as one of the Arlington rapes four years earlier. Both Horgas and Fahey knew they had just caught a serial killer but Fahey had to convince a jury of Spencer's guilt based upon fledgling scientific evidence that she needed jurors to understand and accept in order to obtain a capital murder conviction. In fact, due to the relative infancy and lack of knowledge about DNA evidence, trial judge Benjamin Kendrick held a special hearing to determine whether the evidence was even legally admissible. After considerable inquiry Kendrick decided that the evidence was credible and would be admitted into trial.

Trials

On 11 July 1988 Spencer went on trial in Arlington for the murder of Susan Tucker. On 16 July after only six hours of jury deliberation, Spencer was found guilty of capital murder and sentenced to death. This was the first case in the United States in which a defendant was found guilty of capital murder and received the death penalty based upon DNA evidence; a noteworthy distinction, indeed.

Spencer's Richmond trials began in the Circuit Court of the City of Richmond, Manchester Courthouse on 17 January 1989 and ultimately, on 22 September 1989, he was found guilty of rape, burglary, sodomy, and capital murder and was unanimously sentenced to death following several unsuccessful appeals of his conviction and death sentence at both state and federal levels. It didn't help his case any that when the jury was shown crime scene photos Spencer was very eager to look at them as well; essentially wanting to revisit the excitement he experienced when he brutalized the victims. Aside from this display of enthusiasm Spencer demonstrated absolutely no remorse or other emotion.

In his first appeal with Supreme Court of Virginia, Spencer raised five issues: that the DNA evidence was unreliable; that his defense team was denied the opportunity to adequately defend against said evidence because the trial court denied a discovery request for Lifecodes' notes and memoranda, that the trial court refused to provide funds for an expert DNA witness for the defense, and that the prosecution failed to reveal any evidence of problems with Lifecodes' testing process; that the trial court wrongly admitted the DNA evidence; that the prosecution improperly removed a juror for alleged racially-motivated reasons in violation of Batson v. Kentucky, 476 U.S. 79 (1986); and that the attached aggravating factor of "future dangerousness" is unconstitutionally vague. The Court upheld the lower court's ruling. The United States Supreme Court denied certiorari.

On 10 September 1990 Spencer filed a petition for a writ of habeas corpus with the state trial court which was ultimately dismissed on 15 November that same year and subsequently affirmed by the Supreme Court of Virginia. Next, Spencer filed another habeas corpus petition in the United States District Court for the Eastern District of Virginia which was also denied. He then requested a Certificate of Probable Cause to appeal which was also denied by the United States Court of Appeals, Fourth Circuit. An additional Notice of Appeal and request for Certificates of Probable Cause were filed in district court on 29 April 1993 and 25 May 1993 which were met with the respondent's motion to dismiss. The Fourth Circuit Appellate Court granted Spencer's application for Probable Cause.

In this appeal Spencer's legal team raised seven issues: ineffective assistance of counsel at the original trial because they failed to obtain a defense DNA expert; that he is "actually innocent" of the crimes for which he received the death penalty and would not have been convicted had he been able to challenge the DNA evidence and if the "prejudicial injection of astronomical probability ratios" had not been introduced at trial; that his trial counsel were ineffective due to their failure to conduct voir dire on the subject of racial prejudice; that Virginia's proportionality review is unconstitutional and does not allow "rational exceptions"; that the jury instructions regarding mitigating evidence were constitutionally inadequate; that his trial counsel were ineffective due to their failure to present certain mitigating evidence; and that the DNA analysis was unreliable, should not have been admitted, and, thus, his trial counsel were ineffective with respect to this evidence.

The Fourth Circuit considered some of Spencer's issues. First, with respect to ineffective assistance of counsel, the court turned to Strickland v. Washington, 466 U.S. 668 (1984), in which the United States Supreme Court stated that in order to prevail on an ineffective assistance of counsel claim the petitioner must demonstrate that not only did counsel perform deficiently but that the petitioner suffered prejudice as a result. Both factors must be present and the burden of proof rests with the petitioner to prove whether there was a reasonable probability that if it were not for counsel's alleged errors the result of the trial would have been different and whether there was a reasonable probability that the sentence would have concluded that other mitigating evidence would not warrant death.

Spencer's claim of ineffective assistance of counsel because of their failure to provide a defense DNA expert was dismissed due to evidence that the court not only discussed with Spencer's counsel about procuring an expert but that because no experts interviewed were willing to testify on the defense's behalf does not make his counsel ineffective. Further, his attorneys had a blind DNA test run by an independent laboratory which corroborated the evidence against Spencer.

As to the voir dire allegation of racial bias, because of the publicity surrounding Spencer's first trial in Richmond, a change of venire—wherein a jury is selected and brought in from another county due to the fear that pretrial publicity would prevent the empaneling of an impartial jury—was granted and the jury was from Norfolk. The Court held that the change of venire eliminated race as an issue with which to be concerned and that it had no reason to believe that any prospective juror had any racial bias against Spencer and this allegation was also dismissed.

With respect to the mitigating evidence concerns, Spencer contended that had his counsel adequately investigated his background that they would have discovered that his school history, presentence report, and Department of Corrections reports all stated that he was troubled; that he was emotionally damaged by being erroneously told that his father was dead when, in fact, he was not; that he regularly ingested PCP; and that he may have some degree of organic brain damage and that his counsel failed to appoint a psychologist to evaluate his mental state. The Court said that the record reflected that Spencer's counsel did, in fact, conduct a thorough background investigation which yielded evidence that Spencer's attorneys in the Arlington trial had hired both a psychiatrist and psychologist who mutually found a complete lack of any mitigating circumstances and ceased any more investigation because of fear that more incriminating evidence might have been uncovered. In fact, per the recommendation of the Richmond criminal defense bar, Dr. Robert Mullaney conducted a pretrial evaluation of Spencer and Spencer's attorneys decided to not utilize Dr. Mullaney as a witness because the sole "plus"—Mullaney's opinion that Spencer's future dangerousness would be minimized if kept in prison—was far outweighed by the potential negatives which would ensue had Dr. Mullaney testified: these being the jury finding out that Spencer committed the offense, denied his guilt, and had shown no remorse whatsoever. Further, the defense counsel stated that if they had used Dr. Mullaney then the prosecution would have been entitled to have Spencer evaluated by its own expert.

As for Spencer's claim of defense counsel's deficiency in handling adequately DNA evidence, the Court argued that his counsel did, in fact, conduct a thorough investigation and contacted several experts, some of whom assisted throughout the trial but were unwilling to testify and, therefore, determined that counsel was not ineffective simply because they could not find an expert willing to testify. Further, regarding his "actual innocence" claim and that he would not have been convicted if the "prejudicial injection of astronomical probability ratios" into the trial record had not occurred, because a claim of "actual innocence" is not a constitutional claim then—and differs from a claim of "factual innocence"— the Court's discretion was limited. Ultimately, the Court held that Spencer failed to demonstrate any constitutional error that could have affected the jury's verdict. Further, the trial judge heard all of the information regarding DNA analysis including its statistics and limitations and still decided to admit the evidence into court.

Spencer's execution date was set for 26 August 1993.

Execution

Desperate last-minute appeals for a stay of execution were denied by the United States Supreme Court and Timothy Wilson Spencer was executed on 27 April 1994. He was pronounced dead at 11:13 p.m. He was 32 at the time of his death.

Virginia author and veteran detective Lee Lofland attended Spencer's execution and described, on his website, the atmosphere at the prison as "nothing short of surreal." He stated that Spencer entered on his own, calmly took a seat in the chair, and permitted the "death squad" to secure him and attach electrodes. His face was completely devoid of any sign of fear, regret, or sadness. When asked whether Spencer had any final words it appeared that he might say something but then stopped, silently. Lofland described how Spencer made eye contact with him and even made a two-thumbs-up gesture until the leather mask was placed over his head and he was executed.

On execution day, Davis' friend Lorna Wyckoff called Spencer a "monster" and the "personification of evil." Spencer's brother Travis said it was the most difficult day of his life, hugging his brother for the last time.

Post-Execution

Whereas DNA evidence proved critical for finding Spencer guilty, it was far more difficult procuring David Vasquez's exoneration since the samples from the Hamm murder were too degraded. Vasquez would need a pardon from the governor. Fahey formerly requested the assistance of FBI Special Agent John Douglas who had founded the Behavioral Science Unit in the early 1980s after interviewing some of the most notorious serial killers in history such as Ted Bundy, Charles Manson, and David Berkowitz, and identifying patterns in their behavior; their unique "signatures." Douglas' agreement to assist was the first time FBI profilers had ever been asked to prove a suspect's innocence.

Douglas said that one must look for a signature to link similar cases and that a signature was a type of ritual performed by a suspect that is truly unique. Douglas believed that the nature of how Spencer bound his victims constituted a distinctive signature in the five homicides and that use of ligatures and ropes exceeded the necessary amount of force necessary to control the victims was also part of his signature. On 4 January 1989 Vasquez was pardoned and became the first person exonerated, albeit indirectly, by DNA evidence.

Spencer's conviction was such a landmark case because it broadened the public and professional knowledge about DNA and that the jury understood its significance and was able to convict a serial killer of capital murder was a major revelation. The case also prompted Virginia to open the first state DNA laboratory in the United States in 1989 and to set up the first DNA database.

Shortly thereafter, in 1992, the Innocence Project came into being. A nonprofit founded by New York's Benjamin Cardozo School of Law, the Innocence Project has worked to free 179 of the 337 people exonerated by DNA evidence, including 20 who were on death row. The most common reason cited for wrongful convictions is erroneous eyewitness identification with mishandling of forensic evidence due to faulty tests and/or procedural errors the second reason. DNA is not completely infallible, however. The Innocence Project states that approximately four percent of those exonerated were originally convicted as a result of improperly conducted DNA tests which have prompted virtually all defense attorneys in criminal proceedings to request retesting on their clients' behalf.

In addition to Paul Mones' (1995) book Stalking Justice: The Dramatic True Story of the Detective Who First Used DNA

Testing to Catch a Serial Killer that focused upon Detective Horgas' efforts to link his cases in Arlington to those in Richmond and, ultimately, to Spencer, Spencer's case provided the basis for Patricia Cornwell's first crime novel Postmortem (1990) as she, at the time was employed as a computer analyst in the Richmond, Virginia's Office of the Chief Medical Examiner. Former FBI profiler John Douglas devoted chapter 11 of his 1996 memoir Journey into Darkness to Spencer. His case also inspired the forensic science documentary Medical Detectives which first aired on 31 October 1996.

THE SUFFOLK STRANGLER

JASMINE GREY

Steven Gerald James Wright was considered to be an ordinary, everyday English barman. Friends and family thought that his gambling addiction and his relationship issues were the brunt of his problems, but little did they know that was only scratching the surface of his nasty habits. He followed into the footsteps of the British serial killers that had come before him, like the legendary "Jack the Ripper", by primarily preying on the prostitutes of the red light district. Steven Wright is better known as "The Suffolk Strangler" or "The Ipswich Ripper" and he is currently serving a life imprisonment for the murders of five young women: Tania Nicol, 19-years-old; Gemma Rose Adams, 25-years-old; Anneli Sarah Alderton, 24-years-old; Annette Nicholls, 29-years-old; Paula Lucille Clennell, 24-years-old. All of these innocent women were murdered while working the corners of the red light district in Suffolk. The two-month-long murder spree received mass media attention and pushed the entire Suffolk area into utter panic. The heinous nature of the Suffolk Strangler's crimes, the mystery of his identity, the body count, and the mass hysteria pushed the police department into a full-scale investigation. After hard work, persistence, DNA evidence, and a few false leads, the police finally linked Steven Wright to the Ipswich Ripper.

Early Life

Steven Gerald James Wright was born on April 24, 1958, in Erpingham[1], a Norfolk village in the United Kingdom. His father Conrad was a military policeman and his mother Patricia was a veterinary nurse. As the second eldest of four children, with one older brother and two younger sisters, Wright claimed to live in an unhappy household. Patricia Wright divorced Conrad on the claims of domestic violence and abandoned the family when Steven was only 9-years-old.

After he was arrested for the murders of five women, Steven sent a letter to his father that suggested a childhood full of violence and anger that could explain his violent nature: "Dear Dad, this is a reply to your letter you are right you have never seen me angry before because I am a quite [quiet] and placid person whenever I get upset I tend to bury it deep inside which I suppose is not a healthy thing to do because the more I do that the more withdrawn I become because I have seen to [too] much anger and violence in my childhood to last anyone a lifetime. But what really makes me sad is the fact that I thought all the family feuds were behind me now I really thought we had made a step forward I just wish everyone would get along and work towards a family unit because all the bickering and point scoring against each other is really getting me down it seems you are pulling me one way and Pam is pulling me the other and in the end, something will give and it just seems to me that person will be me and that is the last thing that I want at the moment has I am sure you do as well because if I start to fall apart at the seams I don't think I could cope in here I need to be strong to cope with this nightmare like that but you said in the paper that when you looked into my eyes you would know whether I was guilty or not that really hurt me it was like a knife in the heart

---

1.   https://en.wikipedia.org/wiki/Erpingham

for you to even contemplate that I could even be capable of such a terrible crime."

Conrad Wright, his father, claims that he does not know what his son is talking about. He denies the abuse that Steven refers to and insists that he had a partially normal childhood. He was known to bottle up his anger and hyperventilate until he passed out. "He must be a raving lunatic," Conrad admitted after attending every trial in his son's defense. Conrad recalls his son during childhood as being quiet and introspective. Steven was also known to love horror films, Conrad explained later, "I was watching a film about a stranger and I thought how Steve loved horror films. He'd be jumping up and down, really into it."

Soon after he left school in 1974, Wright joined the Merchant Navy and became a chef on the ferries that sailed from Felixstowe, Suffolk. He developed a name for himself as a "ladies man" because he was always seen with women and rarely without a girlfriend. When Wright was only 20-years-old he met his first wife and the mother of his first child, Angela O'Donovan. They married soon after they met, in 1978, but the couple separated just ten years later, in 1987. This would start a pattern of failed relationships that would slowly chip away at Wright's mental stability. Wright would later make three suicide attempts after splitting with his wife and/or girlfriend.

After the divorce, Wright worked many odd jobs, including at QE2, where he soon used prostitutes to heal the pain from his recent split. Wright claims that this was when his indulgence with sex workers truly began; he would begin visiting specific parlors and ports whenever he "got the urge". He was working in the onboard shop on QE2 when he met a young stewardess named Diane Cassell. In August of 1987, Wright married Diane Cassell at Braintree register office. Not unlike his first marriage, his marriage to Diane did not turn out to be a happy one. Wright and Cassell's marriage was full of abuse and neglect. Elizabeth Roche, a former next-door neighbor, explains that abuse nature that Steven Wright did not attempt to hide from friends and family, "Steve used to strangle Diane right in front of us. He would pin her up against the wall and put both hands around her throat. There were, at least, three times when he did it in front of witnesses. It would end when either my ex-husband or I would pull him off or he would come to his senses." Steven Wright seemed to often portray sudden, violent mood swings and fits of aggression, Roche went on to explain her former neighbor, "He had an ability to have a violent row one minute and then have a calm conversation with you straight afterward as if nothing had happened. The only way I can describe it is to say he was a real Jekyll and Hyde character. He definitely had a psycho side to him." Due to their dysfunctional and violent relationship, Wright separated from his second wife nearly a year after their wedding date – they divorced in 1988. "The marriage was a nightmare," Diane Cassell later stated, "It was an awful time which I would rather forget. I was glad when it ended. It didn't even last a year and he went off with someone else."

In 1989, Wright was working at the White Horse pub in Chislehurst when he began his four-year-long relationship with Sarah Whiteley. They moved to Plumstead where they had a daughter in 1992. Sarah described Steven Wright as a kind, generous, loving father. While in Plumstead Wright managed the Rose and Crown Pub. Wright had finally managed to be in a stable environment for the first time in his life, but it didn't last very long. This all came crashing down when the weight of Wright's addictions became too much for him to control. Steven lost his job and his newly found family due to his heavy drinking and frivolous gambling. After he lost the pub, Steve moved back to Felixstowe, where he worked odd jobs, but never accumulated much wealth because of his spending habits. Most of his hard earned money went to prostitutes and sex workers.

It was pretty well known that Wright's mental condition was not very stable after his second split up. Wright drowned his emotional and financial issues with gambling, drinking, and engaging with prostitutes, which only increased the mountain of debt that was hanging over his head. Steven Wright tried to commit suicide for the first time in 1994, when he locked himself in his garage, in a running vehicle, in hopes of carbon monoxide poisoning. This attempt was a failure and he was pulled out of the car by police before it was too late. His family and loved ones were in shock. Steven's half-brother Keith Wright explained the reasoning behind his brother's brash actions, "He just got himself into so much debt. I suppose he couldn't find a way out." Wright's financial issues were increasing at a dramatic level, falling apart as he tried to fund his addictions. In an attempt to earn money, Steven Wright bought a £13,000 car on hire purchase then sold it. Simultaneously Wright continued to charge his credit card, creating huge bills and adding to the debt that would eventually get him arrested for stealing £80 from the cash register at work. Nearly £40,000 worth of debt was racked up before he fled to Thailand and declared himself bankrupt.

The most interesting part of Wright's life was the very short time that he spent in Thailand to run away from the debt he accumulated in England. In Thailand, Steven spent most of his time spending money on Thai prostitutes. Somchit Chomphusaeng was a Thai woman who claimed to marry him while he was hiding away in 1999. After their two week honeymoon, Wright flew back to Britain and never returned to see his wife again. She received a letter shortly after his departure from a woman who claimed to be his mother. The letter told Somchit Chomphusaeng that Wright had been murdered, or in more gruesome details, had been stabbed to death. She saw her husband again years after his untimely "death" when photographs of Wright were released from his arrest in Ipswich. Upon first seeing the photograph, his "widow" claimed that she fainted from pure shock. Later, when she was in the proper mindset, she explained her husband's deception: "It must be his ghost. I was told he'd been murdered."

A Life shared in Ipswich

Steven Wright met Pamela Wright in 2001 in Felixstowe, Suffolk. Their shared last name have no hereditary connection, but they immediately hit it off and Pamela stayed by his side throughout the guilty verdict of the murder trial. In 2004, Steven and Pamela moved into a rented apartment in the center of Ipswich, Suffolk, which was very popularly known as the red light district where sex workers sold their trade for anyone who had the money. Steven worked as a forklift driver on the docks of Suffolk as Pamela worked at a call center. Soon after the move, Pamela took up the night shift at her job, which gave her partner plenty of free time to indulge in his habits. The increased and late night hours made Steven and Pamela's sex life virtually nonexistent. His girlfriend was completely unaware that the change in their sex life, and the increased about of time that Steven would be alone, would result in the deaths of five innocent women. Wright now had the freedom visit local prostitutes any time that he "got the urge" and he took advantage of the situation. After Steven dropped his unsuspecting girlfriend off at work, he spent the late night hours prowling streets of the Ipswich red light district, which was where he captured and preyed on his victims.

Steven created quite a name for himself in Ipswich, as he frequently visited the girls in the red light district. He was nicknamed by the sex workers as the "Mondeo Man" because of the car that he drove, the "Silver-backed gorilla" because of his hair color, and the "Soldier" because he wore camouflage pants from time to time. Most of the women didn't feel comfortable engaging with him because of his out of the ordinary behavior. He was very unlike most of their clientele because he seemed too angry and he seemed to ask too many questions, claimed a former sex worker in a later documentary interview. Some of the sex workers went into vivid descriptions on how he would cruise the red light district dressed in high heels, a PVC skirt, and a wig, masquerading as a woman as he tried to pick up prostitutes. One Norwich worker explained from personal experience, "If you didn't get in the car he would get naked and just sit there with the headlights on. He freaked me out. The police knew about him." Her statement was proven right when Detective Chief Superintendent of the Ipswich murder investigation Stewart Gull stated that Wright was a pretty well-known curb crawler around this point in his life.

The Murders and the Investigation

Between the dates of October 30th and December 12th of 2006, Steven Wright murdered five sex workers from the Ipswich area. This string of murders took Suffolk by storm and sex workers everywhere were terrified that the Suffolk Strangler would pick them up next. These girls had few similarities despite their location, their occupation, and the drug habits that forced them to put themselves in an extremely vulnerable set of circumstances. All of these women were down on their luck and none of them were over the age of thirty when they made the fatal mistake of getting into the black Mondeo that belonged to Suffolk Strangler.

Tania Nicol was only 19-years-old when she encountered the Suffolk Strangler. On the freezing cold night of October 30th, 2006, the young girl left her home at eleven o'clock to service the curb crawlers of Ipswich's red light district. Sometime during that night, Tania willing stepped into Steven Wright's vehicle without hesitation, which hinted that Tania already knew him and did not expect anything unusual out of the situation, but when they pulled away from the curb the 19-year-old girl was never to be seen alive again. Usually, when Tania had a client she always made a point to keep her friends and colleagues updated on her whereabouts at all times. This night, however, Tania's friends did not receive the usual update. Tania didn't come home that night or any night after that. Tania's mother, who was unaware of her daughter's lifestyle at the time, reported the disappearance to the police 48 hours after she'd gone missing. The Suffolk police department regarded Tania as a high-risk target because of her profession and immediately took steps to discover her whereabouts. Detective Chief Superintendent Stewart Gull explained her disappearance in a documentary interview later, "She had literally disappeared off the face of the earth. Her phone record showed us a very flat line from the 1st of November. No incoming or outgoing movement of data at all..."

The Suffolk police had absolutely no leads to point them towards the missing girl, so they took to the public to find anyone who knew the whereabouts of Tania Nicol. Little did they know that while they were investigating the disappearance of one woman, another was in danger of falling into the same trap that caught Tania.

The name of the second victim was Gemma Rose Adams. Gemma was last seen on the night of November 14th when she boarded a train after visiting with her mother. She was only 25-years old. Much like Tania, Gemma always kept people updated on her location through texts and calls, but on that cold November night, the calls stopped coming. Her boyfriend, worried because Gemma wasn't answering his text messages, reported her disappearance on November 15th. The similarities between Gemma and Tania's profession, location, and disappearance, drew police to the conclusion that these cases were linked, and were most likely done by the same man, or same group of men. Upon this realization, the Suffolk police immediately stepped up their efforts to find the young girls and began to question random, passing motorists in the red light district for information on the girls' whereabouts. One of these random, passing motorists was actually Steve Wright. When he was stopped and questioned on his relationship with Tania Nicol and Gemma Adams, he claimed that he didn't know them. "We distributed some 20,000 leaflets around the area," Andy Henwood, an investigator, explained in an interview, "...we set up road checks at periodic times after the disappearances. We interviewed some 400 people in respect to Tania's disappearance and some 300 people in respect to Gemma's disappearance." Despite the efforts of the Suffolk police, they never received any leads to the whereabouts of these two missing women. As the weeks passed by, the investigators who had been hopeful to find the two girls were beginning to give up the notion that they were alive.

On the morning of the December 2nd, Gemma's body was found in a Hintlesham river by water bailiff, Trevor Saunders. "I noticed what I'd thought, at first, was a dummy, a mannequin. So I got down into the water to get it out," Saunders described his encounter with the body that he found upon checking the creek, "So I got down to pick it out, to clear the blockage, and when I got down to her, that when I realized that it [weren't] a dummy. It was a real body and I immediately thought to myself that I had found one of the missing girls." Due to the deposition of her body, Gemma's cause of death could not be established. She was naked when they discovered her, but there were no signs of sexual assault.

After Gemma's body was found, the police began a full-scale investigation to find the body of the assumed dead Tania Nicol. Despite the freezing cold temperatures, a team of divers swept through the disposition spot to find at least one strand of evidence. Less than a week later, Tania Nicol's naked body was discovered in a brook near Copdock Mill, less than two miles away from where Gemma's body was discovered. "Not in my wildest dreams did I anticipate that they would uncover the body of Tania Nicol," DCS Stewart Gull recalled, "We were no longer dealing with two missing persons. This was now a double murder inquiry."

A post mortem took place on both of the victims, but there were no concrete causes of death, due to the terrible shape of the bodies when they were discovered. It was obvious that the women died from lack of oxygen, but no tests could be made to find the culprit of the heinous crime. Ray Palmer, forensic scientist, explained the difficulty he had with retrieving evidence from the bodies, "...because it had been present in flowing water for a number of weeks, any prospect of recovering fibers or other debris for the skin, or any DNA from the skin, in that period of time was virtually zero."

The Suffolk Police department, which investigated an average of six murders per year, was not prepared for the two murders that took place in a matter of six days. The way that the bodies were disposed caused extra issues for investigators, "The bodies of Gemma Adams and Tania Nicol were found in fast flowing, very cold water, and the problem that presented from our perspective was because of the emersion of water, any trace evidence that was present was most likely to be destroyed or washed away." The Ipswich Ripper's choice of deposition location made investigators extremely wary about who they were dealing with, as they realized that they were dealing with a cold and calculating murderer. "The fact that he had placed the bodies in water so as to destroy any forensic evidence, suggested to me that this was a very, what criminologists would describe as an 'organized' killer. By 'organized' I mean that he carefully thought through how he's crucially going to avoid being detected by the police," explained criminologist, Prof. David Wilson.

Anneli Sarah Alderton was 24-years-old when she was last seen on the night of December 3rd. Her body was discovered just days after the first two victims, in a woodland near Amberfield School on December 10th. Alderton was the very first body to show up on dry land. She was found naked and sexually assaulted, but the most disturbing part of the scene was that her corpse was posed in a cruciform position. Unlike the other victims, Anneli Alderton's body had not been deposited in water, so it might've had traces of evidence that could actually lead investigators to the murderer. Forensic scientists immediately combed the scene for any shred of DNA they could find. Investigator Gull explained how he felt after the discovery of Alderton's body in an interview, "Once Anneli Alderton's body had been found, we were clearly into a different realm. It looked very much like we had a serial killer on our hands. It clearly had very obviously linked murder investigations in a very close area around Ipswich and all the indications of that stated that it was the work of one man, or men working together."

The discovery of three murder victims in less than a week lead criminologist, David Wilson, to the conclusion that they were dealing with a serial killer, "When the third body turned up I think I was the first person to say there is a serial killer on the loose in Ipswich and I think those words, I chose with a great deal of care because they were, as far as I was concerned, accurate and they also should've suggested, which I think they did, the gravity of the circumstances." Reporters all over the world flocked to Ipswich upon the news of three bodies. "What happened overnight as this crisis was developing was that the streets became filled with only one group of people and that group of people was journalists. Journalists seemed to be bumping into each other desperately hoping to find a prostitute that they could interview. "

Despite the fact that there was a serial killer in the area, targeting only prostitutes, business did not slow in Ipswich's red light district. Ipswich was a prominent area for drugs and the majority of prostitutes worked the streets so they could fund their drug addictions. This provided an ideal situation for the Suffolk Strangler. The police put out a clear message that warned all sex workers against putting themselves in a life threatening situation, but not many listened. All the working girls that were interviewed admitted that they were scared, but that did not stop them from working. These women had addictions to feed and bills to pay, and sadly, even a murderer wasn't enough to keep them away from the curb crawlers of the red light district.

"Is it my turn, tonight? Am I not going to come home tonight? But what choice have I got but to go out there?" Sarah, a woman who worked the streets of Ipswich, explains the terror that she experienced during this time, "Cars would come by and you'd be praying that they would pick you up to get money, but you're praying that they wouldn't because you don't want them to do what they're going to do." Paula Clennell, the Ipswich Ripper's final victim, was interviewed by an Anglia News reporter only a month before her body was discovered. Paula agreed that she was afraid of the disappearances, but she admitted that it was not enough to keep her away from the money that she desperately needed. "I need the money," She shrugged with her back turned to the camera. Paula Clennell died less than two months later, at the hands of the Suffolk Strangler.

Annette Nicholls was 29-years-old when her body was found on December 12. Nicholls was naked when she was discovered by investigators in the same woods that Anneli Alderton was found. Her corpse was posed in a cruciform position, just like Gemma Adams. Police searched the woodland overhead when an observer from the helicopter inspecting team, Maggie Williams, made another shocking discovery: the body of a 24-year-old Paula Lucille Clennell. A post mortem confirmed that Paula Clennell died from compression to the neck, but the cause of Annette's death could not be established.

After finding five murdered women in the matter of six weeks, DCS Stewart Gull reluctantly announced to the public that they were dealing with a full-fledged serial killer, "Although we only had the cause of death for two [women], in all probability they all died as a result of some form of interference with the airway. So you put all of that together and I think quite rightly, we drew the conclusion that we were looking for just one or more persons, who were involved together in the abduction and murder of all five women." Gull stated. The 600 officers and staff of the Suffolk police department were joined by 500 members from all over the country. It was the biggest manhunt that had ever been conducted in eastern England.

Media presence increased in this area tenfold, which eventually drew the attention of a very odd character named Tom Stephens. The 37-year-old man admitted in an interview with a newspaper that he personally knew all of the victims. It wasn't long after the interview when Tom was taken into custody. "The police had to arrest Tom Stephens on that occasion because he said, 'I knew all of these five women, they've all been back to my house, I do not have an alibi for the nights that they went missing," Explained Professor David Wilson, "In those circumstances the police would've been bonkers not to arrest somebody who is openly saying that."

Tiny amounts of DNA were retrieved from the bodies of Anneli Alderton, Annette Nicholls, and Paula Clennell. The DNA all link back to the same person Steve Wright. Wright used gloves in an attempt to keep all his crime scenes clean from his DNA, but he didn't consider the DNA sample that he left in Birmingham from his previous offenses. This sample sat in a national database until it matched the fibers that were found on the victims. Eventually, this forensic evidence released Tom Stephen's from custody and shined a light on the true Suffolk Strangler.

The Trial

After Wright was identified he was put under 24-hour investigation where the police followed his every move. Early in the morning on December 19th, the police arrested Steve Wright from his Ipswich home. When he was questioned by the police Wright refused to speak. Any questions would be answered with the phrase "no comment". During the first eight outs of interrogation, he recited that line over and over again. Even without a confession, the forensic evidence was enough to charge Steven Wright for the murders of all five women on December 21st, 2006.

Wright's trial began on January 16, 2008, at the Ipswich Crown Court. The only case in Wright's defense was the argument that Wright was a frequenter of prostitutes in this area, although he denied using prostitutes during the interrogation, which would explain why his DNA was found on three of the young girls' bodies. He focused on Tania Nichols, telling a story about how he picked her up with the intention to have sexual relations, but changed his mind and returned her back to the red light district. Again, this account differed from the one that he originally gave to investigators. On February 21, 2008, Steve Wright was charged as guilty on all five counts of murder after eight hours of deliberation. He received a life sentence without any chance of parole. On February 22, 2008, Wright was taken to prison, where he'll be forced to live out the rest of his years behind bars.

Wright is still alive to this day and he is having a terrible time in prison. His twisted state of mind after imprisonment is outlined in his letter to his father: "...I just wish everyone would get along and work towards a family unit because all the bickering and point scoring against each other is really getting me down it seems you are pulling me one way and pam is pulling me the other and in the end, something will give and it just seems to me that person will be me and that is the last thing that I want at the moment has I am sure you do as well because if I start to fall apart at the seams I don't think I could cope in here I need to be strong to cope with this nightmare like that but you said in the paper that when you looked [in] my eyes you would know whether I was guilty or not that really hurt me it was like a knife in the heart for you to even contemplate that I could even be capable of such a terrible crime. You say you want to help me the only way that will happen is if you make the effort to work together because all this he said she said you must understand is not doing my frame of mind any good I just want it to stop I do love you dad..."

arm. Lastly, there was John Sharpe, a compulsive gambler who suffered from short term memory loss.

"Dorothea took Bert Montoya under her wing," Orange said. "Moreso than the other tenants. He liked the fact that he could call her 'momma' and she called him her 'honey bear.' The social worker was surprised at how well he had adjusted to living under Puente's care. But Dorothea used him as a trophy. She used him to show everyone how compassionate and nurturing she could be."

The other tenants began getting jealous of Bert, in particular, John McCauley.

"The other tenants were paying upwards of $300 a month," Orange said. "They would get room and board plus two hot meals. Bert would get all that for free. All because Dorothea had taking a liking to the kind yet simple-minded man."

Dorothea went so far as to set up Bert with a running tab at the local bar. Bert would come in to the tavern, drink no more than three beers, then be on his way.

As much as Dorothea took to Bert as her showpiece, Ben Fink was a thorn in her side.

Fink would drunk himself into a stupor and had an uncanny ability to achieve alcohol levels that would be enough to kill an elephant, let alone a human being.

One night, the compulsive John Sharp was watching a horror movie in his room when he heard a large thump. The sound came from the upstairs bedroom that belonged to Ben Fink. Then he heard large bumps coming down the steps, as if someone were dragging a body. He thought it creepy at the time but didn't investigate.

Ben Fink would then disappear from the boarding house.

No one thought anything of it, however, as boarding house occupants were a transient group of people. Dorothea herself would kick people out after a few weeks and sometimes tenants themselves would leave on their own accord.

Dorothea never liked Ben Fink. Bert Montoya was until one night he did something to get into her doghouse.

Bert had went to the local tavern and this time he had gotten so drunk that he passed out inside the bar. Three of the other tenants had to carry him back to the boarding house.

"The group of men that brought him back described Bert as 'blowing bubbles' through his mouth," Orange said. "So that opens up the possibility that he had something else in his system aside from alcohol. We could easily surmise that Dorothea had begun to drug him up and the alcohol only exacerbated his symptoms. But something had spooked Bert. Something prompted him to drink more than his usual amount. He was trying to medicate himself and forget something he had seen at the boarding house."

Bert then ran away from the home, walking miles in order to return to 'Detox', the homeless shelter downtown.

"I don't want to go back," Bert cried out when the Detox manager allowed him back into the home. "I don't want to go back."

WHAT IS THAT SMELL?

Tenants in the boarding house began complaining about a rancid smell that was coming from the empty bedroom upstairs.

This would later be labeled as the "Death Room".

When the owners of the home, the Odoricos, came to do their monthly inspection they couldn't help but notice the odor themselves.

"It smelled rotten," Ricardo said. "It smelled rotten in there."

"I thought it was the tenants," said Laura Arebalo, Ricardo's daughter. "because some tenants they would not bath on a daily basis."

Dorothea deflected the complaints as expected. She would blame the neighbors, saying they must be cooking something that's "not right." Then when that sounded lame she would blame a broken sewage line.

But late at night, Dorothea would shampoo the carpet in the room, awaking John Sharp.

When tenants and the owner asked about the room, Dorothea would simply say it was a room that was "cursed."

It was the same room where her friend Ruth Monroe had died only a few years earlier.

Neighbors complained to the city and the Department of Health was called in. They did an inspection of the house and made Dorothea sign a few documents.

But the smell remained.

And Bert Montoya returned.

After over two weeks on the streets and sleeping at "Detox" he arrived back at Dorothea's door steps.

Bert wanted to slip back into the house unnoticed but Dorothea saw him.

"When they cross me," Dorothea said. "They don't cross me a second time."

Then Bert disappeared.

"There was a reason why Bert didn't want to go back to the house to begin with," Orange said. "He openly told the people at the Detox that he didn't want to go back. I think he saw something there. Mostly likely he saw them disposing of a body. Chopping up a corpse. Something had freaked him out and Dorothea knew he would eventually say something."

"Bert had become a problem for Dorothea," Sacramento Police Detective Cabrera said. "He might even bring the police. She couldn't allow Bert to bring attention to her. She apparently felt that there was only one thing to do."

MORE SUSPICIONS

Neighbors began taking note of the strange doings of a man only known as "Chief."

Dorothea thought of Chief as the resident handyman of the boarding home. She had the man do odd jobs around place even though he was an alcoholic. Neighbors saw that Chief carted off dirt and junk away in a wheelbarrow after digging in the basement of the boarding home. He then tore down a garage in the backyard and put in fresh cement.

Then Chief disappeared.

And the owners weren't pleased that Dorothea had put in a concrete patio without any consent on their part.

"One time I went to the house," Ricardo Odorico said. "And I found a concrete patio."

"I used to have lots of roses," Veronica Odorico said. "I liked roses. Then I went and saw that everything was different. I said (to Dorothea) 'What happened? You took out the roses. She said 'I don't like roses.' I used to tell my husband he gave her too much freedom. He said it was to improve the house. I said I liked it better like I had it before."

By May of 1988, neighbors no longer complained of a smell coming from Dorothea's home. Now they were complaining of a stench coming from Puente's backyard. Dorothea dismissed their concerns, telling them that she was using "fish emulsion" to fertilize her soil.

"We couldn't stand it," one neighbor said. "There was a sick smell in the air, and there were lots of flies in the area."

In November, of that same year, social worker Nickerson would arrive at Puente's boarding house to do a welfare check on her tenant, Bert Montoya.

Montoya had been last seen in August and Dorothea would tell the police that the man had "gone home to Mexico."

"Dorothea gave this huge elaborate story," Orange said. "But the social worker knew that Montoya would not have picked up and left without notifying her. Smelling something fishy, she notified the police."

Police initially believed Dorothea's story but returned after Nickerson stated that another one of her clients went missing after being in Puente's care.

"Dorothea was accommodating when the police came to question her," Orange said. "They could not do anything without her permission. They couldn't search the premises or even come inside her house. But she was very polite and allowed one of the detectives to look around the home. He found some medicine vials that looked suspicious. They had names of different tenants on the vials but they were all in one drawer of Dorothea's. Then the asked if they could look around in the garden. To his amazement, Dorothea remained cooperative and said it was okay."

The police began digging up Dorothea's back yard. Initially, the dig did not go well. The police unearthed eggshells, food and other articles of garbage. They discovered some leather-like material, with the detective describing it as "very opaque, leathery."

One of the detectives dug further and came upon what he thought was a tree root. He pulled on the "root" and broke it away.

It turned out to be a human leg bone.

And the leather-like material turned out to be decomposed flesh.

The police then discovered the first of several corpses on November 11th, 1988. They found two more the next day.

"It wasn't uncommon for old Victorian homes to have human remains in the backyard," Orange said. "People have dug holes in their backyards and have found bones that date back to the early 1900s. There were occasions where folks didn't have enough money for a proper burial so they buried bodies in the backyard to save money. Initially, that is what the police took the bones for. A case of an old time burial."

But news quickly spread throughout the town and people lined up around the home to gawk. The crowd swelled so large that the police had to cordon off the street. Hot dog and t-shirt vendors began to show up to sell their wares. One of the t-shirts had an elderly grandmother holding up a shovel. The caption on the shirt read "I dig Sacramento."

Dorothea then inquired with Detective Cabrera that she was going to "go for a cup of coffee" at the hotel. Cabrera himself walked her to the hotel to ensure that no one harassed her on the way.

The detective returned to the site and within twenty minutes, he unearthed another body.

"Where's Dorothea?" his Lieutenant asked.

"Dorothea would pay a cab driver sixty dollars to take her to Stockton," Orange said. "From there, she took a bus to Los Angeles."

The police remained on the premises and continued to dig. Three days later, they would unearth seven bodies. They would identify Ben Fink by his swastika tattoo. Dorothy Miller, an elderly alcoholic would be identified as well as Betty Palmer.

"One of the more gruesome finds was that of Betty Palmer," Orange said. "She had her hands and feet chopped off as well as her head. Police searched far and wide for her different body parts to no avail. They dug and even checked under the crawlspace of the house. It is believed that Palmer was Dorothea's second victim and she was perfecting her technique, removing whatever evidence of identification she could."

THE AFTERMATH

The police continued to search the boarding house but found no other bodies. They still believed that other murders took place and Puente had used other means to dispose of her victims.

"We are getting a large number of calls from people with relatives who have stayed there," the Sacramento Police said in an official statement. "There are a lot more than seven names."

Twenty five tenants of Puente were missing and unaccounted for as the police did forensic work on the seven corpses.

Meanwhile, Dorothea Puente remained on the run.

The search began for Puente and by November 17th, she had been spotted in a Los Angeles bar. She had introduced herself to a patron as "Donna Johansson" and began questioning the man about his disability income. She offered to move in with him and fix him "Thanksgiving dinner" despite only meeting the man.

"She invited the man back to her hotel," Orange said. "He found her charming but declined. She got up and left and he's watching television in the bar. A news report comes on and he sees Dorothea is wanted for murder."

The bar patron called the LAPD and Dorothea was arrested at her hotel. Detective Cabrera and other officials from Sacramento Police arrived in Los Angeles to take her back.

"I'm sorry, Detective," Dorothea said while sipping on a cup of coffee.

"Dorothea, I knew if we dig we're going to find more," Cabrera said. "I know that. I know that."

"Well, I didn't put them there," Dorothea said. "I couldn't drag a body any place."

"I believe that. But I believe there's somebody else involved here."

Cabrera knew that there was a distinct possibility that Dorothea had an accomplice.

"Bert Montoya weighed about two-hundred and fifty pounds," Cabrera said. "How does a person that's five-foot-three, five-foot-four, one hundred and thirty-five pounds carry somebody like that."

Resident John McCauley was arrested and questioned by the police. He was later released for lack of evidence.

The police went on to believe that Dorothea had unknowing accomplices, employing her tenants to dig the holes. She would cut the body into pieces. For the pieces she needed help with, she would roll the body part up in carpet or plastic and have someone carry it out.

THE DEATH ROOM

In December of 1988, forensic police work had positively identified four more victims that were uncovered at the Puente boarding home. The victims were Bert Montoya, Vera Martin, Dorothy Miller and Leona Carpenter.

There was evidence to believe that Carpenter was buried alive.

"She (Leona) was put in the ground shallow," Cabrera said. "It appears that her legs, the victim kicked her legs up. And in doing so compacted the dirt around her legs forming a little bridge."

The mystery remained about the smell of the "Death Room". There were no remains found in the room.

Yet the smell never went away.

"One thing I'll never forget is when I pulled the carpet back," Cabrera continued. "When I pulled it back, the most grotesque odor came out and I knew that it was putrefying body fluids. The thing is there was other people living there. And it (burying the bodies) was based on opportunity. When was the best opportunity to put the people in the ground. So these bodies would have to lie there (in the room) until a period or a time when she could get them into the ground. I was in those graves. There was no odor. There as no smell. But in the 'Death Room', the carpet. The body fluid had a smell that would knock you over....This was nothing more than a house of horrors."

THE MOTIVATION

The sum total of Puente's scheming and killing netted her more than $5,000 per month. In turn, she would take the clothing of her victims and donate them to charities.

"We would get calls from local charities," Cabrera recalled. "And they said they were given bags of clothing from Dorothea. Well, what a great way to get rid of evidence."

Dorothea would be brought to trial and prosecutors would describe her as one of the most "cold, calculating" serial killers in American history. No one ever witnessed her kill anybody but Dorothea would later reveal that she would use drugs to overdose her victims. Forensics would discover traces of a prescription strength sleeping pill in all of the remains.

The social security checks would continue to arrive at the residence despite the tenant being deceased.

Dorothea used part of her ill-gotten gains to get a facelift.

On December of 1993, Dorothea would be convicted on three counts of murder of the nine bodies discovered.

"The tragedy in looking back at this story is that it could have been prevented," Orange said. "No one took the time to investigate Dorothea's background. Different agencies knew different information about her yet no one collaborated. The true victims are, of course, the deceased. They were referred to Dorothea as the 'throwaway people'. People that when she dumped into the ground, no one came looking. The tragedy is that Dorothea was right. But for the circumstances surrounding the disappearance of Bert Montoya, who knows how many more murders she would have committed?"

She was sentenced to life in Chowchilla State Prison and she died in 2011.

THE COPELANDS

OLIVIA WATSON

Chapter One

Ray and Faye Copeland are often known as the oldest couple ever to be sentenced to death in the United States. At the ages of 76 and 69, the couple was sentenced to death in separate trials for the murders of five vagrant men that they had taken in, hired, forced to commit fraud, and then finally killed to keep quiet.

While Ray's guilt in the crime was indisputable, Faye's role in the crimes is muddled as she was the victim of severe physical abuse at the hands of Ray. Was she truly involved in the crime? Or was she simply a victim herself?

Ray Copeland was born in Oklahoma in 1914. He had a tough childhood—his family was struggling to survive the Depression and moved around a lot. To help support his family, Ray began a life of petty crime as a young man. He would forge cheques and steal livestock every chance he could.

In the late 1930's, this life of crime caught up to Copeland and he was arrested and sentenced to a year-long jail sentence. After his release in 1940, he met Faye Wilson, a young woman who belonged to a simple family. The two connected and Ray won Faye's heart by promising to always protecting her.

Ray and Faye married only a few months after first meeting. They decided to move from Oklahoma to Missouri and Ray quickly found them a property on the outskirts of the small town of Mooresville. The property was a small plot of farmland that had a simple farmhouse and a few barns, but lots of space for bringing up cattle.

Ray had spent his whole life taking care of cattle, and was convinced that raising and selling cattle would be his fast track path to building a proper life for himself and his family. Ray and Faye had several children in quick succession, which meant that they needed money fast. It wouldn't be long until Ray returned to his old ways, and began to use crime as a means for obtaining money.

Chapter Two

In the late 1980's cattle auction houses throughout the state of Missouri were frequently being swindled. Buyers would show up, make their purchase, pay by cheque and then disappear. The cheques were inevitably worthless.

To combat this problem, cattle auctions in the area began to keep track of buyers who were known to not be good for their money, and they shared these names with other cattle auction houses. If you were blacklisted by one auction house, you would be blacklisted at all the others in the area as well.

Ray Copeland quickly made it onto the cattle auction blacklists. After returning to a life of crime, he quickly built up an increasingly bad reputation. This caused a lot of problems—his whole livelihood was raising cattle and now he couldn't purchase any cattle to raise unless he paid in cold hard cash, something he didn't often have.

Faced with the realization that he could no longer buy cattle himself, he lacked the means to move his family to a new area, and that he was tired of wasting time in jail, he came up with a new plan: a way to use his illegal money-making methods that would allow him to remain undetected.

Ray Copeland began to hire vagrant men from the area to go to cattle auctions with him. He would have the men bid and pay for cattle using his own bad cheques and then sell the cattle before the auction houses realized the cheques bounced. This way, if the auction houses came after someone in relation to the bad cheques, the vagrant men would be responsible, not Ray Copeland.

This scheme worked for Copeland for quite a while. It confused a lot of auction houses and the local police forces for quite some time. As Leland O'Dell, a former sheriff from rural Missouri explained: "It was so odd that so many of them would have cheques but when we went to go look for them, we couldn't find them. We would enter them into the computer, but they never showed up."

Copeland's scheme was smart. No one would expect a man with cheques to be vagrants, and most vagrant men were incredibly difficult to track down.

Eventually, this scheme caught up to Copeland. After police were able to find and interview some of the vagrant men they found out that they had almost all been hired by Ray Copeland. Ray was arrested for his involvement and spent his later incarceration determining how he could further improve this plot.

A while after Ray had been released from jail, the instances of successful cattle fraud scams occurring began to rise again. This time though, all the buyers were repeat customers of the auction houses and none of them could be traced down to be questioned. The only thing that connected them was that at some point in time, many of the buyers had all worked on the same farm owned by 78-year-old Ray Copeland and his wife Faye.

But who exactly were Ray and Faye Copeland, and why had so many of their previous employees seemingly disappeared without a trace?

The answer to this would shock police and Missouri's rural community to their very cores.

Chapter Three

To most, the Copeland's were a regular family living a simple life on their small farm. They appeared to be just a regular elderly farm couple that was a bit shy. They didn't like to socialize with a lot of other people, but that was never really a problem. They seemed completely ordinary.

The Copelands had a difficult life though. Their small farm wasn't enough to support the family so Faye took jobs in local factories and worked as a maid in local motels. When asked why she stood with her husband through all of this difficulty, Faye Copeland simply answered, "Because he was my husband. I was taught from childhood that when you married someone, you stayed with them. The husband was the boss. Ray was always the boss."

The whole family, including Faye, also was required to help out on the farm. They were in way over their heads with the amount of chores and work that needed to be completed everyday, even though none of them earned the family any extra money. Faye would wake up early to go muck out cattle stalls before work.

The family was so poor that when Faye did this, she did it barefoot despite the season. She had one pair of shoes and didn't want them destroyed. She needed them clean to keep up appearances while she spent the rest of her day working her other jobs in town.

When the Copeland children left the farm, Ray looked for farmhands. He was up in age, deaf, and not a great businessman. He was also illiterate. He couldn't read or write which made it difficult for him to keep track of how the business was going. He needed someone to help out with the chores, but also the business side of the ever-struggling farm.

To find these workers, Ray would visit local homeless missions. He would come in and ask people if they would like to go out and make some money and get paid at the end of the day. He would even offer to help the men get set up with bank accounts for their new finances.

These men were almost always vagrants. They were men who were usually on the run, they had addictions, family problems, and mental illness. Most had been arrested for vagrancy or petty theft. Ray Copeland would pay them $50 a day for their labour and would provide them with room and board if the workers wanted to stay on at the farm long-term. For someone who had been previously homeless, a steady paycheque and a place to live in a quiet rural setting would have been paradise. Many jumped at Ray Copeland's offer.

One of the men who went to live and work on the Copeland's farm was 27-year-old Dennis Murphy. Murphy was a drifter from Illinois who was down on his luck when Copeland offered him steady work and a place to live. Murphy was also wanted in connection to writing bad cheques to cattle auction houses.

In 1986, a sheriff's deputy following up on Murphy's several instances of fraud visited the Copeland farm after hearing from other vagrant men that he had gone there to work and hadn't been seen since. The deputy asked Copeland if he knew Murphy's recent whereabouts. Copeland replied that the man had simply took off one day, and he hadn't heard from him since.

Copeland claimed that most of the workers he hired would leave in the middle of the night and he would never see them again. Murphy was only one example of this. When Copeland was told that Murphy was a thief, he said he wasn't surprised. He had been swindled too. Copeland also had a cheque from Murphy that had bounced due to insufficient funds.

Unbeknownst to Ray Copeland, seven other men in addition to Murphy were currently being investigated in connection to local cattle auction scams. The police had been having an incredibly difficult time tracking down any of the eight men and were getting close to determining that all eight must have left town immediately after committing their crimes.

One day however, a call from an unlikely informant in Nebraska opened up a whole new path of investigation for the police—a path with a sinister turn. What if none of the men could be found because after committing their own crimes, they all became the victim of a heinous serial killer.

Chapter Four

The unlikely informant from Nebraska was Jack McCormick, a drifter and small time conman who had at one time worked on Ray Copeland's farm. He liked to tell stories and told police that he thought he had seen human remains including a skull on the Copeland's farm during his time there.

Due to the extensive criminal past Copeland had, and the fact that many of the missing men had worked for Copeland as well, police decided to follow up on McCormick's story.

The Copeland's farm covered 40 acres and included a pond, a barn, fields, and woods. A major search was launched on the property by police. They surveyed the area looking for possible burial sites, human remains, or crime scenes. Scent dogs and backhoes were both used in the search which lasted for weeks. Searchers even poked holes in the walls to find any hollow hiding spots.

After nine days of searching without success, police began to doubt McCormick's story so they decided to bring him back to his former employers farm.

Former sheriff O'Dell was one of them men who brought McCormick back to the Copeland's farm. He remembers telling the man just point to where this skull and leg bones were.

When confronted with this, McCormick got nervous. He told police he could've been mistaken. Perhaps he had actually just seen a discarded pan or other large object poking the bushes. He asked to be taken away from the farm right away—he didn't want to spend a minute more than needed to there.

After this frustrating experience, police decided to launch an in-depth investigation into the background of Ray Copeland. What they found showed an interesting coincidence. Twenty years earlier, Copeland had been arrested several times for the same thing his vagrant workers had—writing bad cheques.

Copeland had seemingly calmed down since then, though. It had been over 20 years since he had wound up in jail, and he had never been arrested for a violent crime. Police soon learned that Copeland worked on some other farms in the area to earn extra money.

One such farm was only a few miles from Copeland's own farm. These properties now needed to be searched as well. Although they weren't quite sure how all the pieces fit together yet, police were almost certain that the disappearance of Murphy and the seven other missing vagrant men were somehow connected to Copeland.

When police searched this secondary location, they made a startling discovery in the barn were Copeland worked moving around large bales of hay. In the back corner of the barn, hidden underneath and behind several large hay bales was a shallow grave—in it, were the bodies of three men lined up head-to-toe-to-head. They had probably been in the grave for two or three years, and were now completely unrecognizable due to the amount of decomposition that had taken place.

The bodies were wrapped in blankets, which kept them dry so they had not decomposed down to skeletal remains. To help this, the soil was also clay, which helps to ward of decomposition as well. Instead, the skin of the bodies had dried out and shrivelled like a mummy.

The three men had been killed by single gunshot wounds to the head. But there was no evidence linking Ray Copeland or anyone else to the crimes. A few days later in another barn on the same property police removed hundreds of bales of hay and found another body under a floorboard.

Six weeks later in a nearby well was yet another body. This man had been wearing a belt that read *Dennis* across the front. But was this Dennis Murphy? And was his killer Ray Copeland?

Chapter Five

After police found the remains of five different men on a farm connected to Ray Copeland, they reinterviewed McCormick. This time, McCormick was more confident in his memories of his former boss.

McCormick told police that Ray Copeland had been running a cheque fraud scam. He said Copeland had given him a few hundred dollars to open a chequing account and told him to list a post office box as his address. He then took McCormick to cattle auctions and sat in the stands, signalling to McCormick when to bid on the cattle.

When he won the bidding, McCormick would pay for the cattle with a cheque. After a couple of his cheques cleared he would be in good standing with the auction house. They next time they returned, he was able to spend more money and write even larger cheques under the pretence that the cheque would be good as well when it was brought to the bank. It almost always bounced the second time.

Copeland would sell the cattle bought under McCormick's name and kept the profits himself. But before the cheque had a chance to bounce, Copeland confronted McCormick with a gun.

Copeland told McCormick that there was a raccoon living in a hole in his barn and he needed the worker's help to get rid of it. He wanted McCormick to crouch down next to the hole and poke the raccoon with a stick while Ray waited with his gun. At this time, McCormick was already nervous around his large, aggressive boss who he knew was orchestrating a fraud scam at the time.

The skittish McCormick bent to Copeland's will and began to crouch down in the barn and poke at the hole with a stick. When nothing happened, Ray told him to keep going. McCormick felt a chill go up his spine and quickly looked back up at his boss to see him pointing his '22 rifle not at the hole where the raccoon was allegedly going to be running out of but directly at his own head.

McCormick promised Ray he would leave the area and never come back if he spared his life. Ray agreed, and McCormick immediately left Missouri behind him. For five months the vagrant man was quiet about his ordeal, and Ray's scam plot, as he still feared Copeland. He knew his former boss had no problems taking lives, so he did what he felt he needed to do to protect his.

When Police searched the Copeland's home, they found a '22 rifle and an assortment of men's clothing, none of which belonged to Ray. They also found several pairs of men's shoes in a range of sizes, none of which fit Ray or their sons, and a bunch of empty suitcases.

Most damningly though, hidden in a camera case was a list of names. The list was a record of men who had worked for Ray Copeland in the past. Next to four of the names was an X, which corresponded with four vagrant men who were wanted in connection to bad cheques that had been given to pay for cattle at nearby auctions. One of which, was Dennis Murphy.

Four names were marked with an X on Copeland's list, and five bodies had been found hidden around a farm Copeland had worked on. It was obvious to investigators that they needed to find a way to have the four bodies positively identified as soon as possible.

Chapter Six

Investigators working on the Copeland case sent the skulls of the five bodies to a forensic odontologist who photographed and x-rayed each of the skulls to compare the dental markings to dental charts from each of the men whose names had been marked with an X. Although this is a common practice in the world of forensic science and criminal investigation, this instance proved difficult.

All the men on Copeland's list were vagrant and homeless. While they all had dental records on file from their childhoods, they were now extremely out-of-date. None of the men had received recent dental care. Without recent records, and with a lifetime worth of damage due to improper care, it was difficult to determine whether the dental records didn't match the skulls because they weren't the same people, or if they didn't match any more because of the outdated records.

One of the skulls, however, was easily matched to previous records because of irregularities in the bones around the teeth. This skull had been from the body found in the well on the farm, and it was positively identified as being Dennis Murphy.

Eventually, the four other skulls were able to be positively identified. Three of the four had been names marked with an X on Ray Copeland's list.

The five bodies were sent to Coroner Scott Lindley to be autopsied. In each case, the cause of death was found to be from gunshots fired from a close distance.

"If the shot is fired from close range, the inside of the skull tends to break or flake away and there is more small fractures and damage done to the skull altogether," Lindley has explained.

Inside each of the skulls Lindley also found bullets and bullet fragments. Markings on the bullets were later conclusively determined to have been able to come from only one gun—Ray Copeland's '22 caliber rifle.

Faced with this information, police confidently arrested Ray Copeland for the five men's murders. In a move that shocked many, they also arrested Ray's wife Faye, who they believed had been his accomplice.

But what role exactly did 68-year-old Faye Copeland play in the murders?

Chapter Seven

Faye Copeland claimed she knew nothing about Ray's crimes. She knew about his previous convictions for fraud, of course, but had no idea that Ray had been murdering their employees in a more modern cattle fraud scheme. According to Faye, when the workers disappeared Ray told her that they had simply run off or that he had fired them and they left right away. She had no reason to doubt her husband's stories, the men were vagrants after all, and Ray had emotionally and physically abused Faye their entire marriage so she wasn't about to question him for details.

While in prison, Faye wrote a letter to her husband assuring him that things would calm down soon. While it was meant to be a calming gesture to the man she was married to, Faye's letter was taken by police and used as a known handwriting sample to be compared to the list of names found in the Copeland's home. Faye's handwriting matched the list of the missing men.

While police saw this as damning evidence Faye maintained her insistence that she had no idea about the murders. She explained to police that Ray was illiterate so he often got her to write lists and notes for him all the time. She never asked any questions, it wouldn't have done her any good. When Ray felt like she was questioning his thoughts or choices he simply slapped her across the house to get her to stop.

No one outside of the family had any indication that Ray may have been abusing his wife, but Ray and Faye's children could recall thousands of times Ray lost his temper and took it out on his wife or his children. Al Copeland, one of Ray and Faye's sons, once recalled to police a time when Ray smacked Al's younger brother with a frying pan because he had been scraping the last few mouthfuls of oatmeal out of his bowl with a spoon and Ray didn't like the noise.

Violence had been an everyday occurrence in the Copeland household.

Ray and Faye Copeland were tried in court separately. Prosecutors believed that Ray had acted alone in orchestrating the fraud schemes, including murdering the men afterwards to keep them quiet, but that Faye had known what was going on the whole time, which would make her criminally responsible as well.

There was no questioning Ray's guilt in court. Investigators were able to prove that each of the five men had died at the other end of Ray's gun after being lured to work for the man and then used as pawns in a cattle fraud scheme. It was irrefutable evidence.

Ray was quickly found guilty on all five counts of murder and other related charges including fraud. He was sentenced to death by lethal injection. Even his own children celebrated Ray's death sentence, viewing it as justice served for the horrible way he treated everyone around him, and for the horrible acts he committed simply to make extra money without having to do extra work.

Throughout her trial, Faye continued to claim she had no involvement and no knowledge in Ray's actions—he had committed his crimes all by himself. Faye was simply an abused wife her put her head down and did what she was told to do. Throughout her life she had carried bruises and broken bones for nothing and had spent most of her life doing everything possible to avoid Ray's violence. Her greatest crime was not asking questions.

The list of workers in Faye Copeland's handwriting, however, sealed her fate. It was the smoking gun of the prosecutor's case, and it got Faye convicted for all five murders as well. She also received a sentence of death.

Before Ray Copeland could be executed he died in prison in 1993. Six years later, in 1999 Faye's attorneys appealed her conviction on the basis that Faye had been too terrified of her former husband to admit her life long abuse at his hands. The abuse had been the reason Faye had written the list, but jurors had never heard this before. The only previous explanation previously could have been that she was involved.

On this basis, the courts commuted her death sentence to life in prison, but her convictions remained. Three years later, Faye suffered a stroke which left her partially paralyzed and unable to speak. She was released from prison a week later on medical parole, fulfilling her final wish not to die in prison. Faye passed away from natural causes less than a year later on December 23, 2003.

DEATH ROW GRANNY VELMA BARFIELD

Georgia Johnson

It never ends.

No way.

No way am I letting this man demean and degrade me another day.

He's just like my father.

A binge drinker. And the binges were happening more and more.

He's on the road to nowhere and taking me with him.

It never ends.

First my father. Now him.

Fuck it.

I threw the cigarette on the blanket. I knew it was flammable.

Then I watched the smoke rise and smiled.

In Lumberton, North Carolina, Thomas Burke fell victim to a house fire which was caused by a burning cigarette. Investigative authorities thought that he had fallen asleep while smoking, leaving thirty-eight-year-old Velma Burke as his widow.

They didn't know that the fire was set by Velma.

Velma knew how to play the part of the grieving widow. She cried and gave the authorities the requisite crocodile tears. No one would believe that the murder of Thomas Burke would set off a series of killings performed by the seemingly kind and harmless church-going woman with the soft voice.

But Velma was a killer...

EARLY LIFE

Velma Bullard grew up as the second of nine children in the rural part of Sampson County, North Carolina.

Times were tough for the Bullard family. They would live on a small farm with no electricity, running water or an outhouse.

"They had to go outdoors," forensic psychologist Paula Orange said. "The entire family had to endure the indignity of going into the woods or using pots to shit and piss."

The home was small and cramped for the nine children. Velma would be forced to sleep in the same bedroom with her parents until the age of five.

Her father was a loom repairman (fixing an apparatus that was used to weave clothing) and an abusive alcoholic. Velma had an older brother, Olive, who were subject to his nightly beatings. Lillie, her mother, was too meek to protect her children from her husband's violent outbursts.

"She had the type of father who would not need any provocation," Orange said. "He would take out the pettiest frustrations, like not being able to find something around the house, and take it out on the children. Velma would become resentful toward her mother who was too weak or indifferent to stop her father from beating on the kids. She accepted his discipline as 'the way it was.'"

Velma would find school as a welcome escape from her dreadful home life. She loved her teacher and was an excellent student during her early grade school years. When she would return home from school, she took solace in the fact that her father would always arrive home late as he worked long hours at the textile mill.

"Her father Murphy had that Protestant work ethic in him," Orange said. "He accepted the long hours and low pay, seeing a kind of nobility in that. Only problem was, he would binge drink. Not store bought alcohol but homemade moonshine. After a couple of shots, he would be 'lit' and inflict his wrath on everyone in the house."

By the age of eleven, Velma would be forced to take on various chores around the farm. She would clean up the house, washing and iron everyone's clothing (eleven people). Her father would chastise her for not mending or sewing his work clothes properly as well.

"Her father was a stern taskmaster," Orange said. "Hell, you can say 'slave driver.' He would have Velma come home early from school days when the laundry got too backed up. Velma hated this and felt embarrassed. Her family didn't have much and as she grew older her classmates began to see her for what she was, a poor girl that was an easy mark for teasing."

Velma would grow to be 5'3" but gain weight as she got older. She would be mocked about her obesity, her shoddy clothes the gap between her two front teeth. She would also be called "knot head" after she ran head first into a boy at school which left a permanent contusion on her forehead.

By the age of twelve,Velma seemed to have taken on all of her mother's duties. She would cook all of the family meals in addition to performing cleaning around the farm house. She would miss school for days at a time as her father forced her to complete chores around the home before she could continue her education.

"Academic achievement was not at the forefront of her father's mind," Orange said. "Her mother was of little use because of her depression and mental illness. Velma was the oldest girl so she took on the duties of mom at an age where she should have been playing with dolls."

ANGER, ABUSE, AND CHURCH

Despite her father's verbal abuse and alcohol-fueled beatings, the family kept up a face of religious interest. Velma would be sent to Bible school every year until the age of thirteen. During her last year of Bible school, her father marked the occasion by buying Velma a silk pink dress with ribbons. Velma recalled the day as one of the happiest of her life.

The happiness would be short-lived.

Velma would claim that her father raped her when she was thirteen years old. She revealed this only to her pastor in her later years before she stood trial. Velma did not even tell her mother whom she did not think would believe the molestation took place.

"Things that went on inside our home when I grew up," Velma said. "Were kept inside."

At the age of fifteen, Velma continued to excel in school. Despite her chubby physique, she becomes adept at basketball and is pegged to be the team's star player for the upcoming season. But her father did not allow her to play.

"Who is going to iron these damn clothes?" he snarled.

The family then moved to Robeson county and switched from the Presbyterian denomination to Baptist. It was here that Velma would meet Thomas Burke and the two made it clear that they wanted to date. Once again, Velma's father would intervene, telling Velma that she had to wait until her sixteenth birthday until she could date.

The two waited patiently for her birthday to arrive and the following year Thomas would propose to her while they went to the movies.

Knowing that her father would not approve, Velma and Thomas eloped, moving to Dillon, South Carolina. Neither Thomas or Velma had any money as they both quit high school to get married. Thomas then went to work at a local textile mill.

"At this point, I believe that Velma began to realize that her life would not be that much better with Thomas," Orange said. "He literally has the same job as her father."

Economics forced Velma and Thomas to move in with his parents. This arrangement would last for a year until Thomas got a better paying job at a soft drink company.

At the age of nineteen, Velma would give birth to her first son, Ronnie. The couple would then move back to Parkton, North Carolina where they would remain in the same home for eleven years. Two years later, the young couple would welcome a daughter named Kim.

A CYCLE OF RELIGION AND ABUSE

The Burkes would be fixtures at the local Baptist church with Velma taking the reigns to teach a Sunday school class. But the prayers and sermons would do little to offset the growing ennui in the Burke home. Two years after giving birth to Kim, Velma would get hit by a drunk driver while crossing the street. She would be hospitalized for an extended period, suffering both physically and mentally.

Thomas' job at the soft drink company would not be enough to provide for the family. Velma would be forced to leave her small children at home and work in a textile mill just like her father. The couple would have different work hours, with Velma working nights and Thomas working days as they would take turns watching the children.

Velma would fall victim to the hard work at the mill and the stress of raising two young children. She began bleeding and her doctor performed a hysterectomy.

Velma's mother would take pity on the couple and give them one acre of land near their old farm. Thomas would build a three-bedroom home for the family but Velma was already going down a slippery slope. Her personality changed after the hysterectomy, claiming that she always felt "nervous and afraid."

Things would get worse as Thomas suffered a head injury in a car accident. He then began to drink heavily and begin to beat Velma.

"It was deja vu," Orange said. "Velma had, in essence, married her father."

One night, the couple argued and Thomas punched Velma in an alcohol-fueled tantrum. The police are called to the home and Velma sent Thomas to the state hospital to get treatment for his drinking. Her husband remains there for three days but when he returns home, his behavior is worse than behavior. He's angry at Velma for sending him to the "drunk tank". His alcoholism worsens and he would go on to lose his job because of absenteeism.

"Velma is thirty-five years old at this time," Orange said. "But she's an old thirty-five with crow's feet under her eyes and a hangdog look. She's had a rough life, not necessarily by her own design, and it has taken its toll."

Velma leaves the textile mill but then finds two different jobs in order to support the family. During the day, she works as a sales clerk in a Belk department store. At night, she goes to work as a machine operator in a cotton mill.

Thomas, meanwhile, would continue to drink.

He rages on a daily basis, on one occasion he pinned son Ronnie up against the wall and threatened him with a knife. Velma would faint during the encounter and be transported to the hospital. She was diagnosed as having a nervous breakdown and lapsed into a serious depression. The medical staff gave her tranquilizers to calm down. Velma believed that it was during this stint in the hospital that she became addicted to the painkillers.

"The drugs were helping," Orange said. "When nothing else did. So she wanted more and more."

Velma's children acknowledged that their mother's mood swings were due to the drugs.

Over the next three years, Velma would go in and out of the hospital for drug overdoses. After each visit, her addiction only grew as did her prescription list.

"She fell through the cracks in her own family," Orange said. "And in the system itself. Her family had their own issues to deal with as Thomas would abuse everyone on a daily basis. Finally, Velma did something she could control. She killed her husband."

On April 21st, 1969, Velma would drop a cigarette on the floor of her home and waited until her husband inhaled enough smoke to die.

His death, however, would do nothing to solve Velma's problems.

Her addictions and anxiety would only get worse.

A HOSPITAL FREQUENT FLYER

Velma would have another nervous breakdown after killing Thomas and lapse into a guilt-ridden depression. But seven months later, a co-worker at the Belk department store would introduce her to fifty-four-year-old Jennings Barfield. Jennings had emphysema and diabetes but Velma would marry him anyway. Unlike her marriage with Thomas which started out well, Velma's marriage with the older Jennings would be troubled from the start. Her drug addiction would escalate and Jennings would express his own regret at marrying her.

"I don't know why I married her," Jennings said. "All she does is pop pills all day."

After less than three years of marriage, Velma decided to part ways with Jennings. She didn't file for divorce, however, she decided to poison him with arsenic. She would later claim that she only meant to "make him sick."

Jennings Barfield was already ill and doctors had no suspicion that Velma was behind the death. Arsenic was a slow burn poison that could kill without detection. The autopsy called for no arsenic test and Velma had gotten away with murder once again.

But Seven months later, Velma would overdose on her prescription meds and become hospitalized. Her family recognized the pattern but could not wean Velma off of the drinks. She would remain hospitalized for three weeks.

Her personality seemed to change after the hospital release. She returned to work at Belk department store but kept being combative and argumentative with customers. Her boss knew of her circumstances and tried to coax her to do better. He took her away from the public contact and into the back stock room where he had her put pricing on the clothing items.

Her boss soon realized that Velma's addiction had gotten out of control. Velma would not be able to function in the back room, leaving tasks uncompleted as she would have her prescription medications delivered to the store.

"It is a hopeless situation," the store manager told Velma's son Ronnie before he fired his mother.

BROKE AND DESTITUTE

With no income, Velma would lose the family home as she no longer paid the mortgage. She would be forced to move back in with her parents and face the two people she blamed everything for.

Her father had grown ill, however, and would die from lung cancer shortly after Velma moved back into the home. She would feel bad about her father's death and admit that she had a love/hate relationship with him.

"I had learned to love him as much as I had hated him," Velma said. "He was so good to my kids. I think he tried to do with my kids like he wished he had done to us. He could not stand to see me correct them. If I would pick them up and spank them, he would ask me, 'Isn't that enough?'"

But after her father's death Velma self-medicated once again. She overdosed and was hospitalized for two weeks. Her family didn't judge, they instead thought she was "cursed."

"Velma needed psychiatric help," Orange said. "So she began medicating herself with deleterious results. She would "doctor shop" for different physicians who would be manipulated into giving her the drugs she wanted. Her addiction eventually grows until she becomes desperate for money in order to fuel the drug habit."

A MURDERER AND A THIEF

Velma began stealing from those closest to her, starting with her mother. Her mother confronted Velma about a missing check and Velma went ballistic.

"She had violent mood swings," Orange said. "The medication had completely changed her personality as she needed the drugs above all else. The people around her were not familiar with how to handle a person who had this kind of mental illness. So this made for a very dangerous cocktail for her and anyone close to her."

Hitting a new low, Velma took out a $1,000 loan under her mother Lillie's name. She put up the family home as collateral and forged her mother's signature on the documents. Velma then blew through the money and a month later took out another loan, once again using her mother's house as collateral. The following month, she emptied the checking account on her now deceased husband, Jennings. Two months later, the loan company began sending Velma overdue notices as she had not been paying off the loan.

"In Velma's mind," Orange said. "She had no other choice but to kill off her own mother."

Velma went to the local pharmacy and looked for bottles that had the warning of "fatal if ingested." She put the poison into a drink for her mother and watched as she drank the fatal elixir.

Her mother then began vomiting and lost control of her bowels. Within a few hours, her mother could not so much as walk and an ambulance was called.

Velma came to visit her in the hospital to finish the job. Armed with a Thermos, she made a special concoction of chicken soup and arsenic.

"Drink it slow," Velma said as she tenderly lifted the cups to the lips of her ailing mother. "Slow."

Her mother would eventually die of "natural causes" as no one suspected Velma of committing murder. Instead, she received sympathy.

"So sorry for your loss," hospital staff said.

"The thing with arsenic is that it shuts down the whole system," Orange said. "So hospital staff just chalked up her mother's weakness to old age. Checking for arsenic poisoning would be the furthest thing from their mind."

Velma showed the necessary emotion and received sympathy from friends and family. She then moved in with her daughter Kim and son-in-law Dennis who lived in a trailer park. She could not evade the authorities for long though as the authorities caught wind of Velma's check forgeries.

Velma reacted as she always did. She would run away and medicate herself.

"Her drug addiction kept pushing her into a corner and she saw no way out," Orange said. "So, this time, she goes to her son Ronnie's house and overdoses again, trying to kill herself. She falls and breaks her collar bone which laid her out in the hospital another three weeks."

But the police find her situation unsympathetic.

"We're sorry, Velma," the deputy informed her at her hospital bed. "But once you have been cleared for release, we will arrest you."

Velma would not have that. She tried to overdose again but this go around the hospital staff pumped out her stomach.

She was sent to court the next day and sentenced to six months in jail for the forgery. She is released after four months for good behavior.

NO REHAB HERE

Her addiction still unchecked, Velma returned to live with Kim and her son-in-law. She rummaged through the belongings of her son-in-law and stole a check, forging his name so she can get more prescription meds. Her daughter Kim now has caught wind of her mother's addiction, pleading with her doctors to stop prescribing her.

"In some ways," Orange said. "The doctors were just as guilty as she was. But back in the day, there was no way to cross-reference this stuff like we do now. Once she had her fill with one doctor she would go to the next and the next."

Velma's addiction prevented her from taking a forty-hour a week job. So she looked for alternative forms of income.

She would find a job taking care of the elderly.

Montgomery and Dolly Edwards would be her first clients.

"She found herself some easy targets," Orange said. "There didn't seem to be any legislative body in place that prevents sociopaths from caretaking the elderly. So Velma doesn't slip through any cracks, she just befriends the elderly couple and begins taking care of them."

Montgomery was blind and unable to walk. He was 93-years old and his 83-year old wife was too feeble to take care of him. They paid $75 a week for Velma to become their live-in caretaker.

All was good, at least in the beginning. But Dolly had a sharp tongue and would criticize Velma daily. Velma would keep a nice exterior unless confronted, saw Dolly has yet another wheel in her cycle of verbal abuse.

"It seemed to be a never-ending loop for her," Orange said. "Being forced to deal with verbally abusive people. Velma had long since snapped and Dollie simply had no idea who she was dealing with."

Velma began to plot out Montgomery and Dollie's demise until she meets their nephew, Stuart Taylor.

Stuart was already married but was blown away when he met the caretaker of his Aunt Dollie.

Velma would play it cool, stealing what she could from the couple in terms of petty cash and household items that had value. They outlived their usefulness to her within a year as Montgomery died of "natural causes". One month later, Dolly also passed away.

And again, no one suspected the sweet and soft-spoken Velma to have had anything to do with their deaths.

MOVING ON

Velma saw being a caretaker as a perfect front for her. She could steal as much money as she could and when the old folks detected something amiss she would simply poison them. After killing the Edwards' couple, she set the word out at church that she as available to be a caregiver. The pastor would refer her to Margie Lee Pittman who was seeking for a caregiver for her elderly parents, John Henry and Record Lee.

"She comes here twice a week," the pastor reassured Pittman. "She's a nice, kindly woman. You can't go wrong."

Pittman's father, John Henry Lee, was eighty years old when he discovered that his new caregiver had forged a $50 check on his account. He then fell violently ill, suffering through a spastic spell of vomiting, diarrhea, and convulsions. The doctors would chalk up his quick death to gastroenteritis but in fact, he had been poisoned with arsenic.

Velma played the caregiver role until his end. She attended his funeral and cried with the family, sending an ornate wreath (with money stolen from the dead man) to the proceedings.

For whatever reason, Velma spared Lee's wife and moved back to Lumberton, North Carolina to live in a trailer park. She began working as an aide in a nursing home and received word from Stuart that he was now a widow. The two began dating and she moved part of her belongings into his home.

"Stuart is a nice guy," Orange said. "He has no idea what kind of woman Velma is. She is so manipulative and cunning that the younger man is putty in her hands. So the relationship starts great as she reels him in with kindness and charm."

The couple are happy cohabitating until Stuart Stuart finds a letter addressed to Velma from the state penitentiary.

Curious, he began reading the correspondence and realized that is from a former cellmate of Velma.

Stuart became enraged. He threatened to "expose" Velma to all of his family and friends. Somehow, someway, however, she was able to calm him down.

He then found out that she had forged over $200 in checks on his account. The two argued but stayed together for the next two months.

"Velma had the Christian facade down pat," Orange said. "She asked Stuart to forgive her and the next thing you know they are going to a Rex Humbard revival. But before they went, she poured arsenic poison in both his beer and tea. She made sure he drank every drop."

Returning home from the revival, Stuart started to vomit on the drive home, the poison kicking in.

Velma had to keep the con going. She had to appear like a concerned girlfriend so she called up Stuart's daughter, Alice, later that night and told her that Stuart had came down with the flu.

Stuart's daughter expressed concern but Velma kept her at bay.

"Don't you worry now, honey. I'll take care of everything."

Stuart died the next day.

Velma would speak at Stuart's funeral and tearfully asked for his wedding band. His family graciously allowed her to have it and gave her $400 to help her cope with the grief.

But Alice knew her father was a picture of health. She vociferously argued for more tests beyond the standard autopsy and sure enough, arsenic had been found in Stuart's tissues.

On March 10th, 1978, the sheriffs arrived at Velma's home to bring her in for questioning. She was interrogated for over three hours, holding her ground. But she knows the evidence will trump her denials and tries to commit suicide after being released. This go around, however, her son Ronnie stopped her.

The sheriffs come to visit Velma again and she has one more surprise up her sleeve.

But Velma has one more surprise up her sleeve.

She would confess. Not only for the murder of Stuart but of six others.

"I set my first husband on fire," Velma confessed without an attorney present. "And I killed the rest of them."

"It was almost as if she wanted to be free of the guilt she had been carrying," Orange said. "Her confession seemed to take a burden off her back."

"The last ten years were like that," Velma said. "A drug nightmare. It was a case of not knowing where you are or what you've done."

The bodies of her victims were later exhumed and all tested positive for arsenic.

FACING THE GRIM REAPER

Velma's case would be prosecuted by Joe Freeman Britt, who was listed in the Guinness Book of World Records as the country's "deadliest prosecutor."

Velma would plead not guilty by reason of insanity but the court denied her plea.

"I needed to keep them sick until I could pay back the money I had stolen from them," Velma said. "I wanted to earn their thanks by nursing them back to health. I needed the money. I was addicted to pain killers. Anti-depressants. Amphetamines."

On November 23rd, 1978, Velma's trial would begin in Elizabethtown, North Carolina where she would be charged with the first-degree murder of her boyfriend, Stuart Taylor. The trial lasted seven days and the jury reached a verdict of guilty, placing her on death row at the age of 47. She was scheduled to be executed on February 3rd, 1979 but received a stay.

Velma would be sentenced to death and the verdict was appealed all the way to the U.S. Supreme court. Her attorney maintained that the jury had never been presented with the full extent of Velma's "addiction and background." Velma remained tight-lipped about that to everyone but her pastor. Her attorney felt thought her horrific background could have been used as part of her defense and the jury would have found her to be more of a sympathetic case.

CHANGING SPOTS?

"She's not the same person who went to prison in 1978," Kim Burke Norton, Velma's daughter said.

While in jail, Velma became a model prisoner.

"The first week I was here was the worst week," Velma recalled. "Everything about it."

Velma no longer had access to her drugs in prison and she began to dry out. With daily visits from two different pastors, Velma began to discuss her anger and repressed issues that fueled her addiction and murders.

Velma would claim that as she was awaiting trial in 1978 she came to a "meeting with Christ" that caused her to "change inwardly."

Velma heard a broadcast by radio evangelist JK Kinkle. "Jesus loves you, prisoners, too," Kinkle said. "He died for you too. No matter what you've done, the Lord will forgive you."

After Velma heard this sermon, she dropped to her knees and cried out to God.

She would then become the "go to" counselor for young inmates in the prison.

The inmates would nickname Velma as "Mama Margie" because of her wisdom and she would in turn think of them as her "adopted children."

The prison guards and counselors would take the most incorrigible prisoners and place them in a cell next to Velma. Velma would invariably counsel the young prisoner and advise them on the correct path.

"They'd come in ready to kill themselves," Sister Mary Teresa Floyd said. "And here she was with a death sentence, mothering and helping them."

"Living in prison is a struggle," Velma said. "Even at its best. And I know that without Him and His strength that has sustained me, I couldn't have made it even this far."

Her stay on death row soon became a part of the news brief. During this time, a phalanx of evangelists would take her cause to the mainstream. The Reverend Hugh Hoyle would become Velma's personal minister as she received stays of execution in September, October and December of 1981. She would also have a letter correspondence with Ruth Graham, Billy Graham's wife as well as meeting their daughter Ann.

While Velma impressed the Christian do-gooders, the family members of the victims were not taken in by her "conversion."

"She's got religion now, they say," Margie Lee Pittman said. "Well, she had religion before. So we all thought."

A few more stays were granted until 1984 when the U.S. Supreme Court justice Warren Burger granted her a stay until August of that year. At this point, however, her execution seemed inevitable. In an ironic move, Velma would choose poison rather than the gas chamber and enjoyed the final visits from her children and grandchildren.

During the final week before her execution, the Reverend Hoyle, and his wife came to the prison with a battery-powered portable keyboard. His wife played the little organ then the Reverend sang "He Hideth My Soul" and "He is So precious to Me" in the cramped visitor booth.

Velma sang along, whistling in the graveyard before the reaper came for her.

She then wrote letters to each of the victim's family asking them for forgiveness. Reverend Hoyle would deliver the letters to the families, all of whom would refuse them.

MEET THE HANGMAN

As her execution date neared, Velma was placed in a solitary cell that stood directly across from the death chamber.

"It's total isolation," Velma said. "From everyone I had been with for six years."

North Carolina Governor James B.Hunt would reject her final plea for clemency.

On the day of her execution, the jail house would turn into a media frenzy. Death penalty advocates gathered outside the prison and chanted "Hip, hip, hurrah...K-I-L-L" while some sloganeered with "burn, bitch, burn". The protesters held up a few placards that quote Romans ch.13 which ironically was a verse that Velma would repeat to guards during her prison stay.

"For rulers are not a terror to good works, but to the evil...(The ruler) beareth no the sword in vain, for he is the minister of God, a revenger to execute wrath upon him that doeth evil."

The execution was scheduled to take place at 2:00 a.m but the protesters remained outside, their chants reduced to a simple "Kill her! Kill her!"

On November 2nd, 1984, Velma would be executed by lethal injection. The prison official came out and addressed the press, giving out copies of Barfield's statement of apology. The reporters then eagerly anticipated what Velma requested for her last meal. Initially, Velma just wanted the normally scheduled prison food; chicken livers, collard greens and a sheet cake with peanut butter icing. The last meal was delivered but Velma immediately lost her appetite. Instead, she opted for Cheese Doodles and a glass of Coca-Cola.

"Her attorney believed that Velma could have done some good in life," Orange said. "He stated that she could have become a teacher, counselor or a pastor. But her father set her on a path of self-destruction that she couldn't escape from. By the time she the left that road to ruin, she was too far gone in terms of her murderous acts. Justice had to be served in the end. In the end, the law doesn't care how genuine you are in your pleas for forgiveness. It only cares about the rule of law."

"I'm sorry for the hurt that I've caused," Velma said before her execution. "So many people, today if it were possible, I wish I could take every bit of hurt on myself."

THE CULT OF SANTA MUERTE

ANA BENSON

Silvia Meraz Moreno and the Cult of Santa Muerte

What is our picture of the perfect grandmother? Surely, they should be loving, spoilers of their grandchildren. Grandmothers should be a source of advice and support to their own children. Being a parent is a tough job, and the experience and skills that the older generation can offer can be a life-saver during the good times, let alone when things get tough.

But in the case of Silvia Meraz Moreno, we see a different side of the loving Grandma. Life taker is a better term to describe this grandmother than life saver. She led her family to slaughter her own grandson, sacrificing him to the altar of Santa Muerte, a bizarre and frightening cult whose base in Mexico is spreading, like some cankerous disease, to other parts of the world. In particular, to the United States.

Mexico is, of course, a strongly conservative and Catholic country. Religion might be playing an ever-decreasing role in the lives of its people, but for all that, it remains more influential than in most countries of the world. But Santa Muerte, despite the sound of its name with its suggestion of sainthood, is a cult that plays no part in the Catholic Church.

Indeed, the Church's leaders work hard to lessen the attraction of this strange and frightening cult, attempting to educate the poor members of society who are drawn to it. At the moment, they are not doing a very effective job

Santa Muerte is known by many names – Holy Death, Flaquita, which translates with a dark irony to 'skinny girl', or even Huesuda, or Bony Lady. For Santa Muerte is presented as a skeleton. A fleshless body often dressed in a white shroud, one whose presence is slowly, and disturbingly moving out of the dark recesses of private homes into mainstream life.

Effigies of 'Saint Death' now appear on the streets and market places of the most deprived, dangerous parts of Mexico. This trend began following the erection of a statue of the 'saint' on the sidewalk outside the home of Enriqueta Romero in the crime ridden Barrio of Tepito, one of the most impoverished parts of Mexico City. Pilgrims flock in their hundreds to offer gifts to the skeleton, which is bedecked in bright gowns and long, disturbing, hair. A moment's prayer, and the devotees are moved on to ensure the flow of people. Meanwhile, disinterested assistants spray holy water from a can onto the effigies the followers carry.

Fellow leader of the cult, Enriqueta Vargas has a seventy-five-foot fibreglass statue of Santa Muerte in her 'temple' in Tultitlan, where she conducts baptisms and weddings. The Skeleton Saint has even appeared on the television series, Breaking Bad and it is believed that there are upwards of two million followers of this angel of death in Mexico, and perhaps as many as six times that figure worldwide.

The cult that has grown up around this figure has taken on quasi-religious connotations. People, mostly young, offer sacrifices to the skeleton, and in return believe that she will grant wishes. Those sacrifices are typically the treats of the poor – cigarettes, sometimes food, alcohol along with fruit and flowers. She is inclusive in the granting of her gifts, treating the poor in the same way as the rich.

And, in a country where the poor and marginalised feel judged and out of touch with the Catholic Church, she is seen as one who will not judge the poor because of their circumstances, who values everybody irrespective of their background and wealth. It is a powerful message to hold in a country of such extremes of living standards as Mexico.

The 'religious' side of Santa Muerte's following has developed from the Catholic practices under which many of her devotees grew up. Rosaries, prayers and candles feature heavily in prayer to her, and physically, she bears an unmistakable similarity to the Virgin of Guadeloupe. In fact, her roots are not clear. Many believe that she rose from a combination of the practices of Spanish Catholicism, and the legends surrounding Mictecacihatl, the queen of the afterlife and underworld worshipped by the Aztecs.

Nowadays, she is the queen of the downtrodden, the marginalised, the criminals and the organised drugs cartels that are far too prevalent in many parts of the troubled country of Mexico. Prisons are crowded with her devotees. These people feel that they can ask for the granting of any favour, from better health through to protection from drugs trafficking, and as long as they pray, show gratitude and make an offering such wishes will be granted. Her attraction, though, is not limited to just the poor – to the dismay of the Catholic Church, she is attracting ever more followers from middle class homes.

But for all this, what she has not attracted, at least to the latter part of the first decade of this century, are human offerings.

It seems as though her cult originated in the Gulf or Mexico area, before taking a hold in Tepito and spreading from there to the barren border towns of Sonora, then north into the US and south towards Central America. Candles and prayer cards, along with other paraphernalia of Catholic religion, such as figurines, can be found in New York, Los Angeles and Chicago. For a short spell, the Cult of Santa Muerte was even recognised as an official religion in Mexico, but the authorities retracted the status after a couple of years.

Growth of cults such as Santa Muerte are not uncommon in Mexico, which has long had a tradition of worship for local folk heroes as well as devotion to Afro-Cuban and Aztec customs. But few, if any, have had the impact of this particular one.

Yet for a belief system so associated with the underworld of Mexican society, there has been little crime associated directly with the 'saint'. A bishop in the belief system was arrested for corruption in 2011, along with some of his congregation, although his supporters believe that he could well have been framed to bring a bad name to the cult and further disadvantage the downtrodden. David Romo was the bishop of a bright, many might say tasteless, shrine in the dangerous area of Tepito in Mexico City. Of course, the term 'bishop' is something of a misnomer. Any official status was self-appointed, because an organisation that is not officially recognised, and is not allowed to raise money or own property cannot, by definition, hold accredited positions in its hierarchy.

Romo was accused of money laundering and kidnap. The authorities claimed that he led a team of assistants (four men and three women were arrested at the same time as Romo) who collected ransoms through their bank accounts. Romo would organise the kidnaps, the ransoms would be paid to the 'assistants', who would take a small cut of the fee, and the rest would go to the bishop. Although he paid the kidnappers a small amount from that income, he was still making around 25000 pesos, which equates to about $1800, per kidnap.

Members of the Santa Muerte community are split on his guilt. Most feel that he is simply another easy victim of authorities seeking to discredit their cult. Others, though, suspect that the accusations might be true. They dismiss Romo and his followers as disloyal to the cult, people interested only in profit rather that true supporters of the unofficial saint.

But if it is true that the authorities simply framed him to discredit the cult of Santa Muerte, those in authority need only to have waited a little longer, because in 2012 the case of Silvia Meraz Moreno brought infamy to the cause, and all the publicity both the cult's followers, and its opponents, desired.

The State of Sonora in North West Mexico is a barren area, dominated by a mixture of the hot, dusty desert and crumbling mountains. Within that, there are touches of beauty; some of the beaches on the Gulf of California Coast are wonderful, and attract visitors from around the world. Silvia Meraz was born in the region's capital, Hermosillo, in 1968. It is a relatively wealthy city, liberal by Catholic Mexican standards, although even today gay and lesbian couples will attract stares or mistrust, although rarely outright opposition.

But mostly it is a friendly place, where visitors are welcomed, and the majority of the region's population can be found. We know very little of Silvia Meraz's background, but it appears as though education was minimal, and her upbringing was tough. This hard upbringing no doubt contributed to the strength of will that would later lead her to convince her family to participate in the vilest of acts.

At some point, she moved to Nacozari de Garcia, a small town close to Hermosilla, but a little to the north. This town existed on its copper mining. Meraz was already a grandmother by the age of 34, the father of her children certainly not on the scene, even if he were known. It is thought that Meraz ran a brothel, although the authorities were not that concerned about the matter.

In fact, the local community held Meraz's household in some sympathy. They were clearly very poor, had no obvious means of income and lived quietly on the edge of town in a crumbling shack of a home. There were only a couple of unusual events that caused some twinges of concern among the people of the town. Firstly, the number of strangers who seemed to visit – that was the basis of the authority's feelings that the home was a base of prostitution. Secondly, Meraz was the local leader of the cult of Santa Muerte.

People come and go in this part of Mexico. It is very rural, and extremely impoverished. While the nearby State capital is more liberal and cosmopolitan, the small town of Nacozari de Garcia liked to keep to itself.

So even when a ten-year-old boy disappeared, the investigations were cursory. Martin Rios disappeared in July 2010. The police spoke to the boy's mother, and also to her boyfriend, but they seemed unconcerned. Friends had reported that Martin had been seen in the town of Agua Prieta, a bigger community on the border with the US, close to the town of Douglas, Arizona. He had been begging there.

The daughter and the boyfriend promised to go and collect him, and the police were satisfied, and investigations ended. How the boy covered the 150 miles from Nacozari de Garcia to Agua Prieta, and who was tending for him in the bigger city were questions that were either not asked, or the responses were not fully investigated. No more was heard of Martin Rios for another two years.

Then, twelve months or so later, another ten-year-old went missing. Jesus Octavia Martinez Yanez was the grandson of Silvia Meraz. Local people noted that Martin Rios had been a regular visitor to the home of Meraz. Less surprisingly, of course, so was Jesus. Suspicions began to raise their heads. But there was no evidence for any wrong doing, just a vague feeling that things with the Meraz family were not all that they should be.

Searches in the locality led to no sign of the boy, nor any witnesses to his disappearance. Had he too left the small copper mining community to stay with friends or relatives, or on the streets, in a larger town? Was he begging on some street corner, vulnerable and alone? Or worse, had he been forced into the drugs trade – youngsters were often used as carriers and messengers, they were less suspicious than adults, many of whom would already be well known to police. Perhaps he too had been forced into prostitution, or the human trafficking trade.

A year after the disappearance of young Jesus, the link with Martin Rios was made, but still the Meraz family were not under suspicion. Certainly, it was known that that not only Silvia, the family matriarch, was a local leader for the Santa Muerte cult, but that her son was also heavily involved in the underground 'religion'. Yet, as we saw earlier, although many involved in the drugs trade followed the teachings of Santa Muerte, they had been no violent crimes directly tied to the belief system. There was no reason to suspect that the Meraz clan were responsible for a first.

Back in the 1980s, fifteen bodies had been discovered in Mexico, apparently slain in ritual killings. However, although suspicions had been present that there could be a link to the 'Holy Death' cult, it had seemed more likely that it was a drug's fuelled slaughter. The defence had claimed that the killers believed that by sacrificing the dead, which included 21-year-old American student Mark Kilroy, they would be protected from arrest. But no direct link between the slaughter and the Santa Muerte cult was proved.

Therefore, there was no particular reason to associate the family of Meraz with the disappearance of either of the young boys. However, the question of prostitution remained. Many in the town were convinced that this was going on at the house, but lack of evidence (and, probably, resources and time) had prevented any investigation. This, after all, was a town with a major drugs problem, where cartels were omnipresent, and where poverty presented plenty of problems of its own to the local law enforcers.

But now the authorities had an opportunity to investigate. The disappearance of the boys gave them a legitimate reason to search the collection of outbuildings and shacks where the Meraz family lived. Investigators felt that there was little or no probability of finding any evidence of the boys, but they expected to find evidence of other, less nefarious, activities.

But what they did discover shocked even the hardened investigators of the Mexican police.

One of the barns had been turned into a kind of place of worship, complete with altar. To their surprise, and horror, polices found evidence of blood spread for thirty square metres around that altar. Maybe it was ignorance on the part of Meraz and her followers, but it seems as though little effort was made to hide the blood. Perhaps the family believed that the Santa Muerte would protect them from prosecution.

Even then, police wondered more about the traces of blood. The area is notorious for violent crime, most of it emanating from the drugs cartels. But it was soon established that in this case, the perpetrators seemed likely to be based closer to home.

Although the Santa Muerte cult was growing fast, in the tiny town of Nacozari such interest as there was stayed close to home. Indeed, close to the family of Silvia Meraz Moreno. Then a breakthrough occurred. Police dug up the bedroom floor of one of Silvia Meraz's daughters, and there discovered the remains of Jesus.

With there seeming to be no other probable perpetrators of whatever crime had occurred, the police arrested the cult members. Along with Silvia, her partner Eduardo Sanchez, was taken into custody, and a link was soon found to the missing

Martin Rios. It turned out that Sanchez had once been in a relationship with the boy's mother, Zoyla Hada Santacruz Iriqui, who was also arrested, and was later found to have agreed to her son's sacrifice. Silvia's three daughters were also arrested – Francisca Magdelana, the eldest at twenty-five, twenty-one-year-old Georgina Guadeloupe and Silvia Yahaira, who at fifteen is a minor under Mexican law, and would not be able to face trial until she turned eighteen.

Munro Palacio, an investigator in the case reported the disturbing news that the fifteen-year-old 'sees the religious practices of the family as normal.'

Others arrested were Meraz's son, Ramon Omar Palacios Meraz, and the grandmother's father, Cipriano Meraz Aguayo who was 83 at the time. But police were very clear that it was Silvia who was both leader and driving force behind this particular branch, a family branch, of the Santa Muerte devotees.

Once in custody, any sense that the family had prepared for discovery disappeared. Almost immediately. Discrepancies emerged between their stories. The police realised that they had on their hands a serious criminal event. Back at the Meraz's home they continued to search, and soon discovered that their gruesome discoveries were not over.

Cleotilde Romero was a 55-year-old woman, who had been a friend of the Meraz family. She had been reported missing back in 2009, but nothing had been found of her, until now. The extent to which the police searched for her at the time is difficult to say. A poor, marginalised woman in rural, poverty hit Mexico? The police would have had other problems which demanded their time. Her body too was discovered roughly buried in the vicinity of the home.

But it was not just that these three people, two of them young boys, had been murdered, it was the manner of their deaths that caused the greatest distress. It was clear that their demise had been ritualised. Slashes and cuts covered their bodies. It was soon obvious that the wide spread of the blood around the altar had been a result of the nature of their deaths.

The fear and horror that faced these victims is impossible to imagine, the pain would have been devastating. And two of the victims had been young children. In fact, Jesus Martinez had been virtually decapitated. It suggested a frenzy of violence, with no regard to the suffering it was causing.

As for those held in custody an entire raft of crimes was laid at their feet: first degree homicide, corrupting minors, illegal burial, robbery and conspiracy.

A spokesman for the prosecutors in Sonora state put the scale of the crimes into perspective. Jose Larrinaga said: 'They sliced open the victims' veins and, while they were still alive, they waited for them to bleed to death and collected the blood in a container.'

He went on to explain that the killings had taken place late in the evening, in a candle lit ceremony. Silvia Meraz herself had fallen into a delirious state, either genuine, or manufactured to influence the others involved.

'We all agreed to do it. Supposedly she (Cleotilde Romero) was a witch of something,' she said later. She would not comment on the deaths of the children.

Jose Larrinaga continued in his explanation of the ritual which saw the death of the three victims. He said that once the victims' blood had been collected, it was poured around the altar, and smeared into it.

The reason behind the murders was that Silvia believed that such a sacrifice would earn the family the favours of Santa Muerte. That she would act benignly on the family, and bring riches to them. She would take them out of the poverty of their lives.

It needs to be remembered that by the time of the killing, the cult of Santa Muerte had lost its briefly held official recognition in Catholic Mexico. In Nueva Loredo, a beautiful but crime ridden city to the east of the country, city workers had bull-dozed the many shrines to the false saint. But attempts to banish the cult from the country were not succeeding. Believers claimed that they had received all kinds of benefits from the skeleton deity. One convicted murderer told journalists that she protected the various items of contraband he kept in his cell by shielding them from the authorities. Presumably, following telling his tale, that shielding was short lived.

It is easy to see why a poor, disadvantaged family in a small copper mining town in northern Mexico might seek the support of anything that could help them out of their dismal existences. But to place riches above lives demonstrates a moral shallowness that cannot be defended.

When those lives are of a friend, as in Clotilde, and two young children, any lingering sympathy dissolves to nothing. Then, on top of this, we know that these children are, were, the sons and grandson of members of the sect.

Back in 2012, the State President of Sonora expressed his sadness that the power or Santa Muerte had led to these events in his region. 'As far as we know there are no more perpetrators,' he said, 'but we will see what information these people (the accused) provide, but the important thing is that they are already detained, and we will look to the full weight of the law to go against it.'

Following her arrest, Meraz appeared before the cameras with her daughters. Looking worried and deeply downcast, nevertheless she held true to her belief in Santa Muerte, holding a poster celebrating the saint of death.

And so, what can we conclude of this woman? It is hard to be sure of the state of her mind, as she sits in her prison cell, where she will remain for the rest of her life.

It is difficult to find much to say in her defence. It is probably the case that in her deluded state she did believe that a sacrifice to the 'white lady', as she is sometimes called, would help the family, offering them protection, wealth and health. It is also seemingly the case that during the sacrifices she did lose reason, hacking at the still living bodies with an axe and knives. It is certainly the case that the family lived in absolute poverty, and that most probably Silvia had been the victim of abuse herself. Perhaps she had been a prostitute, and had grown up without the guidance and support of her family which might have enabled her to develop a moral framework.

But we continue to come back to the horrific nature of her crimes, and that she dragged her own children into them. This was a family with a severely dark side.

And perhaps it is that which gives us the best insight into the actions of Silvia Meraz. This is a woman who is mentally unstable, who lacks any kind of empathy with others – it seems more than likely that she employed her own daughters in prostitution. In the end, the authorities ceased to pursue this investigation at the Meraz home, because the crimes they discovered where so much more insidious, but we know that it was widely believed the house was used as a brothel.

We also know that her fifteen-year-old daughter believed the kind of worship the family pursued was the norm. She had been infiltrated into the belief system so fully that she was able to participate in the murder of her own nephew. Therefore, we can deduce that the practices followed by the Meraz family were well established.

Although Santa Muerte seems not to have induced many killings and abuses directly – despite the fact that many of the followers of the cult have committed serious crimes in other circumstances – many other types of cults have. Unstable, sociopathic people are drawn to such organisations, and often rise to the top of them. In a situation where their behaviour is unchecked, they flourish. We have seen this in large scale events, such as the mass suicide of Jim Jones' cult in Guyana, and we see it on a smaller scale in abuses carried out in the name of satanic rituals.

Silvia Meraz Moreno was such a woman. Her individual sect was small, consisting of just her family. Who knows, had she lived in a larger community perhaps her individual branch of the cult of Santa Muerte would have been much bigger, attracting followers from outside her family. Perhaps in those circumstances, where she would no longer be the matriarch, others with less demonic moods might have tempered the actions of the cult, with sacrifices being no more than flowers, fruit and candy.

In that case, three people, including two young boys, would be alive, and eight others would not be sitting in prison.

But that was not how things turned out for Silvia Meraz. Poverty, an unsatisfactory upbringing, and a failure in the Catholic church to understand the extent of the impoverishment facing the underclass in Mexico were the factors in her life that could have been different. Living in a small community, where crime was rampant through the drugs cartels, added to the recipe that would lead to death. A different home town might have attracted the authority's attention to what was happening in the Meraz household, and the extent of the crimes committed there might have been limited to running a brothel or hosting prostitution.

We do not know if she enjoyed killing, if she felt remorse or if it was the failure of Santa Muerte to deliver the benefits she sought that drove her on to kill children.

But whatever, the crime is inexcusable. There are few who will argue that Silvia Meraz did not get exactly what she deserved.

SARA ALDRETE AND THE SERIAL KILLERS OF DEVIL'S RANCH

AARON GRIFFIN

EARLY LIFE

Sara Aldrete was born on September 6, 1964 in Matamoros, Tamaulipas, Mexico. As a teen, Sara was allowed to cross the border and attend Porter High School in Brownsville, Texas while her father supported the family working as an electrician. Teachers were fond of Sara as she was a well-behaved student who excelled academically. Her guidance counselor advised her to attend college immediately after graduation but Sara opted to marry instead. At the age of nineteen, she tied the knot with thirty-year old Miguel Zacharias on Halloween Day in 1983. The union did not last last, however, as they were separated and divorced within five months.

Two years later, Sara gained legal status as an American citizen. She enrolled at Texas Southmost College, a two-year school in Brownsville. She had been admitted on a work study program that minimized some of the tuition costs as she worked as both an aerobics teacher and assistant secretary in the school's athletic department.

Sara started classes in January of 1986 as a physical education major. At 6-feet-1 and with model good looks, she was a striking figure around campus.She became one of thirty-three students selected from over a 6,500 member student body to be included in the school's Who's Who directory for 1988. An active student on the campus, she organized a Booster club for the school's soccer squad as well as playing for the girl's volleyball team.

After the dissolution of her marriage, however, she had to move back home with her parents in Matamoros. They had constructed a patio/stairwell outside her second floor room so she could have some semblance of privacy. Sara came home on weekends and during the school breaks, hoping to transfer to a four-year program wherein she could receive a teaching certificate.

Her height and lithe physique caught the eye of many men, in particular Gilberto Sosa, a drug dealer who had ties with the powerful Hernandez family. She began dating Sosa while nurturing an interest in the religion of *Santería*. She learned about the religion's rituals and history during an anthropology class, immediately becoming obsessed. Ironically, this interest would coincide with meeting the man who would take her on a trip into darkness that she would never escape from.

"She would cross that border to Mexico," Lt George Gavito said. "And she would become somebody else."

GODFATHER AND GODMOTHER

Sara was driving through Matamoros on July 30th, 1987 when she nearly got into a car accident with a young man driving a luxury Mercedes-Benz. The young man got out of the car acting apolegetic. Sara was immediately taken by his good looks and well-spoken nature. His introduced himself as Adolfo Constanzo. They exchanged information and Adolfo expressed excitement when he learned that Sara shared the same birthday as his mother.

What Sara didn't know was that the near miss on the Matamoros street was carefully choreographed. Adolfo had been stalking Sara's boyfriend, Gilberto, assessing how much power he had in the drug dealing Hernandez organization.

Adolfo quickly befriended Sara and seduced her with his knowledge of the occult. In a subsequent meeting, Adolfo met the couple together, completely ignoring Gilberto's offer of a handshake and focusing his attention exclusively on Sara.

Later, an anonymous phone call informed Gilberto that Sara was dating someone else. The drug dealer went into a jealous rage and confronted Sara. She denied the allegations but he broke off the relationship anyway.

Sara then turned to Adolfo for comfort. He told her that he knew that Gilberto would break up with her as he had seen her future in a tarot card reading. Adolfo proceeded to "comfort" Sara by seducing her but their physical relationship would not last.

"Sara started dating Constanzo until she found out he was gay," Gavito said. "She said 'no problem'. But he told her what was he was involved in and she introduced him to the Hernandezes. So it was Sara that was the one that connected all of this people together."

Adolfo wanted a meeting with the leader of the Hernandez family, Elio, and Sara arranged for that to happen. Adolfo saw that he could influence drug dealers with his dark magic and earn a nice living for himself. Charming Elio Hernandez would be step one toward that goal.

When Sara returned to the college, her classmates noted that her demeanor changed significantly. Sara obsessed on witchcraft and magic in every conversation. She wanted to argue on the merits between good and evil.

Sara eventually left her studies behind and Adolfo welcomed her into his growing cult. He christened her as "La Madrina", the Godmother. He himself was "El Padrino", the Godfather.

WHO WAS ADOLFO CONSTANZO?

Adolfo was born in Miami, FL on November 1st, 1962 by a fifteen year old girl who would subsequently have three children by three different men. His mother, named Delia Aurora Gonzalez, had her son blessed by a Haitian priest who practiced *palo mayombe*, a form of witchcraft that owes its origins to the Congo but was passed down to Cuba and Puerto Rico with the settlement of slaves.

The boy's mother was excited when the Haitian priest pronounced that her six month old child was "chosen" and "destined for great power."

Delia moved the family to San Juan, Puerto Rico shortly after his baptism. Adolfo's childhood was steeped in the teachings of the dark imaginings of his mother. She taught him the rituals of her bizarre religion even as he became an altar boy at the local Catholic church.

When Adolfo was ten, his mother moved her growing family back to Miami. They once again met with the Haitian priest and young Adolfo began an apprenticeship under the man.

A MOTHER FROM HELL

Adolfo's mother Delia was arrested over thirty times. Her rap sheet included shoplifting, passing false checks, grand theft and child neglect. Her punishment, however, was always lenient and she was never sentenced to anything more than probation. She attributed her ability to escape jail stints to the spells she cast under *palo mayombe* and she passed down this belief system to her son.

A true tenant from hell, she left every apartment she stayed in a vandalized mess. Delia left the walls and floors bloodstained with the remains of animals that she sacrificed. Living in a section of Miami known as the Coral Park Estates, Delia lorded over her neighbors in a reign of terror. Earning her reputation as a witch, Delia was vindictive with anyone who dared inspire her wraith. Neighbor Elena Menendez found a dead goose on her door step with its head wrapped in a red handkerchief. Carmen Reiganda opened her door to find a decapitated chicken on her porch after her son had gotten into an argument with Delia.

Mother and son left a legacy of fear behind in the small Miami neighborhood and the majority of the people were afraid to talk about them.

"Everyone here is worried (Adolfo)will come back to get them for talking," said one man. "I've completely protected my house, and if they come by, I'll blow them away."

LIKE MOTHER, LIKE SON

Adolfo inherited both his mother's religion and criminal ways. He indulged in Miami's gay bars during his teens and earned a living through petty theft. He found school to be a burden and was only interested in learning about black magic. The boy barely graduated from high school and dropped out of junior college after one half-hearted semester.

He continued to obsess about witchcraft with his Haitian priest mentor. They formed a team to rob graves at midnight to stock the priest's lair with dead bodies. They created voodoo dolls and sprinkled blood over them to curse people that crossed them.

The philosophical tenets of *palo mayombe* laid the foundation for Constanzo's future drug dealing endeavors. The belief system places no value judgments on the individual, there is no "good" or "evil" magic. Criminals familiar with the practice used it to protect them from the law but the Haitian priest had a solemn warning for his young student.

"Let the non-believers kill themselves with drugs," the priest said. "We will profit from their foolishness."

By the age of fourteen, Delia became convinced that her son had psychic abilities. Adolfo claimed to have predicted that President Ronald Reagan would be shot by John Hinckley. Adolfo had a murky vision for his own future, however, as he was arrested twice for shoplifting in 1981, including one incident where he tried to steal a chainsaw.

Two years later in 1983, Adolfo had sworn his allegiance to *Kadiempembe*, the name for Satan in *palo mayombe*. The Haitian priest gave Adolfo his blessing as the boy vowed to worship evil in return for financial gain. The priest initiated Adolfo into the fold with a ritual scarring as he took a knife and sliced arcane symbols into the body of his young student.

"My soul is dead," Adolfo said at the end of the ceremony. "I have no God."

BEGINNING OF A CULT

Blessed with good looks, Adolfo landed a modeling gig in 1983. He traveled to Mexico City for a photo shoot and earned some extra money telling fortunes with tarot cards in the city's dangerous Zona

Rosa (Spanish for "Red Zone", a strip of prostitutes, bars and drug dealings.)

The trip to Mexico netted him his first cult followers which included Martin Quintana Rodriguez, Jorge Montes, and Omar Orea Ochoa. Adolfo had affairs with Quintana and Orea, wherein he would be the "woman" or the "man" in the relationship depending on his mood.

In 1984, Adolfo moved his base of operations to Mexico City permanently. He lived with both Quintana and Orea, engaging in nightly homosexual ménage à trois. He began offering his psychic services around the city, developing a reputation for seeing into the future and offering *limpias*. These were ceremonial "cleansings" for those who thought they were cursed by life or wanted some enemies taken care of.

Adolfo kept records of his dealings with the townfolk and his journals revealed that he had thirty-one regular customers. Some of his patrons would pay up to $4500 for one single ritual. Adolfo gave his customers a menu in which they had a choice of sacrificial animals to choose from. Roosters went for $6, goats $30, boa constrictors $450, zebras $1100, and African lion cubs were $3100.

Adolfo began to target the more successful drug dealers in the area. He would help them schedule shipments and customers based on his own alleged "visions". He would charge exorbitant fees for his "magic" to make dealers and their henchmen invisible to police and remain bulletproof against would-be assassins.

Most of the drug merchants had upbringings that paralleled Adolfo's in that their parents were poor peasants who believed in the supernatural. They made for easy dupes for the charismatic cult leader who had one dealer pay him over $40,000 for his supernatural blessings over a period of three years.

Adolfo always delivered, however, as he realized that at such prices his magic would have to be just that, a magic show spectacle. On one occasion he and three of his followers broke into a Mexico City graveyard and excavated numerous graves for bones. His reputation grew as his stage show became more elaborate. He was soon entertaining physicians, business men, fashion models and a host of transvestite cabaret singers. In a bizarre twist, there were several high-ranking police officials that joined Adolfo's cult. The most notable was Salvador Garcia Alarcon, a lead narcotic investigator and Florentino Ventura Gutierrez who was the head of the Mexican branch of Interpol.

The devotion of these individuals clearly went beyond mere bribery or charm. It soon became apparent that they worshiped the young Satanist as he led them on a tour to all of the pits of hell he could dream up.

A year later, Ventura would introduce Adolfo to the infamous Calzada family, arguably Mexico's biggest drug cartel at the time. Letting his charisma do the work for him, Adolfo won the gang over with an elaborate ritual and they repaid him for his blessings of "magic". By 1987, Adolfo had amassed enough cash for a luxury condo and a slew of high-end cars which included an $80,000 Mercedes-Benz.

"Constanzo made these people believers," Gavito said. "I think it could happen to anybody. Most of these kids came from good families. And they're already involved in moving narcotics. So I think it was easy to graduate into the cult part of it. Because they saw the wealth and they saw the power that Constanzo had."

Adolfo liked to push the envelope, however. Not satisfied with his payments from the drug dealers, he disguised himself as a DEA agent and relieved a Guadalajara dealer of his cocaine stash. He sold the coke through his police connections for a $100,000 profit.

As the stakes rose, so did Adolfo's need to have more over-the-top rituals. It was during this time that he began incorporating human sacrifice into his ceremonies. His callousness in both torturing strangers and his closest friends scared both the dealers and police officials into remaining on his good side if they could.

The Calzada drug cartel bought into Adolfo's act hook, line and sinker. The simple minded drug dealers attributed their continued prosperity and survival to his magical powers. Adolfo sensed his influence over the family and realized that he had became a necessary "good luck" charm to them. In the spring of 1987, Adolfo called for a meeting with the heads of the Calzada family. He demanded to become a full partner in their drug dealing enterprise.

The Calzada family rejected the notion immediately.

Adolfo, however, realized that if he was not going to be given power then he would take it.

On April 30th, 1987 Guillermo Calzada Sanchez and six members of his family disappeared under suspicious circumstances. They were reported missing on May 1st with the authorities discovering remnants of what looked like a Santería ceremony at Calzada's office as they found as melted candles and bones scattered about. A week later, mutilated remains washed ashore on the Zumpango River. The police trolled the river and recovered the seven bodies. All of the corpses showed signs of severe torture: fingers, toes and ears were removed, genitals slashed, a spinal column was excised from one body, two others had their skulls opened with their brains missing.

The body parts of the Calzada drug cartel were now part of Adolfo's growing *nganga* or cauldron, a large iron kettle where he stirred up his "witch brew."

His primary drug competitors now eliminated, Adolfo believed that he was growing stronger in his dark magic and began setting his sights on bigger targets.

The Hernandez family became next on his to do list. Adolfo set up a meeting with the powerful Elio Hernandez through Sara who had been dating his son. Adolfo had received word that the Hernandez cartel had dissension in the ranks and were becoming more vulnerable to competing drug families.

During their talk, Adolfo convinced Elio of the efficacy of the *palo mayombe*. He seduced him with the idea of taking his enemies and sacrificing them to his Satan God. In return, Adolfo promised that his family and drug enterprise would be blessed by the dark forces, that they would become invisible to police and bulletproof.

"Give me fifty percent of the profits," Adolfo said. "And I'll control things."

THE BELIEVERS

In 1987, Adolfo became obsessed with a film called the *The Believers* which starred Martin Sheen and Jimmy Smits. It was a movie that showcased the Santeria and voodoo possession and Adoflo saw himself in the characters. He sought to replicate what he saw on the screen into his own rituals.

"It is not at all surprising that Constanzo and Sara Aldrete were infatuated with the movie *The Believers*," said occult researcher Carl Raschke. "The magical practitioners in the film are portrayed as insuperable and almost all knowing."

Adolfo saw the film as validation for what he was doing, specifically conjuring up the spirit realm to aid him in his crimes. Sara, on the other hand, used the movie as a recruiting tool for prospective members.

"[There is]...a story making the rounds that tells of the night Aldrete persuaded three male friends to screen a video of *The Believers*," Rolling Stone magazine reported. "After the film, say the students, Aldrete stood up and began to preach in strange tones about the occult. 'They had been drinking and they just thought she was trying to be spooky,' said one of the students who knew the boys. 'but they look back on it now and think she must have been serious.'"

THEY MUST DIE SCREAMING

Adolfo's thirst for more power and wealth required that his rituals become more specific and gruesome. He moved his cult to a place called Rancho Santa Elena which was about twenty miles away from Sara's hometown of Matamoros.

On May 28th, 1988, Adolfo murdered a drug dealer named Hector de la Fuente and a farmer named Moises Castillo in sacrifices to his demon God. Not satisfied with the level of sadism he achieved in those killings, he then tortured and mutilated a transvestite named Raul Paz Esquivel. Paz was a former lover of one of Adolfo's original followers, Jorge Montes. The level of torture was extreme as they dismembered Paz's body, turning him into a bloodied pretzel. Paz' dismembered body was then left on a city street only to be discovered by school children.

Sadism and torture became foremost on Adolfo's mind as he sought new ways to increase his depravity. Invariably, he would sodomize his victims before their death, giving them one last indignity. Blood and guts fed his cauldron where Adolfo turned the "stew" like a modern day witch. He believed that the devil he worshiped would be more pleased if his sacrificial victims suffered as much as possible.

"They must die screaming," Adolfo intoned to his followers.

THINKING BIG

On August 10th, 1988, rival drug dealers kidnapped Ovidio Hernandez and his two year old boy. They wanted revenge for being ripped off on an $800k deal.

Adolfo, feeling the need to show off the efficacy of his *palo mayembe*, kidnapped a random stranger off the street and brought him to the ranch. They tortured the man, offering him as a sacrifice to their Satanic God while praying for the safe release of the Hernandez family member and his son.

Three days later, the dealers released Hernandez and the boy without any ransom money being exchanged. The Hernandez family gave full credit to Adolfo and his use of witchcraft.

He had them under his spell...

NO SAMPLES FOR YOU

Three months later, a 35-year old ex-policeman turned cult member named Jorge Valente de Fierro Gomez was caught using drugs, stealing from Adolfo's stash.

Adolfo decided to make an example out of his follower as he didn't want any of his members to partake in the drugs. The ex-cop became yet another sacrificial offering to *Kadiempembe*.

On Valentine's Day of 1989, Adolfo's group captured three competing drug dealers and tortured them to death. They dismembered the bodies and added them to the gruesome brew. A week later, another sacrificial victim had been kidnapped but the man put up such a lengthy fight that the group was forced to kill him before he could be tortured. The followers continued their quest to acquire victims. They came upon a 14-year old boy and killed him before realizing that the teen was a cousin of Elio Hernandez.

The boy cried uncontrollably as Adolfo's henchmen had the knife to his throat. Adolfo decided that the boy could be added to the brew because he was too sad. If they sacrificed the boy, then the demon god would be sad. So they killed the boy and went out to the streets to find another young boy.

Adolfo did this because he wanted to acquire the boy's youth. When he wanted "youth" he would have a young boy kidnapped and sacrificed. When he wanted "strength", he would have a strong man kidnapped and dismembered into his brew.

SPECIAL BLESSING NEEDED

By this time, Adolfo had amassed over 800 kg of marijuana that his followers had stolen from another gang. He thought he needed a special blessing to ship the large amount across the Rio Grande. His followers kidnapped another stranger off the streets but Adolfo was not satisfied with the level of sadism they had achieved in torturing the man. He felt that his demon overlord, *Kadiempembe*, would require a new benchmark in torture and pain.

"Bring me someone I can use," Adolfo said. "Someone who will scream."

He also wanted someone smart, someone who had medical training. He instructed his followers to keep their ears out and find an American college student who was going into the medical field.

The next morning, his followers brought in a young college student named Mark Kilroy.

SPRING BREAK HORROR

Matamoros had been a popular hangout for college students on spring break for decades. Students would come upon the small Mexican city looking to let loose in the uninhibited foreign soil that offered prostitution, nudie bars, booze and drugs.

By March of 1989, however, the town had over sixty unsolved disappearances over the course of three months. Unfortunately, this did not deter the usual contingent of American collegians from descending upon the town and enjoying the nightlife.

Mark Kilroy was one of those tourists.

A popular high school student, he played on the basketball and golf teams. He served on the student council and graduated 14th in a class of 210. He initially enrolled at Tarleton State on a basketball scholarship but transferred to the University of Texas after two years, giving up his basketball aspirations to concentrate on his pre-med courses. He was, by all accounts, an upstanding young man.

His father, Jim Kilroy, recalled that when his son was in high school, he would sometimes go to Mark's bedroom to make sure he was studying. He would find the young man reading his Bible instead. "What do you do?" Kilroy asked as he recalled the memory of his son. "He needs to study. But do you go in and tell your son to quit reading the Bible?"

Mark had trekked to Mexico for the spring break with three friends who were all his former classmates at Santa Fe High in Texas.

"The whole semester," a friend recalled. "That (the trip) was all we talked about."

They spent the night enjoying the Mexican food and drinking. They chatted with some girls visiting there from Kansas then returned without incident to their rooms at the Sheraton Hotel on South Padre Island over 20 miles away.

The second night would be quite different. They spent the evening drinking and then around 2 o'clock in the morning they began walking toward the bridge which connected Matamoros with the Texas border town where they had parked their car. Two of Mark's friends walked ahead while Mark and Bill Huddleston lingered about twenty feet behind. Huddleston briefly stepped into an alley to urinate. Mark waited on the street.

When Huddleston came back onto the street he could not find Mark anywhere. There were no signs or sounds of struggle.

THE ABDUCTION

Four of Adolfo's followers had kidnapped Mark. They had been driving a red pick up truck along the main drag of Matamoros, tailing the group unnoticed.

When they spotted Mark alone, they offered him a ride.

"They all had badges that said 'state police," Gavito said referring to the fact that Adolfo's followers disguised themselves as cops. "They all had jackets that said police on them. They had red lights in their car. They ran around Matamoros like they were police officers. When (Mark) went off to use the bathroom that was the perfect time. They went up to him, they badged him, they put him in a car, they told him he was under arrest for being drunk. They drive down about two blocks. They pull over, they all get out, the policemen, the guys 'acting' as policemen. They wait for the other car to show up. (Mark) jumps out and starts running."

Mark Kilroy ran for two blocks. The Constanzo crew chased him down yelling "freeze".

"(Mark) being the well educated boy that he is," Gavito said. "Who was brought up to respect the law, when he heard the word 'freeze', he stopped. He was half a block from getting back on the main drag where there was two thousand kids partying. And he stopped, they handcuffed him, they threw him back in the car, they took him back to the ranch. They tied him up and they put him in the back of the Suburban."

He was given food and told he would not be harmed.

Twelve hours later, however, he would be sacrificed.

Kilroy was the only American kidnapped by the cultists. He also came from an affluent family including an uncle that worked for the U.S. Customs Service. His father was a chemical engineer and his mother a volunteer paramedic. The family were devout Catholics, active in their local church.

The response from from the public was immediate. There was a $15,000 reward for information leading to his return or the arrest of his kidnappers.

Yellow bows graced the churches of his hometown and beyond. Dozens of people joined the search for Kilroy, with hundreds of flyers being handed out around the town. San Antonio Mayor Henry Cisneros lobbied Mexican authorities to find the young man.

"I had worked with the Mexican police for over twenty years," Lt. George Gravito recalled. "Best cooperation you've ever had in your life. All of a sudden, I ran into a wall. No cooperation. The state police was telling us that (Mark) was involved in narcotics. But they wouldn't tell me where they're getting the information. This guy was corrupt. What we're meeting with right here on the border, one day you're investigating a crime in Brownsville, Texas and tomorrow morning you're investigating it in Matamoros, Mexico. It's not your jurisdiction and you have to know how to move around. You can't step on the wrong toes because they're gonna kick you out of the country."

The Matamoros police interrogated over one hundred known criminals in the area in the search for Kilroy. They beat their legs with clubs and sprayed soda water mixed with hot sauce into their nostrils.

They came up with nothing.

ONE MORE SACRIFICE

Adolfo had used the sacrifice of Kilroy in his mind to ensure the safe shipment of his marijuana. But now, he thought he needed yet another special sacrifice to his palo mayombe overlord.

Adolfo decided to target Sara's former boyfriend, Gilberto Sosa.

On March 28th, 1989, Sosa became the cult's final sacrifice as the marijuana made its way across the Rio Grande on April 8th.

Adolfo's alleged psychic abilities would fail him, however, as his depraved empire would soon come to an end in a way that he didn't foresee...

PURE LUCK

The police drew no leads for two weeks until they came across a "happy accident" on April 10th of that year...

"We were lucky," Gravito recalled. "What helped us in this investigation was, we had been working on some narcotic cases. DEA Brownsville had been working real close with *un commandante* in Matamoros. That *commandante* was Juan Benitez Ayala. He was the head of the federal police assigned to the Matamoros area. This man, Juan Benitez Ayala, I'll say was about five feet tall. But he probably stood about eight foot tall. I mean when this guy walked in anywhere people were scared of him. He worked and that's all he did.

"You didn't see him in bars. You didn't see him in restaurants. And the reason he didn't go to bars or restaurants, one, he was afraid someone might put something in his drink and kill him. The guy was taking down some powerful people in Mexico and we went to talk to him."

"I told him we got this problem with this state police guy, he says these kids were involved in narcotics, and I assure you that they weren't. We had helped them on some cases, we had busted some big people (because) we had shared some information. So he put his people to work. And every time we had a lead, we'd call him, we'd go over there, we'd kick doors down, you know, you don't need a search warrant, the search warrant IS the federal police and nobody gets in your way."

The Mexican police had erected roadblocks and began a random drug roust in areas of Matamoros unrelated to the Kilroy disappearance. They had a policy of targeting only the low level runners and leave the heads of the drug operations alone.

Serafin Hernandez was the epitome of the low-level drug dealer. He was the twenty year old nephew of Elio Hernandez and a well known trafficker. During this drug roust, Serafin came across the police checkpoint and was followed. He unknowingly led the officers to the innocuous looking cattle ranch. A shabby looking corral marked the front with a tar paper and wood shack that stood in the rear of the winding, unmarked road.

It was Rancho Santa Elena, the home of Constanzo's cult.

The police waited a week and returned en masse, arresting both Serafin and another dealer named David Serna Valdez. The interrogations began and the two dealers proved to be cocky witnesses. They claimed they were "protected" by supernatural powers, of course referring to the spells that Adolfo had cast.

Inside, the police found a horror chamber beyond the imagination of any snuff film. The 15x25 foot shed was saturated with blood and smelled of rotting flesh. They found human brains, hair, teeth and skulls. Some spines had been crafted into necklaces. Scattered around were machetes and white votive candles in a box that bore a picture of *Our Lady of Guadalupe*.

The press nicknamed Rancho Santa Elena as the "Devil's Ranch."

"I thought in my twenty two years of law enforcement I had seen everything," a Texas deputy said. "I hadn't. As we drew near, you could smell the stench...blood and decomposing organs. In a big, cast iron pot there were pieces of human bodies and a goat's head with horns."

MAKING THE CONNECTION

"About two o'clock in the morning I get a call from *el commandante*," Gavito recalled. "We found (Mark) he said. 'You found (Mark)? You kidding?' he said no. We found (Mark). Where? He said he's buried in a ranch outside of Matamoros. I asked him how? Or who? He said there was a caretaker that also lived near the ranch. When he arrested Serafin, he picked him up too, the caretaker, but he didn't file charges against him. But he kept him under house arrest and the caretaker saw a picture of (Mark) on top of the table. And he pointed to it and said 'I know that boy'. 'How do you know him?' 'I was feeding him. I was giving him bread. I untied one of his arms so he could sit up and eat' because they had him tied to the back of a Suburban."

El Commandante then began interrogating Serafin. Without prompting, Serafin began offering information on how he knew Mark Kilroy, admitting that he was the one who kidnapped him.

"This guy was volunteering all of this information," Gavito said. "I mean usually in Mexico you have to go, you know, I guess its something you have to know when you get arrested, that they're going to torture you to get the truth out of you. But I've never heard of anybody just confessing this easily as Serafin. And we kinda talked a little bit and the name Constanzo had come up on his investigations. Serafin had said that they had kidnapped (Mark) because the *Padrino*, Constanzo, wanted somebody who was studying medicine because they were doing some kind of witchcraft."

"They were going to use Mark's brain to give it to this pot that they had. And I didn't understand what he was talking about and I said did you have to torture this guy and he said 'no, this guy (Serafin) thinks that bullets do him no harm and the police can't hurt him he thinks that this guy, this Constanzo is gonna come in here and take him out of here."

"It's our religion," Serafin said. "Our voodoo."

George Gavito recalled that during Serafin's confession he repeatedly made reference to the aforementioned film, *The Believers.*

"I remember I didn't understand what he was telling me," Gravito said. "I said, 'Is it Santeria?' And he said, 'Yeah, yeah, Santeria, voodoo, man.' And then he kept on saying, 'The Believers, The Believers, The Believers.'"

"Elio made [Serafin] Garcia a priest, but Garcia didn't really know what he was practicing because all he had on his mind was the movie."

Serafin told the authorities about El Padrino, the Godfather, as being Adolfo Constanzo. He revealed the details of Adolfo's ritual of African magic, palo mayombe. "Adolfo ordered the slayings," Serafin said. He revealed that the Godfather had tortured and sodomized his victims before killing them. They would then mutilate the bodies and harvest the organs for his witches brew.

SCENE OF THE CRIME

Serafin was brought back to the Devil's Ranch with Ayala and Gavito, both police officials not expecting the level of depravity they were about to investigate.

"We asked him where the body was," Gavito recalled. "And he said 'which body?' Just like that. 'Which body?' 'Man,' El Commandante says. 'Man, if you're playing games with me' and he got pissed off. And he (Serafin) says 'hold on, which body you want?'"

"'What do you mean, which body!'" El Commandante screamed.

"There's a bunch of bodies out here," Serafin said. "Which one do you want?"

"What do you mean?"

"Yeah," Serafin began walking through the corrals. "There's one buried here, there's one buried there."

"How many?"

"I don't know."

"Where's Mark?"

"Over there in the corner."

"Where?"

"I don't remember exactly," Serafin said as he started walking to a corner of the corral. "But I think it is where that wire is."

The police looked down and saw a coat hanger half-buried in the dirt.

"Why a coat hanger?"

"Oh, because Constanzo wanted to make a necklace," Serafin said. "With Mark's backbone. So after we killed them and everything we ran wire through his back, through the spinal cord, so that later on we could just come and get it out and he could make a necklace."

Disgusted and angry, Benitez-Ayala handed Serafin a shovel, forcing him to dig up the body of Mark.

During the dig, Serafain revealed that Constanzo had killed Mark with one machete slice to the back of his head. He began revealing more details of other killings, matter of factly and without feeling. At one point he even asked if the police we're going to order food because he was getting hungry.

El Commandante Benitez-Ayala became enraged. He took out his Uzi and fired the weapon into the air out of frustration.

"You don't think bullets can hurt you?" he asked Serafin.

"No," Serafin replied.

El Commandante then began emptying his entire clip.

"That's when the kid's eyes opened up," Gavito recalled, remembering how frightened Serafin became. "I mean his eyes opened up when he heard that sound, I mean it freaked us all out because we didn't realize what was going on. He (Serafin) went from being a believer to being a disbeliever pretty quick. He went back to being a normal person."

Serafin suddenly snapped out of his brainwashed state.

"I don't know why they got us to do this," Serafin said.

"All of a sudden it was 'why' they got us to do this," Gavito said. "It just changed."

His body unearthed, Kilroy's skull had been split open and his brain removed. The police then found a nearby shed wherein they located Adolfo's *nganga*, a cast-iron cauldron that was stained with blood, body parts and numerous sticks, the "palos" of *palo mayombe.*

Inside the kettle were spiders, scorpions and the brain of Kilroy. His brain had been boiled in blood over an open fire along with a turtle shell, a horseshoe, a spinal column and other human bones.

FAILING MAGICAL POWERS

Adolfo was surprised at the reaction to Kilroy's disappearance. He was used to his killings not gaining any notoriety at all. Even after the fact, three of the unearthed victims have never been identified and only a handful were reported missing.

The next day, all hell break loose for the cult members. Four members of the Hernandez family were arrested and the cash from their big marijuana sale was confiscated. The police began unearthing bodies from the ranch on April 11th, finding more bodies in a nearby orchard.

Feeling the heat, Adolfo went on the run with Sara, and his two lovers Martin and Omar. A Hernandez family hit man named Alvaro De Leon Valdez, nicknamed "El Duby", came along as well.

Adolfo's first instinct was to go to Miami where he could be with his mother. He decided to stay travel to Mexico City, however, using the homes of followers and friends of followers to hide.

The gruesome discoveries made the rounds in tabloid television. Geraldo Rivera produced a segment on the murders. There were false sightings of the cult being reported in the United States. Adolfo was claimed to have been seen in Chicago where people mistakenly labeled him as part of the Windy City Mafia. Sara was reportedly seen skulking around schools throughout various border towns, threatening to kidnap and kill ten white kids for every one of her followers that were jailed in Mexico. There was a church located in Pharr, Texas that was burned down after rumors that some if its members were connected to Adolfo's cult. Serafin Sr, a drug dealer and follower of Adolfo, was found and arrested.

The national news did little to shed light on the whereabouts of Adolfo, however. They successfully hid from sight as if their Devil God had swallowed them up and welcomed them into hell...

BETRAYAL IN THE CARDS

Adolfo did a tarot card reading on April 18th, 1989 and supposedly foresaw a betrayal among his followers. He knew that any of the many low level drug runners could have ratted out Serafin Sr and he now looked at his followers with a suspicious eye. He kept a gun close by and did his best to avoid sleep. His paranoia led to angry outbursts against his acolytes.

"They cannot kill you," he warned. "But I can."

The Commandante, Juan Ayala, meanwhile, took the threat of Constanzo's *brujeria* (witchcraft) very seriously.

"He flew in his own brujo (male witch), to take care of him and to take care of all his agents," Gavito said. "To make sure there was not 'bad vibes'. And not only that, but to help him in the investigation. To find out what was the best way to catch Constanzo. He (the witch) told Benitez, 'you wanna catch him? Burn their hut! Burn their nganga! Burn where they were worshiping.'"

"So we got out there one Sunday morning. Took one Mexican television station to cover it because he wanted Constanzo to see this. The brujo puts gasoline around it. They light it up and it starts to burn and we sit there while the whole thing burns to the ground."

Adolfo watched the scene on television as Ayala had hoped. His screen police sifted through what was left at the ranch. He then went into a rage inside the small hideaway apartment, smashing furniture and flipping over the couch for starters.

"He felt raped," Gavito said. "He felt that we had invaded his privacy. That we had done something we shouldn't have. He started losing it."

MOVING ON

Adolfo made one last move with his followers as they found an apartment on Rio Sena in Mexico City.

Sara, finally realizing her life was in danger or needing to now play the role of the victim since the authorities were no doubt closing in, made a handwritten note. She threw it out the bedroom window in the hopes that a Good Samaritan would come along and find it.

The note read:

Please call the judicial police and tell them that in this building are those that they are seeking. Tell them that a woman is being held hostage. I beg for this, because what I want most is to talk—or they're going to kill the girl.

A stranger walking by picked up the note but kept it to himself, thinking it was a joke. Upstairs, however, Adolfo plotted his next getaway move.

"They'll never take me," he said.

MORE RANDOM LUCK

A few days later, police arrived on Rio Sena and began going door to door looking for a missing child. Adolfo saw them from his window and began opening fire with his Uzi not realizing that they were not looking for him.

Over one hundred eighty-police men almost immediately. A fiery battle ensued which lasted almost forty-five minutes. Surprisingly, the only person injured during the crossfire was an officer who was struck by Adolfo's first barrage.

According to Sara, Adolfo ordered his own killing, telling El Duby to shoot him and his right hand man, Martin Quintana Rodriguez.

"He lost it," Gavito said. "He turned on the stove. Put the money on the stove. Started burning money. He started throwing coins out. Just lost it."

"He went crazy, crazy," said El Duby. "He grabbed a bundle of money and threw it and began shooting out the window. He said everything, everything was lost. No one's going to have this money."

"He wanted to die with Martin," Sara said.

Adolfo soon realized he was trapped. He handed his Uzi to El Duby.

"He told me to kill him and Martin," El Duby said. "I told I told him I couldn't do it, but he hit me in the face and threatened that everything would go bad for me in hell. Then he hugged Martin, and I just stood in front of them and shot them with a machine gun."

The police entered the apartment with guns raised but Adolfo and Martin were already dead, their bodies slumped together in a closet. The three remaining cult members, El Duby, Orea, and Sara were captured.

Over twenty rounds were found in autopsied body, possibly indicating that the Mexican police had continued to shoot him port-mortem.

THE TRIALS

El Duby's case was open and shut. He had confessed to the two murders and had no reasonable defense. Sara, however, was a tad different as she initially proclaimed to be a victim but knew too much of the cult's ins and outs to not be considered an accomplice.

After the shootout, fourteen cult members in total were indicted for murder. In August of 1990, El Duby was convicted of the killing of Adolfo and Martin, getting a 35-year prison term. Juan Fragosa and Jorge Montes were convicted to 35 years for the killing of Raul Esquivel.

Omar Orea, one of Adolfo's lovers, died of AIDS before going to trial.

Sara had been acquitted of Adolfo's slaying but was sentenced to a six year term for her criminal associations. She maintained her innocence throughout, stating that she never practiced the *palo malembe* but a "Christian Santeria."

Showing a calm demeanor during her interrogations, Sara expressed sorrow for the murders of Kilroy and the other victims.

American law officials saw Sara as having a split personality. They knew that in private, Sara would lose her "charming aspect" that she revealed when she knew the television cameras were on. She reverted into another self, talking with relish in describing the cult's rituals.

"I would say she has three personalities," a Mexico City attorney general said. "One personality comes out and faces the cameras and denies any involvement in the human slayings, another emerges when she talks to police and the third one comes out when she talks to herself."

American Customs agent Oran Neck spent several days in Mexico City assisting the local police. "Sara has kind of lost touch with reality," Neck said after he questioned her. "Her dual personality is coming up pretty strong right now. When you talk to her without the TV cameras there, she's pretty truthful."

"She gives a lot of data with great detail to investigators. It seems like when the cameras come on, she kind of reverts back to this nice, young, clean-cut kid from Texas Southmost College."

"When the cameras were there, she was real nice," Lt. George Gravito said. "When she was with us, she was the same ol' witch."

SARA'S SENTENCE

"If I had known it (the cult) was like this," Sara said. "I wouldn't have been in it."

Six years after her criminal association sentence was up, Sara was tried again and convicted of several of the murders at the cult's headquarters. She is now serving 30 years in prison.

During an interview with SFGate, Sara claimed that she was tortured by Mexican police after her capture. She said she was stripped, blindfolded, hung upside down, beaten, had her toenails pulled out and was burned inside her vagina in and out. She claims the burns were so severe that a doctor told her she'd never have children.

She also remembers the police shoving her hands into Adolfo's autopsied body at the morgue.

They yelled at her to pull out his heart.

"There is your devil," they mocked. "There is your prince. Kiss him. Kiss him."

The Mexican authorities have denied these claims.

"The witch deserves everything she got," Lt. George Gavito said.

Mark Kilroy's parents have said they have forgiven her but do not want her released. "You have to control a mass murderer," said Jim Kilroy. "What are you going to do? Let her loose and have her murder other people?"

Even after the convictions, some murders from the time period have remained unsolved. Between 1987 and 1989, there were 74 unsolved ritual murders in Mexico City. 14 of these involved children. Adolfo's cult is connected to 16 but there has been no evidence to connect them to the rest.

"We would like to say, yes, Constanzo did them all," prosecutor Guillermo Ibarra said. "And poof, all those cases are solved. And the fact is, we believe he was responsible for some of them, though we'll never prove it now. But he didn't commit all of those murders. Which means someone else did. Someone who is still out there."

SUSAN ATKINS & THE MANSON CULT

Susan Atkins was one of the more notorious female members of the "Manson Family" headed by Charles Manson. She was part of a gang of serial killers that terrorized Southern California in the summer of 1969. Known as "Sexy Sadie" because of her occupation as a topless dancer, Susan was involved in eight of the nine Manson killings including the gruesome Tate/Labianca Murders. She would be sentenced to death which was later commuted to life in prison. Susan would be denied parole over eighteen times in becoming the longest-incarcerated female inmate in the history of California.

CHILDHOOD OF A KILLER?

Susan was born May 7th, 1948 in San Gabriel, California. She was the middle child of three children born to Edward and Jeanette Atkins. Susan grew up in a middle-class area in San Jose, California. Her personality was described as "quiet" and she sang in both her school's glee club and the church choir. She appeared to have been the odd one out of the family, however. She had two other brothers and her parents would favor her brothers over her. Her father preferred the company of the eldest son while her mother preferred the youngest child, Steven.

"I didn't like my mother," Susan said. "She tried to get along with me, but I just refused to get along with her. I didn't like my father either. Didn't like either one of them. I didn't like my mother because she was an alcoholic. My father also was an alcoholic, used to beat my mother up."

"The family appeared to be middle-class," forensic psychologist Paula Orange said. "And the claim of the parents being alcoholics came from Susan herself. But it is evident that she had a normal upbringing for that era in that she was taken to Sunday school, sang in the church choir and was a member of the Girls Scouts. Not exactly a recipe for a future serial killer."

Her mother would die of cancer when Susan was fifteen. Susan and members of her church choir sang Christmas carols under her mother's bedroom window right before she would be hospitalized for the final time. Susan's relatives, however, remarked at how indifferent Susan was about her mother's death.

"As is the case with a lot of serial killers," Orange said. "There is a traumatic event in their lives that numbs them. They lose the ability to feel empathy for others. When Susan's mother died, it set the stage for her later life and made her vulnerable to the likes of Manson."

Susan was forced to move several times and wound up fending for herself at the age of eighteen. The cost of her mother's medical bills took a toll on her father financially and he was forced to sell their family home. Her father would move to Los Banos, California taking along Susan and her younger brother Steven. He would work on the San Luis Dam construction project but would leave the two teens to look after themselves.

Susan would take a job during her junior year in high school, using the money to support herself and Steven. Academics were not her forte, however, as she was only an average student in Leigh High School in San Jose. When she entered Los Banos High School she had lost complete interest and received bad grades as she bounced from relative to relative.

"She (Susan) just didn't seem to care," stated a friend of Susan's. "Like when her mother died, she didn't show any real sadness about it. I don't think Susan cared about anything very much. There was something wrong with her"

Susan would leave home the moment she turned eighteen. She would work as a waitress in San Francisco and meet a pair of shady characters named Al Sund and Clint Talioferro. She joined the duo as they stole a Buick Riviera and then drove north up to Salem, Oregon.

The trio would hide in the woods and steal food from other campers. A month later, the Oregon State police caught up with the Susan and her car thief friends. She was jailed for three months then placed on two years probation. Susan then returned to San Francisco, once again turning to waitress duties. Needing more money, she began doing some topless dancing as well as doing some housekeeping for rich people on Muir Beach.

While living in San Francisco, she stayed in a communal house and started taking LSD. She then dabbled in Satanism and other alternative lifestyles and philosophies.

She would then meet the man who would change her life forever, Charles Manson.

ENTER THE PSYCHO

Manson was playing guitar at a home where Susan lived with a few friends who were dope dealers. Janis Joplin lived near the house and Atkins enjoyed sitting on the front porch to listen to Joplin practice. Manson himself began singing songs to her when they first locked eyes.

"My eyes landed instantly on a little man sitting on the wide couch in front of the bay windows," Susan recalled. "Without moving his head, he opened his eyes and stared directly into my face. I stared back. It was thought our minds were speaking."

Susan then put on a Doors record and began to dance.

Manson came up behind her and placed his hands on her hips. The two strangers began dancing, with Manson leading his new friend with slow, sensual movements.

"He whispered in my left ear," Atkins would write in her memoir. "That's right. That's good. In reality, there's no repetition. No two moves, no two actions are the same. Everything is new. Let it be new."

Susan then described their dancing as a transcendental encounter. "This stranger and I were dancing, passing through one another. It was as though my body moved closer and closer to him and actually passed through him. I thought for a second that I would collapse. What had happened? Was I crazy? It was beyond human reality."

They made love and Manson told Susan to pretend that he was her father as they had sex. This made Susan even more attracted to him. "You are beautiful," Manson whispered. "You are perfect. You must break free from the past. You must live now. There is no past. The past is gone. There's no tomorrow."

Susan would then describe Manson in messianic terms, comparing the cult leader's treatment of his disciples to Jesus Christ. He washed her feet. He showed her affection and told her to love herself. Manson played the role of savior and father figure to the hilt.

"Charlie had instantly seemed more of a father to me than my own father," Susan said. "He played me like a yo-yo, first hugging me and praising me, then demeaning me in some way."

The house would be raided a few weeks after and Susan found herself homeless. Manson caught wind of her situation and invited her to join his "family". Susan then informed her probation officer that she would be going on a trip with a traveling preacher named Charlie. She and seven other girls, two of whom were pregnant got into Manson's black spray-painted converted school bus on a trip to Los Angeles. The probation officer nixed the idea but Susan ignored the request and was soon traveling down the coast with Charles Manson in the driver seat, singing made-up songs as he made his way down south with the wayward girls of the Haight-Ashbury district.

A NEW NAME

Manson christened Susan with the nickname of Sadie Mae Glutz and had someone create a fake ID for her. Susan then settled in the rest of the "Family" at the Spahn ranch, a former movie set where the followers would get free rent in return for the upkeep of the place.

"There was a semblance of unity," Susan said of her attraction to joining Manson's Family. "An ambiance of family camaraderie. Where everybody supposedly loved each other. There was a surface image of loving one another and caring for one another and being there for one another. And it appeared that way on the surface. And there was a lot going on underneath. You had a lot of different personalities. Lot of different personal problems, conflicting with one another but there was an image of commune."

Susan became one of the female leaders at the commune, often driving around other members. She bought into all of Manson's bizarre theories such as Helter Skelter, the creation of a revolution where the blacks would rise up and kill whites. The followers were subject to daily rantings and pronunciations from Manson as he would brainwash them into accepting his worldview.

"There was a lot of deprogramming that was involved in that," Susan said. "You take away a person's conscience of right and wrong by telling them while they're under LSD or any mind expanding drug, there's no such thing as guilt. And you've already come to a place in your mind or imagination where you don't like the feeling of guilt so its easy to say 'yeah, there's no such as guilt, I believe there's no such as guilt, therefore, I could do anything and not feel guilty about it.'"

PREGNANCY

Susan would bear a child by a man named Bruce White aka Bluestein. Manson would have the honor of naming the boy and he christened the baby as Zezozose Zadfrack Glutz. Manson was not happy with the pregnancy, however, up until the point, Susan was about to give birth.

"The baby is coming," Susan announced to the family with excitement.

"The baby isn't due for a few weeks," Manson snarled. "Go boil me some water. I gotta shave."

Susan then did as she was told and set up the shaving mirror for him in the bathroom. She then dropped to the ground and went into labor as Manson continued to shave.

The baby was breeched and one of the arms came out first. Manson then broke into song as did the other Family members, using the Beach Boys coda to "Cease to Exist/Resist."

It was after the birth of her son that Susan began to think about leaving the cult. Her rebellion began to be targeted toward Manson himself as she thought about her son.

"Things were getting crazy at Spahn's Ranch," Orange said. "Things were getting nuts. And I had a son. And I wanted to get away, I wanted to take my son away. I, on three separate occasions, went outside Spahn's ranch on my own in an attempt to get someone to come back and get my son."

Manson threw Susan out of the family and kept the baby with him and the Family.

"I had gone into Hollywood," Susan said. "Picked up some guy. I don't even remember the man's name. But he had a car, he had an apartment, I told him I would love him, take care of him, take care of his house if he would help me get my son. I went back to the house which was not at Spahn's ranch at that time, there was a house in Chatsworth. I told the young man if you'll wait out in the car I'm going to go in and I'm going to get my son. I didn't think Charlie was there. And I went into the house and there was different people there. Catherine Sher was there, Mary Brunner was there, Lynnette Fromme was there, Sandra Good was there, Tex Watson, Bruce Davis might have been there. Steven Grogan was there. And when I went in, I asked Catherine Sher, who at that time I called 'Gypsy', I said 'Where's my son?' and she said 'He's right here." And she reached over and someone else had him and I said 'Give him to me!' And I went to the closet where I knew there were diapers and blankets and I had my son and I was going to leave. And at that point Charles came down from the upstairs, it was a two story house and he asked me 'Where are you going?' I remember my heart really starting to pound and he said 'Before you go I want to show you something.' And he opened the bedroom door. And I saw Mary Brunner on a bed, she had two black eyes, her nose was swollen, she had a bloody lip, she was holding her sides and Charlie looked at her and said 'Tell her what you were gonna do this morning.' And she looked at me and said, 'I was gonna take Pooh Bear,' which is what she called her son, 'And leave.' And Charlie looked at me and said, 'Now do you want to go?'"

Susan would leave again, spending some time living at a communal home on the Buchanan Ranch in Topanga Canyon while hooking up with a man named Rory. Susan reportedly began talking bad about Manson to some of the people at the ranch. But one day Manson came to the ranch, standing above a ridge yelling 'Sadie!', his created name for Susan.

Susan then came running back to Manson as he welcomed her back into the Family. He then wrote a song called "Sexie Sadie".

"Sexy Sadie," Manson sang. "You came along to turn everybody on. Sexy Sadie, you broke the rules, you laid it down for all to see."

Susan was relieved of her parental rights after she was convicted of the killings. No one in her extended family sought custody of Zezozose and he was subsequently adopted. The child was renamed and Susan never saw him again.

"He was unscathed by all of this," Susan said. "And I'm so very, very grateful for that."

CRIMINAL WARM-UPS

By the summer of 1969, the Manson Family were pushing the envelope when it came to committing crimes. They started with stealing cars. Susan learned the methods of auto theft rather quickly. She set the Family record for hot-wiring a car as she reportedly could do it in less than thirty seconds. But the Family were also suspected of possibly running a prostitution ring with all of the underage runaways that populated the Spahn Ranch. Manson had his followers sell drugs and during a deal gone bad Manson had an altercation with a black drug dealer named Bernard "Lotsapoppa" Crowe. Manson thought that he had killed Crowe and that the Black Panthers would seek to avenge his murder. He was wrong on both counts but he pressed the need for money on his followers. Manson then heard through the grapevine that one of his old friends, a man named Gary Hinman, had just come into a large inheritance. Manson sent his followers over to Hinman's home in order to entice him to join his cult and be its financial benefactor.

Gary Hinman was thirty-two years old at the time and made his living teaching music. He was on his way to earning a doctorate in sociology at UCLA. A practicing Buddhist, he owned several cars which included the obligatory hippie Volkswagen. He was a popular fixture in the Topanga Canyon area and was well known in the hippie subculture of Los Angeles.

Susan Atkins joined Bobby Beausoleil and Mary Brunner to Hinman's home on July 25th, 1969. Susan knew that their goal was to get money from Hinman and that the possibility of violence was all too real.

"There are competing stories from Susan about the Hinman murder," Orange said. "Initially, she told authorities that she did not know that Hinman was about to be killed. But in her memoir, she contradicts that claim. She comes clean after the fact because it would probably seem pretty silly for someone to arrive at a home with a bunch of knives and guns and not think that something bad was about to happen."

The three family members would confront Hinman about his rumored inheritance. Hinman would be puzzled by their sudden interest, denying that he had come into any riches. Beausoleil then beat Hinman to a pulp but the man would not change his tune.

Manson arrived at the home and wasted no time.

"I got a knife on my leg," Manson said. "And I cut Hinman's ear. I looked at them and I said 'That's how you do it. Don't bring me here, no more.' Then I'm thinking I gotta scare this character. I am what they call in the Underworld a bad actor. So I say, 'Alright, now I got to kill you, Hinman.' He said 'Don't kill me.' I said 'If I don't kill you, you are going to tell my parole officer and sent me back to prison."

Manson then threatened Hinman with more bodily harm if he went back on his word. Agitated and worried that he would be sent back to jail, Manson left Hinman's home with his Family members now in charge of the hostage.

"You guys stay here," Manson ordered Susan and Mary Brunner. "Fix him up a bit. Bandage up his ear."

Susan looked on horrified at the scene. Blood spewed from Hinman's ear as he rocked back and forth in pain, his entire face swollen from the beating. The two women put Scotch tape over Hinman's ear until they received more instructions.

The three Manson associates would keep watch over Hinman for two days until he signed over the registration for his cars. Manson then called Beausoleil on the phone and ordered him to kill Hinman.

Beausoleil would stab Hinman twice, fatally wounding him. He then left a bloody hand print on the wall as well as some Black Panther inspired revolutionary words. He did this in the hopes of pinning the crime on the radical group but he would instead be arrested eleven days later, caught sleeping in Hinman's car. After eleven days, Beausoleil was wearing the same bloodstained shirt that he wore while stabbing Hinman to death. Police would find the murder weapon hidden in the tire well of the car's trunk.

SHARON TATE MURDER

Manson would order Susan, Linda Kasabian, and Patricia Krenwinkel to accompany Tex Watson on the night of August 9th, 1969.

"Where are we going?" Susan asked as the three women piled into the car with Watson at the wheel.

"We're going to a home to get some money from some people," Watson said. "Then we're going to kill them. No matter what they do or say, do not show any mercy. No matter how much they beg, do not give them any leeway."

Steven Parent would be the first victim.

An eighteen-year-old delivery man, Parent was visiting the home on Cielo Drive as the previous month he had met William Garretson who was the caretaker at the mansion. Garretson invited Parent to visit anytime and the young man stopped by to try and sell Garretson an AM radio. Garretson refused but the two had a beer and Parent started to leave in his father's truck. As the gates opened for him to leave, he heard a voice yell "Halt!"

Tex Watson and the Manson Family were on him instantly. Parent put his hands up as Watson sliced down on him with his buck knife. The attack slashed off Parent's watch and cut through tendons on his hand.

"I won't tell!" Parent screamed in vain.

Watson then shot Parent four times and instructed the women to push his car back up the driveway. Watson walked across the lawn. The group then spread out and looked for any open window. Finding none, Watson cut through a screen window and entered the home. Once inside, he opened the front door and let in the three women.

Inside the home were Sharon Tate, Jay Sebring, Voytek Frykowski and Abigail Folger. Watson ordered the four people to lie face down on the floor. Sebring, a celebrity hair stylist, protested to Watson.

"She's eight months pregnant!"

Watson said nothing as he shot Sebring.

Incapacitated from the bullet wound, Sebring was kicked in the head several times by Watson. He would suffer a broken nose and eye socket. Watson would also stab him seven times.

"I remember when we first came in one of the people said 'who are you?'" Susan recalled. "And then Tex said 'I'm the devil and I'm here to do the devil's business. And I remember in my conscience it is so alive in me, I remember I had gone so far and there was no turning back.

Even if I wanted to run, even if I wanted to leave, I couldn't. It was like I was caught in something that I had no control over. I had absolutely no say-so in what was happening there, I was like a tool in the hands of the devil is the only way I can put it

"I tied Voytek Frykowski's hands with a towel," Susan said. "And was instructed to kill him. And I raised the knife I had in my hand and couldn't put the knife down. I couldn't bring it down. It was like there was a force there that held my wrist. I couldn't-I couldn't move. And as he saw that I couldn't move then he very easily undid the ties that I tied his wrist with and he and I remember I was screaming for help and he was screaming for help and then Tex came and helped me and I just remember people scattering into different places." Frykowski tried to escape, running across the lawn. Susan and Tex Watson caught up with him as Watson finished him off with a flurry of stabbing. Susan stabbed at his legs. Frykowski tried desperately to stay on his feet, he grabbed a lamppost to try and remain upright. Susan and Tex were merciless, however. An autopsy would later reveal that he would suffer thirteen separate blunt-trauma wounds to his head, two gunshot wounds, and fifty-one stab wounds. Susan and Tex then returned to the home to finish with the killing of Sharon Tate.

Susan held Tate in a headlock while the rest of the occupants were being sliced and stabbed.

Saving her for last, Tex came upon the beautiful actress.

"Hold her down," Tex said as Susan grabbed Tate's legs.

"Please let me go," Tate pleaded. "All I want to do is have my baby."

"Woman," Susan said. "I have no mercy for you."

Susan would later write the word "PIG" on the front door using Tate's blood.

"We wanted to do a crime that would shock the world," Susan said. "That the world would have to stand up and take notice."

The Tate house had been chosen at random but Manson had known of the home from a year prior as it belonged to a record producer named Terry Melcher. Melcher had given Manson some false hope on a record deal that didn't come through.

The next night, Manson expressed his displeasure at how the murders of Tate and the others in the Beverly Hills home were sloppy.

"I need to show you people how it's done," Manson said. He summoned Susan, Patricia Krenwinkel, Tex Watson, Leslie Van Houten, Linda Kasabian, and Steve "Clem" Grogan to accompany him to their next target.

Manson and his followers would enter the home of Leno LaBianca and his wife Rosemary in Los Angeles. LaBiance was a hard working owner of a grocery store while his wife owned an antique shop. Breaking into their home while both were sleeping, Manson had Watson tie the couple up. Both husband and wife protested but Manson lied to the couple, saying that they were only there to rob them. Getting their compliance, Manson went back to the car and ordered Krenwinkel and Van Houten into the home.

"Do what Tex tells you to do," Manson said to the young women.

The Family would proceed to murder the couple and write revolutionary words on the walls using the blood of their victims.

TROUBLE AT SPAHN RANCH

On August 16th, 1969 the police would raid the Spahn Ranch on car theft charges. They still had not connected the Manson family to the Tate or LaBianca murders. The auto theft charges were eventually dropped and the members of the Family who had been arrested were released.

But Manson saw the noose tightening and decided to move his base of operations to Barker Ranch. Two months later, however, the police would raid the new location and arrest the Family once more.

It was during this time that a member of the family would rat out Susan for the Hinman murder.

Susan Atkins would be charged for that crime.

Now in prison, Susan would talk about her crimes to two of her fellow inmates, Virginia Graham, and Veronica Howard.

"I stabbed that bitch (Sharon Tate)," Susan said. "I said 'Look, bitch, I don't care if you're going to have a baby. You better be ready. You're going to die, and I don't feel anything about it. Then I tasted her blood."

Thinking she was crazy, the two inmates decided to report her confession to the authorities anyway.

Based on this information, the police would proceed to arrest Leslie Van Houten, Tex Watson, Linda Kasabian and Patricia Krenwinkel.

Susan would agree to be a witness for the prosecution if she could be spared the death penalty. But she would testify in front of the grand jury without this deal in place and informed that she might incriminate herself.

"I understand this," Susan said. "My life doesn't mean that much to me, I just want to see what is taken care of."

But before the case went to trial, Susan decided to severe ties with the prosecution. She would backtrack on her initial grand jury testimony in which she would admit to killing Frykowski and helping Tex Watson kill Sharon Tate. Susan would later say that she was influenced by Manson to not testify against him.

Contradictions remain in Susan Atkins' involvement in the Sharon Tate murder. Tex Watson would later state that he was responsible for all of Tate's wounds. He would dismiss Susan's confession as nothing more than an exaggeration to get attention. But another Family member, Barbara Hoyt, would eavesdrop on Susan on one occasion and overhear her cheerfully describe her role in the murders.

Susan would be part of the main Manson trial that commenced on June 15th, 1970. The media would locate Susan Atkins' father, Edward, and he dismissed the notion that Susan was under the influence of Charles Manson. Instead, he blamed drugs and the leniency of her previous sentencing. "I think she is just trying to talk her way out of it," Edward said. "She's sick and she needs help." Edward would reveal that he had tried for several years to get the courts to keep his daughter off the streets but they kept letting her go.

Susan would testify that she stabbed Sharon Tate as well as Tex Watson. She would claim that she did it because she was "sick of listening to her, pleading and begging, begging and pleading." Susan would continue to run interference for Manson, denying him any active role in the murders.

Susan's testimony was given little credence as she and the other "Manson Girls" would show their disdain for the proceedings. They would sing Manson inspired folk songs as they entered the courtroom and giggle throughout the trial.

Jurors were not impressed with her zany courtroom behavior. Susan would be sentenced to death and transported to the newly created women's death row in April of 1971.

HINMAN TRIAL

Susan was then convicted of the murder of Hinman, pleading guilty to all charges levied against her. She would testify that she didn't know that Hinman was about to be beaten up, robbed and possibly killed. Susan would later contradict this in later interviews and a memoir which is why so much of her testimony is given little credibility.

JAIL TIME

Sentenced to death, Susan caught a break in the legal system as the California Supreme Court struck down all death sentences in the state that occurred prior to 1972. Susan's sentence was then commuted down to life in prison.

In 1974, Susan would claim that she saw a vision of Jesus Christ in her jail cell. She converted to Christianity and became active in various prison programs. She began teaching classes and received letters of commendations after she helped out in two medical emergencies inside the prison (she helped intervene in a suicide attempt.) Susan would then publish a memoir and try to serve God with the same fervor that she served Manson. In her letters, she compared herself to the biblical Paul and Moses.

Susan would marry two times during her prison sentence. The first marriage would be with Donald Lee Laisure in 1981. Donald was known as "Flash" as he always carried around a huge wad of cash. He was also a congenital liar, lying about his military service in which he claimed a Navy Cross, Silver Star, and an Air Medal while "serving" 54 years. Susan would divorce him, stating that "he wasn't completely truthful with me." She would be his 35th wife. In 1987, Susan would marry James Whitehouse, a Harvard Law grad who would represent her at her parole hearings in 2000 and 2005.

The two would lobby hard in her final parole hearings to no avail.

"You know a person by their behavior," Susan said. "And my behavior in this institution speaks to the change that occurred over thirty years ago. I'm not the same person I was when I came in here."

Susan's parole hearings would continue to be greeted with deaf ears from the parole board. Sharon Tate's sister, Debra, would speak at Susan's parole hearings. She would read from a prepared statement from her father who described how their family was ripped apart. Tate's mother would spiral into a deep depression while her father, an Army colonel, would grieve in silence.

"There is no argument I can make," Susan said in response to Paul Tate's words. "I can only make every attempt to apologize. Remorse and sorrow for hideous actions is not calculatable. You can't calculate it."

Susan would then make references to her own repentance, using the standard rhetoric on how she should be judged for turning away from her behavior rather than be judged for her past actions.

COMPASSIONATE RELEASE?

Susan would fail once again at her 17th parole hearing in 2005. But by 2008, she had been diagnosed with brain cancer. The prognosis was grim, Susan already had one leg amputated and was given less than six months to live. This prompted a motion for Susan to be given a compassionate release which was denied on September 2nd, 2009. Twenty-two days later, Susan would die at the Central California Women's facility in Chowchilla.

In her final moments, she had someone read Psalm 23 from the Bible to hear.

Her final words were "Amen.

SQUEAKY FROMME & THE MANSON CULT

Covering the tragedy of the Sharon Tate and LaBianca murders of the late 1960's, this book documents the twisted spiral of Lynette "Squeaky" Fromme. This book explores how the relatively normal world of Californian suburbia that Lynette Fromme was born into could lead her into the arms of the most notorious cult leader and cult group in history. Taking into consideration how the warped beliefs of a street hustler named Charles Manson could have such a pull on her and the rest of the Manson Family. Come along with us as we explore Fromme's role in the crime and times of Charles Manson and how this troubled young woman would eventually make an assassination attempt on the life of a United States President. She was an average American girl but something, somewhere along the way went terribly wrong. This book attempts to answer the question; what happened to Lynette Squeaky Fromme?

Introduction: What's the Problem?

The year was 1967. The war in Vietnam was just heating up, the Civil Rights movement was fully mobilized, and protesters were arriving en masse in opposition to the conventions of the day. But even with all of the political axes to grind, in 1967, the 18-year-old "Squeaky" Lynette Fromme was just a lost little girl wanting to find a way back home.

When the ex-convict and aspiring cult leader Charles Manson found her, she was weeping on a bench, depressed and frightened after her latest go round with her authoritarian father had left her homeless and on the street. Manson who—of all things—had taken coursework in prison that was based on the motivational book "How to Win Friends and Influence People" already knew how to win friends and he certainly could influence people.

Manson had finely honed his powers of manipulation and his ability to read others all the way back in his Juvenile Hall days in Indianapolis, Indiana. He developed a great capacity to infer what those around him wanted to hear and see, and then copiously worked to give them just that, as he constantly worked over his guards, attorney's and even court judges with his concerted efforts at charisma.

Seeking to be a heavily refined conman, it was a skill that seemed to serve Manson well, allowing him to charm his way through the parole board on several occasions. It was on his latest get out of jail free card excursion that he found Lynette Fromme drowning in her own tears on that public bench. And knowing exactly what to say, without any pretense or hesitation he instantly inserted himself in this troubled young girls world and cut through everything she was feeling so ill at ease about, by simply asking the question, "What's the problem?"

Chapter 1: The Family Business

The day Lynnette Fromme met Charles Manson she began a lasting partnership with the convict turned mystic. In truth, she became one of his first followers in what would become the "Manson Family". The group of free love drug addicted misfits who flocked to Charles Manson's promise of an alternative society. Manson often called himself the "Gardener" and fancied himself a caretaker for all of the misfit flower children of the 1960's who wandered his way.

The wacky beliefs that Manson expressed to his followers in the scorching hot heat of Death Valley were as laughable as they were stupidly offensive. Even worse than his wacky beliefs, however, was his inane ability to pull perfectly good rock music down into the derelict dumps with him.

Dropping acid and listening to Beatles records was one of Manson's favorite pastimes, and it was in the midst of this hobby of his that he somehow became convinced that the Beatles were prophets who had chosen to speak directly to him through coded messages in their music.

And the message that Manson fixated more than anything else, was the one he believed to have gleaned from a song called, "Helter Skelter" which Manson somehow believed to foreshadow future civil unrest and even ethnic cleansing. Shortly after the bloody murders in which Manson's brainwashed followers had scrawled the same two words on the walls with their victim's own blood, it would be Helter Skelter that would become the Manson Family's calling card.

Helter Skelter had become so associated with Manson and his crimes that it eventually forced former Beatles John Lennon and Paul McCartney to weigh in on the controversy. They really didn't know how Manson could have developed such a bizarre interpretation of their song.

Lennon contended that the title "Helter Skelter" was taken from an amusement park that had stood across the street from one of the venues they had played. The lyrics were really just a running gag reflecting the rides at the park with lyrics like, "When I get to the bottom I go back to the top of the slide, where I stop and I turn and I go for a ride."

Both John and Paul have always asserted that Helter Skelter never had much of a deep meaning at all, it was just the band getting together and playing a goofy, silly song. But for Charles Manson's disturbed mind it was some sort of twisted revelation. And as Charlie's loose associations with rock music and prophecy continued, his group of devoted followers, including one Lynnette Squeaky Fromme, became just as convinced as he was.

Convinced that the apocalypse was nigh, the Manson Family's original plan was to just wait it out in their own little commune in the middle of Death Valley, while society destroyed itself and then wait for the traumatized remnants of the civilized world to come crawling to them in the desert. Because who would the shattered remnants of civilization seek out to rebuild the world? Why Charles Manson of course.

It's all pure, unadulterated, tripped out insanity that makes as much sense as the paranoid schizophrenic who believed David Letterman was communicating to her through her television set. But for all of Charles Manson's insanity, he had a powerfully insidious charisma that had crept over his followers, and Squeaky Lynnette Fromme soon believed every warped word out of the madman's mouth.

And so it was that Lynette Fromme's new family spent the rest of the 1960's out in the desert waiting for the end of the world to arrive. But the end of their world didn't come in the form of societal collapse, the Manson Family's world would come crashing down around them when they were implicated in the murders of actress Sharon Tate and a couple name Labianca.

Even though his followers and Manson himself always contended that Manson had never actually killed anyone with his own hands, it was quickly believed that the twisted cult leader had inspired his followers to kill on his command. And in the aftermath of Manson's incarceration, it was Lynette Fromme who became his number one advocate, tirelessly showing up at court hearings, dictating his will and testament and incessantly speaking to reporters.

But much more than this, she quickly became the mouthpiece and the de facto leader of the Manson family in Charlie's absence. For the media at the time, it seemed that if Charles wasn't in charge, then well, Lynnette Squeaky Fromme most certainly was. The most well-spoken member besides Manson himself, Fromme quickly became a main focal point of media attention. According to Manson attorney Paul Fitzgerald, it was Lynnette who expressly formed the Manson Family's "heartbeat".

And for a time, even without Manson, Lynnette Fromme and many of her former Manson Family sister's tried to carry on, even recruiting more men who might serve as a surrogate for Manson. Lynnette attempting to emulate her hero preached to drifters and the discontented. But when men heard the words of Charles Manson's philosophies coming out of Lynette Fromme's mouth they often fell flat or seemed more like an offbeat form of amusement than any kind of real alternative in life.

Fromme would try her best to emulate Charles when she spoke of how the women's liberation movement had undercut American men disrupting the order, but when she spouted things like, "American women were wearing the pants, they had taken their men's balls and chained them up" something that would have had converts nodding along if they came from Charles Manson, just came off as absurd, offbeat, drunken humor when they came from petite little Lynette Fromme.

But while Fromme tried to secure her grip on the family, many in Charles Manson's legal team were attempting to secure their grip on Fromme. Manson's main defense attorney, "Paul Fitzgerald"insisted that Fromme was key to defending the case against Charles Manson.

And he began frequently meeting with Fromme, eventually designating her as a material witness in the case.

This was a move happily welcomed by Fromme since it meant that she would finally be able to visit the incarcerated Charles Manson. Fitzgerald meant to use these meetings as constructively as he could in order to bolster his defense, but much more than legal strategizing, for Lynnette Fromme these meetings usually turned into her own debriefing sessions for the family's former head.

Charles would prod her for information about the latest happenings with the family and then before she left, he would give her hundreds of commands and special assignments to carry out on the outside. If he wanted her to contact someone, she would, if he wanted her to discipline another family member she would, Fromme was now Manson's last window into the outside world and ultimately his messenger to the rest of the family and whoever else he wished to speak to.

But all of these seemingly obscure tasks, suggestions, and assignments that Fromme would receive from Manson none of them proved to have anything at all to the case at hand and attorney Paul Fitzgerald grew increasingly disconcerted. But as erratic as Fromme may have seemed, there was one area in which she always served to benefit the defense team and that was in bringing public awareness to the case.

From the beginning, Fitzgerald figured that the only way they could beat the system and win a not guilty verdict for Charles Manson would be to turn public opinion against the legal process itself. And in this task, Lynne Fromme was a ceaseless cheerleader. She once famously announced, "There is no love in that court, no God in the machine—just a lot of big words that swear to God and stagnate life, rather than adjusting justice, they make the court into a gladiator ring."

In her own jumbled and disjointed way, Fromme was making her own case to the public that the courtroom was like a modern arena in which men like her own modern day Spartacus; Charles Manson, were pitted against odds that were purposefully stacked against them. Fromme felt that if she could espouse this unfair treatment to the public she just might be able to shift the balance in Manson's favor.

So Fromme went on her own Charles Manson awareness campaign, and all over California she would proclaim to anyone who would listen, "Come to the trials—your trials—and see what's going on." This publicity campaign did manage to generate interest. And even if it was just out of morbid curiosity, people did come, so much so, that every courtroom seat was filled, and even outside the packed courtroom, curious onlookers crowded the scene.

But as the courtroom began to overflow with observers Fromme soon found herself without a seat of her own. The prosecution detesting the circus that had been created and viewing Fromme as a distraction would not allow her to attend. Since Fromme and her other acolytes were not allowed in the courtroom they decided to take their message to the street.

Practically every single day of the trial they would assemble on the corner down the street from the Justice Hall. Their antics became so much of a spectacle that they themselves became a morbid kind of tourist attraction. With people coming from miles around just to see Fromme and these other strange women who tried their best to keep up the family business.

Chapter 2: The Conviction of President's

For President Richard Millhouse Nixon, 1970 was proving to be an interesting year. The United States had just invaded Cambodia, greatly escalating a war Nixon had pledged to subdue, inflaming protests at college campuses all around the world. Just one month prior to this signing, 4 young protesters had been shot and killed by the National Guard at Kent State in Ohio. And then, of course, there was the ongoing trial of Charles Manson. A media circus that Richard Nixon freely commented upon on August 4th of 1970 when he declared in regard to Manson, "Here is a man who was guilt, directly or indirectly, of eight murders without reason."

Manson's guilty verdict made headlines across the national media the next day. One of the attorneys had brought a copy of of one of the newspapers to the courtroom proceedings that day, and Charles Manson seeing it, went berserk and snatched it up off the table, holding up for all to see Nixon's condemnation of him. Manson's efforts proved to be part out of outrage and out of cunning manipulation. Manson and his followers hoped that Richard Nixon's biased conviction could grant him a mistrial.

And sure enough, the next day, loyal Manson followers took the cue, and asked the judge, "Your Honor, the President said we are guilty, so why go on with the trial?" But trial judge Charles H. Holder was steadfast in his own conviction and suggested that Manson had brought the controversy on himself and then declared the attorney who brought the newspaper in the courtroom was in contempt of court for violating the order against newspaper publications being present during proceedings.

Lynnette Fromme who had already developed a cultivated hatred of the American Justice System was especially affected by Richard Nixon's pronouncement. She now felt it was clear that the system and even the very President of the United States were out to get them. This was a belief that she maintained and nurtured even after Nixon's replacement by Gerald Ford and many contend that this was what planted the seed of her desire to assassinate President Ford. She wanted to get revenge for the wrong she thought Richard Nixon had done them.

Manson himself tried to throw the President's conviction right back at him, when he declared in reference to Richard Nixon, "Here's a man who is accused of murdering hundred of thousands in Vietnam, who is accusing me of being guilty of eight murders." But no matter how Charles Manson tried to spin it, the proceedings would be destined to continue.

And now a new element of the case against Charles Manson began to merit the concern of the Manson followers; the prosecutions new star witness, former Manson Family member Barbara Hoyt. Barbara was a reluctant witness and had been pressured early on to testify. Wishing to hide from the whole affair she had contacted Lynne Fromme and other former family members, seeking advice as to where she could lay low.

Lynne and her cohorts then came up with the idea that she should fly to Hawaii with two other family members so she could avoid her court date. Apparently, Barbara initially agreed to the plan and flew to Hawaii with the two other members. It was here that Barbara began to have second thoughts, however, about whether or not she should truly avoid giving her testimony.

But before she could decide which way she was going to go with it, one of the member's gave her a hamburger drenched with enough LSD to send someone into a complete psychosis. Shortly afterward Barbara was found collapsed in the street mumbling about her courtroom duties to the lead prosecutor, stating, "Call Mr. Bugliosi and tell him I won't be able to testify today in the Sharon Tate trial."

Known as the "hamburger plot" Lynne and her others were quickly apprehended with charges of conspiracy and obstruction of justice. The lead prosecutor Vincent Bugliosi then did his best to convince the court that Lynn and her compatriots wanted nothing more than Barbara to either die or become permanently disabled from an overdose of LSD. Although the more serious charges were later dropped, Lynne Fromme and her cohorts were all hit up with a "conspiracy to dissuade a witness and conspiracy to bribe a witness" and thrown in jail.

It was from the depths of the Sybil Brand Correctional Institution for women that Lynnette Fromme was summoned once again to stand trial as a witness for the Manson defense team. During her testimony, she proved to be quite a burden for the Judge who had to snap her to attention and keep her on track with several yells of "Just answer the question, Miss Fromme".

From the outset, Fromme seemed more interested in using the witness stand as a platform from which to proclaim her views and the Manson family values than any recognizable form of usable testimony for the defense or the prosecution of a murder case. Growing increasingly frustrated, Judge Older soon silenced her words and ordered all counsel to a impromptu meeting with him in which he told Fromme's defense attorney, "this witness is not interested in being responsive to the questions asked her" and informed him in no uncertain terms that Fromme was not to, "use this court as a forum for her philosophies."

Whatever Lynn was trying to accomplish with all of her statements, it was to no avail, however, and all of the defendants charged with murder received an unequivocal pronouncement of death, while Lynne Fromme herself was quietly shuffled off to the Sybil Brand Institute for Women to serve the rest of her conspiracy charge. For most of America, the case against Charles Manson and his family was closed, but for Lynette Squeaky Fromme it was only beginning.

Chapter 3: Life outside the Pen

When Lynnette Fromme was released from the Sybil Brand Institute for Women in the year 1971, it seemed as if the whole world had changed; at least the world of Squeaky Fromme that is. Charles Manson was sitting on death row along with the other Manson Family members who were charged in the Tate and LaBianca murders. But for Fromme, it seemed that it was more than her friend's lives that had received a death sentence because it was her idealistic dreams—dreams that she had shaped with her fellow Manson family members—that seemed forever condemned to death as well.

The world she came back to was now unrecognizable, completely drained and empty of everything that she had previously hoped for. The summer of love which had flourished in Haight Ashbury with all of its promises was now lost forever. And the man who she looked to as a brilliant and wise father, the man they called the "Gardener" in the hopes that he could cultivate their minds for spiritual growth, was now forever ingrained in everyone else's mind as nothing more than a psychopathic killer.

When Fromme hit the streets after her release in 1971 she found a world gone cold that she no longer recognized. Most of her previous contacts had either disappeared or no longer wanted anything to do with her. For the rest of the year, Lynnette Fromme would bounce around from place to place and spend most of her energy writing a book about Manson which she hoped would somehow convince the world of his goodness and grant him a pardon.

Of course, none of this happened. Even when she finally finished her rambling monolog the story was so radioactive, even with the lure of media attention, no publisher was willing to touch it. Meanwhile, the legal system, or as Fromme and her colleagues frequently called it, "The System" seemed to be moving further and further away from them. As was made evident on October 21st, 1971 when Richard Nixon nominated the conservative Judge William Rehnquist to the Supreme Court.

But even so, Lynn still held out hope for a reversal of Manson's fate, one way or another and as a part of this, she started to establish her own contacts in the legal scene. One major part of this was her introduction in the Spring of 1972 to an up and coming San Francisco Attorney by the name of Doug Vaughn. A notorious figure in the region who drove a pickup truck and often sported a strangely Country Western look replete with hat and cowboy boots.

Lynnette maintained a rather superficial relationship with Vaughn and with him found sympathetic ears as she railed against the government she felt so betrayed by. Vaughn recalls one instance in which the topic came to the latest Democratic candidate for president, George McGovern, a conversation that led Fromme to make the blanket statement about politicians, "They're all just a bunch of liars and crooks."

But speaking of crooks it was soon Lynne Fromme who would develop a whole new cadre of crooks, liars, and thieves, who would ultimately implicate her in another notorious murder. Under the influence of Charles Manson who had forged a partnership with the prison gang, "The Aryan Brotherhood" a fresh flood of ex-cons came flooding into the Manson Family world.

During the course of these events, two of Lynne's friends were killed by the gang members and Lynne herself once again guilty by association was rounded up and thrown in jail once again as a result. It was here that her newly established legal consultant Doug Vaughn came to Lynette's rescue. After Vaughn investigated the case he discovered that the charges leveled against her had no weight.

From the police reports, he determined that the only reason the police brought her in was because she had hung out at the suspect's house and of course because of the tremendous reputation she had as the defacto leader of the Manson cult that already preceded her. The police had just hauled her in based on all of that. Lynn would finally have all charges once again dropped on January 2nd, 1973 and released back out on the streets of California.

Her freedom would not last long since the LAPD had a deep suspicion that Fromme had been involved in a robbery at a Seven-Eleven back in October of the previous year. And after being released from one prison system she was simply shipped off to another one, but in yet another amazingly ridiculous turn of fate in the annals of the Manson family, the "X" Lynn had first carved in her face years ago so that she would be spared from the wrath of locusts, managed to help spare Lynnette from serving another jail term.

Because after Vaughn had the witness to the Seven Eleven robbery take a look at the telltale mark, the witness finally conceded that the person she saw did not have such an unforgettable feature. A few days later the actual woman that robbed the store was captured and after she confessed to the crime Lynne was once again released to live life outside of the Pen.

Chapter 4: The Making of an Assassin

With her own legal battles finally settling down Lynette Fromme was struggling to find her place in the world once again. She was living off of $90 a month on welfare and found room and board at another cheap flat. Even though her surroundings were meager, and her outlook seemed bleak, many thought that she was finally trying to move on with her life and leave the Manson Family behind her.

But as fate would have it, a bestselling book would send her scrambling right back into the arms of extremism. Released in November 1974, Vincent Bugliosi published his book "Helter Skelter" which described the events that had become so infamous with the same working title. Fromme was still hurt over the fact that she could never get anyone to publish her own book, and then to find that someone else had beaten her to it was frustrating.

And then when she actually read the book for herself she was incensed to find certain passages that described her own presence and character in ways she found very upsetting. In one passage Bugliosi even seemed to call into question her mental capacity as he described Lynette Fromme and Sarah Good, "as if they hadn't aged but had been retarded at a certain stage in their childhood."

There it was for the whole world to see; Lynnette Fromme was mentally retarded, irrevocably stunted by Charles Manson who had snatched her up at 18 years old and warped her brain beyond recognition. This outrage spurred Lynnette Fromme to try once again to get her own book published so she could in her own words, "effectively combat the Bugliosi thought syndrome" and she now became utterly obsessed with telling her side of the story.

Meanwhile, President Nixon had resigned in disgrace and was replaced by Gerald R. Ford as the new President of the United States. Despite the seat change, however, it didn't take long for Lynette Fromme to redirect all of her anger at the "system" and Nixon, firmly on the linebacker shoulders of President Ford. She would tell a journalist at the time, "Ford is picking up Nixon's footsteps, and he is just as bad."

Donning her new cult uniform of a red robe Fromme then set out to shut down all of the ills that she claimed had been caused by government bureaucracy from Ford on down the line. One day she barged into a cement factory and demanded them to stop production because it was hurting the environment. In another instance, she even wrote a scathing letter to the Prime Minister of Japan criticizing him for Japanese Whaling.

At this point, calling herself a "Nun of the Earth", Fromme had given up men and embraced the environment, all the while claiming that she was ready to eliminate anyone that polluted the Earth. Even though many of her proclamations were startling with their degree of menace and violence, most people still did not take the petite form of Squeaky Lynette Fromme seriously.

In 1975 she heard that President Ford, the current embodiment of all her perceived evil was coming to town. It was an alignment of events that she just couldn't resist. Fromme remembers how disgusted she was with the excitement of everyone around her that the President was coming. Incensed with what she viewed as a gross and false form of adoration. At the time she intoned to her friend Sandra Good that President Ford was "a dummy, an empty head" and that his adoring fans were, "like sheep looking up to this dead head with dead thoughts."

With increasing rage and hatred that the whole city would turn out to see this "dead head" of a man, Lynette Squeaky Fromme determined that she would be the one to finally silence the object of her hatred once and for all. On September 5th, 1975 waiting with a crowd of, as she would put it, "adoring sheep" Lynette Fromme was the wolf in sheep's clothing, besides the brilliant red crimson of her dress she just looked like a small, pleasant-faced woman, waiting to see the President.

But when he came within just a few feet from Ford, as he was blithely shaking the hands of onlookers, President Ford saw Fromme move toward him out of the corner of his eyes. Ford assumed that she just wanted a presidential handshake as well, but when he stopped to look at the woman, instead of an extended hand to greet him, he saw a gun in his face instead.

After a momentary look of panic, President Ford scrambled to get out of the way of the deranged woman's line of sight, while Secret Service Agent Larry Buendorf screamed the ominous warning, "forty-five"!

Acknowledging the Colt Forty Five that the strange figure in red was waving in her hand Buendorf then pounced on Fromme and ripped the weapon from her hands as a seemingly puzzled and disappointed Fromme cried out, "It didn't go off!" For some reason the gun had failed to fire, granting a sad and dejected Lynette Squeaky Fromme yet another item to her growing list of failure.

Conclusion: Hiding From the Past

By the time of Lynette Fromme's attempted assassination of Gerald Ford, she had actually been quite used to getting arrested, being shuffled through the system and then ultimately being released. She had after all been found implicit with murder on two separate occasions already, and each time she was released.

And so it was that when her gone had failed to go off, preventing her from assassinating President Ford. Squeaky was subdued and believed that her charges would be dismissed since she "caused no harm."

But whether Fromme realized it or not, due to federal legislation enacted shortly after the assassination of President John F. Kennedy, assassination attempts came with a mandatory sentence of life in prison. But as much as she hated the system it would smile on her eventually, and she was released after just 34 years of her sentence in 2009.

Meanwhile, Charles Manson and the other family members are still in prison. Their death sentences were commuted when California abolished the death sentence, but they will no doubt be behind bars for the rest of their lives. But what about Lynnette Squeaky Fromme? Where is Lynnette Fromme now? The last anyone knew she was dodging the media, avoiding the limelight for a change, and trying to avoid anything and everything to do with her past.

LESLIE VAN HOUTEN & THE MANSON CULT

Leslie Van Houten is a former member of Charles Manson's "Family". She was convicted in 1971 for the killings of Leno and Rosemary LaBianca. Leslie's sentencing was part of the main Charles Manson trial but she blamed her actions on the control Manson had over her.

Houten, Manson and two other members of the "Family" were convicted and sentenced to death row until a new California law commuted their punishment to life imprisonment. Van Houten's lawyer passed away during the course of her trial and her convictions were thrown out. She then went to trial again, her primary defense being that she had a diminished mental capacity because of the drugs Manson had given her.

The jury remained deadlocked.

But Leslie would go to trial a third time. She would be convicted and sentenced to two life sentences.

Amazingly, after over twenty different hearings, the California state board decided to make Leslie eligible for parole.

On April 16th, 2016, Governor Jerry Brown agreed.

EARLY LIFE

Leslie was born on August 23rd, 1949 in Altadena, a suburb of Los Angeles. Her father, Paul, worked as a car sales auctioneer while her mother Jane was a former teacher turned housewife. Leslie grew up in a church-going family with one older brother and two adopted siblings who were Korean. A boy and a girl, they were orphaned in Korea and came to live with the Van Houten's in the southern California suburban home which had a pool.

"It was a middle-class experience if there ever was one," forensic psychologist Paula Orange said. "Leslie's family did all the right things. A two-parent household where the father worked and the mother stayed home and took care of the children. They had a home with a pool and would go to church on Sunday. Not exactly the type of background you would expect for a killer. Leslie did not come from an abusive home and seemingly had all she needed to become a happy, well-adjusted young woman."

Trouble started for Leslie at the age of fourteen when her parents divorced. Her mother was forced to go back to school to renew her teaching credentials. Her father left the home but he was no deadbeat dad. He stayed in touch and provided for all of the children financially. Leslie seemed to be well-adjusted on the surface, she was elected homecoming princess two years in a row. But she began dating an older man and by the age of sixteen, she had experimented with LSD for the first time. She would have an abortion as well as begin the drug habit, both of which would cause considerable emotional pain to herself and her family.

"I seemed to what more living out of life then what was expected of young girls at that time," Leslie said. "Drugs, sex, breaking away from the norm."

Leslie met another young man and the two ran away to the Haight-Ashbury district of San Francisco. She eventually returned to Southern California living with her father to complete her high school education. She enrolled in secretarial school, learning shorthand but the career didn't seem to be the right choice for her. Leslie began to study yoga and saw an alternative to her middle-class destiny when she broke up with her boyfriend and began living in a hippie commune in Northern California.

HIPPIES MAN

Leslie would meet Catherine "Gypsy" Share and Bobby Beausoleil, moving in with them in 1968. She would begin a dating relationship with Beausoleil who was a mainstay at the communes along the coast. Nicknamed "Cupid", Beausoleil was a reform school drop-out who managed to get some bit parts in low budget movies. He was also a promising musician, performing in two bands called "The Milky Way" and "Love."

Catherine "Gypsy" Share, on the other hand, was the stereotypical free spirit of the counter-culture movement at the time. Like Beausoleil, she dabbled in acting and got a bit part in a soft core porn called "The Ramrodder." Gypsy would talk of making a pilgrimage to hang out with a man who knew all about love and peace. A man who lived in the moment.

His name was Charles Manson.

"I had gotten to the ranch with people who were traveling up and down the coast," Leslie said. "And prior to that I was neck deep in the hippie movement and I met these people that said they came from a commune in LA where they lived for the day and for the moment and it was a lot of the Leary kind of philosophy of 'be here now'. I was attracted to that."

Leslie followed both Beausoleil and Gypsy to Manson's commune. She was part of the expansion of the "Family" which now included Tom "TJ" Walleman, John "Zero" Haught, Cathy "Capistrano" Gillies and "Simi Valley" Sherri. Gypsy and Leslie had cut ties with Bobby Beausoleil but Manson considered Bobby to be a friend. He didn't want to insult him by taking his women. After much convincing by Gypsy, Manson relented.

Initially, Manson did not want to accept Leslie into the fold. She had an intelligent air about her and he considered that to be a threat. He didn't need smart people. He wanted people who would obey.

Manson eventually saw the positive benefit in having Leslie join the "Family". She was beautiful and he had physical relations with her as part of her initiation. Her beauty would serve in helping recruit more male members. He saw that Leslie also had secretarial skills. He employed her to write in shorthand in order to record the lyrics of the songs that Manson would sing.

"I heard he (Manson) was like Christ," Leslie said. "That he had the answers and that I just really needed to go and meet him. As twisted as it all got I felt that I had met someone that by being around him would have a positive change."

"Leslie stayed for one night at the ranch," Orange said. "Then she returned a little under a month later to stay permanently. Manson, of course, took her under his wing with a lot of his quasi-Buddhist teachings like the shedding of the ego, the giving up of a personal identity. Leslie was at an age where she was vulnerable to that kind of mumbo jumbo. Manson would step in front of her and encourage Leslie to mirror his body movements, to try and anticipate what he would do next. He used these kinds of methods and more to get into his follower's heads."

Leslie called her mother telling her that she was "dropping out of society" and would not be in contact again. She then fully embraced all of Manson's hippie ideals; freeloading, eating out of garbage cans and drop acid.

"Leslie would later claim that she become such an acid head that she could no longer discern reality," Orange said. "She becomes exactly what Manson wanted. Someone who followed without question."

LIFE AT THE SPAHN RANCH

Manson's headquarters were based at the Spahn Ranch. The Ranch had originally been used as a movie set for many Western films. George Spahn was the owner of the ranch at the time. He was eighty years old and allowed the Manson Family to live rent free in return for doing chores and maintaining the ranch. The number of members continued to swell as the hippie movement grew.

"There were about fifteen or so solid members," Leslie said. "There were ten or so transients."

There were also considerably more women than men.

"Manson worked women better," Leslie explained. "I wasn't one of the ones that was physically enamored with him. I was more caught and mesmerized by his mind and the things he professed."

Manson charmed his acolytes with the idealistic philosophy of acceptance and free life. The ranch was isolated and Manson would be the only voice that members of the "Family" listened to. Barbara Hoyt, a fellow follower, would later describe Leslie as a "leader" at the Ranch while Manson was "The Gardener."

"I tend to all the flower children," Manson said.

Leslie became comfortable living at the ranch as she felt a lack of judgment and a kinship with the other followers. There were no clock watches, no sense of time and no sense of personal identities like individual names or birthdays.

"You could absolutely not talk about your past at all," Leslie said. "We started off, in the gentler days, to shed ourselves of our egos and to get rid of our own identity. We were to do what was then called 'become one with one another.' He (Manson) would do this by assaulting our families. Mocking our morals and all of the things we had been taught because all of us were middle-class Anglos."

"Manson's followers were all people who were raised in the church," Orange said. "So it is no coincidence he fostered a 'Jesus-like' look and manner in that he talked in riddles that seemed to make sense to them. He told his followers to love themselves and like Jesus, he would treat them with kindness, even going so far as wash their feet. He would rename his followers like a messiah renaming his family. Leslie would be called Lulu, Lou, or Morning Flower."

ENTER TEX WATSON

Tex Watson was an all-state high-school athlete who was a student at North Texas University. But while working as a baggage handler he began to become interested in the hippie movement and psychedelic lifestyle. His curiosity would eventually lead him to the commune of Charles Manson.

Like Leslie, Tex Watson saw Manson as a God-like figure. Manson would often ask his followers if they were ready to die for him. Watson, like the female followers, had been raised in church. He would later tell his mother that he found God when he met Charles Manson.

"You've always wanted me to be religious," Watson told his mother. "Well, I've met that Jesus you preach about all the time. I've met him and he's here right now with me in the desert."

When Manson asked Watson to kill for him, the former scholar-athlete would not hesitate.

"I didn't even have to think about it," Watson recalled. "(Manson was) like some mystic, so filled with the love of God that nothing is too great to ask, I was filled with Charlie. He WAS God to me."

"Sometimes he (Manson) would re-enact the crucifixion when we were on LSD," Leslie said. "And it was very realistic. He'd go through the whole thing (being nailed to the cross). Then he would make the connection between man's son and son of man. And then the questions would begin 'would you die for me?'"

The brainwashing continued on a daily basis. Manson, while not trained in mind-control techniques knew exactly what buttons to push to get what he wanted.

"One night at the ranch," Leslie said. "We're all sitting around in our little evening get-together. He started to say 'baa, like sheep' and every single one of us, did exactly at the moment that he said."

THE COMING RACE WAR

Manson began talking of a race war. He wanted to stage acts of violence that would propel the black community to follow him into "war" and extinguish the white race. He would have his followers train as if they were about to go into combat. There were guns on the ranch as well as numerous knife stabbing training sessions.

"I believed that Manson was Jesus Christ," Leslie said. "And that it (a race war) was something that had to be done. It was not something that I felt good about or that it was like war. We were going through combat training at the ranch. Prepped like that. He (Manson) believed that the whites had been on top for too long. And all they did was put harm on other people. That we were not like them and that the last time he came he had been crucified and this time he would have to make himself known."

Despite all of the terrorist-like talk, the followers would sit around the ranch all day naked and drop LSD. Manson, a former pimp, kept a lot of his male followers in line with the promise of "free love" from the female followers.

"If a man wanted you," Leslie said. "You went with him. You couldn't resist."

"I looked them in the eye and saw what they wanted," Manson said. "I told them what they had to do to stay with me. If they didn't like it, they left. If they stayed, I had sex with them. I told them to forget their hang-ups and guilt trips. They had to become one with me and my truth. Their wills had to die to become one with me. Sex was their initiation. It was a celebration of life's pleasures. Something to enjoy, not to be afraid of."

MUTINY IN THE FAMILY

Not all the followers rubber stamped Manson's every word. Pat Krenwinkel ditched the communed and hooked up with a biker. Manson tracked her down and ordered Krenwinkel to come back with him. Pat was shocked that she had been found and thought Manson used "special powers to find her." Truth was, Manson had several contacts in the biker culture that he employed.

Leslie herself began to question some of Manson's intentions. Angered, Manson pulled her aside and took her for a ride in his dune buggy. He parked at the top of the Santa Susanas and told her, "If you want to leave me, jump."

Leslie stayed.

There were a few defections in the commune but the primary people Manson needed, like Tex Watson and his "Manson Girls", all stayed.

ROCK STAR WANNABE

Another motive behind Manson's actions were his own failed pipe dreams. He was obsessed with becoming a rock star. He auditioned numerous times and failed miserably. Manson had his hopes for a record deal up when Beach Boy Dennis Wilson introduced him to record producer Terry Melcher. Wilson went so far as to record two of Manson's songs and Melcher expressed cursory interested in producing an album with Manson. He also wanted to make a film about the family and their communal lifestyle. Manson would audition for Melcher but the producer was unimpressed. They remain on cordial terms until Melcher saw Manson get in a fight at the Spahn Ranch with one of his followers. Melcher immediately parted ways with Manson, ceasing all communication.

This enraged Manson and according to Leslie, he "became angry all of the time."

"He felt rejected by the music industry that he wanted so much to be a part of," Orange said. "He adopted a few of the songs from the Beatle's White Album. Songs like Helter Skelter, Piggy, and Revolution 9 became his own personal anthems."

Piggy, in particular, became one of his favorites. The song spoke of white suburbia with their forks and knives.

"He thought one of the songs is supposed to say his name or something," Leslie said. "And we'd listen to it over and over and over. Number nine. Number nine. And you know he was really involved in Revelations 9."

One of his bizarre beliefs was that he believed that the Beatles would join the "Family" and "escape to a bottomless pit where they would becoming the proper rulers of the earth." Manson told his followers that the apocalypse from the Bible was forthcoming. He called the upcoming race conflict "Helter Skelter" from the Beatles' song.

"It was going to be a racially motivated revolution," Leslie said. "And that the blacks were going to control and take over the power."

With a record deal not in the cards, Manson began having his followers commit crimes. They started small at first by stealing cars and robbing homes. Leslie herself had robbed her father's home twice but was caught and served minimal jail time.

Manson would later shoot a member of the Black Panther party named Bernard "Lotsapapa" Crowe. Manson thought he had killed Crowe and began fearing retribution from the Panthers. This led to him training his "Family" members on how to kill with knives.

No longer confident in his ability to acquire fame through music. Manson sought a different route to becoming recognized.

He would become famous by killing people.

And Leslie went along for the ride.

THE FIRST MURDER

Manson's "Family" first targeted Gary Hinman, a music teacher. Details are sketchy on the motives of killing Hinman. Bobby Beausoleil would claim that the Family went to his home because he had cheated them on a drug deal. Another possible motive was that Manson believed that Hinman had money and cars. He wanted him to join the commune and thereby turn over his assets to his growing cult. Hinman refused and Manson sliced off his ear with a sword. Beausoleil stitched the ear back on with dental floss. Hinman was a pacifist and continually asked Manson "why are you doing this?"

After three days of torture, Beausoleil fatally stabbed Hinman two times in the chest. Manson's followers then wrote the words "Political piggy" on the wall with Hinman's blood. A little over a week later, Beausoleil would be arrested driving Hinman's car.

SHARON TATE MURDERS

In August of 1969, two members of the "Family" would be behind bars. Beausoleil and also Mary Brunner who was arrested for credit card fraud. Manson then targeted the residence of record producer Terry Melcher.

Only Melcher no longer lived there.

"Manson knew that Melcher no longer lived at the home," Orange said. "But in some strange, twisted way he probably thought he would be sending a message to the producer who doused his hopes of being a rock star."

The home was now owned by famed film director Roman Polanski who was out of the country at the time. Staying in the home was actress Sharon Tate, Votek Fryskowski, Jay Sebring and coffee heiress Abigail Folger.

Manson followers Tex Watson arrived at the home with three of the Manson Girls: Susan Atkins, Patricia Krenwinkel, and Linda Kasabian. Watson would lead the way while Kasabian stood watch outside.

Breaking through a window, Watson would go on a rampage inside the home. Within minutes would kill Frykowski, Sebring, and Tate who was eight months pregnant. Folger tried to escape but Krenwinkel caught her and stabbed her to death.

The killers stole a total of seventy dollars.

When they returned back to the ranch Manson confronted them at the front. He asked them "if they had any remorse." They said no and Manson reiterated that he and his followers were in a war and that they should not have any remorse for their actions against the enemy.

"Don't tell anyone," were his final words to his minions of death.

LABIANCA MURDERS

The next day, Manson again handpicked some of his followers to commit more murders.

"He (Manson) asked me," Leslie said. "'Do you believe in me enough to know that this is something that has to be done?' Or something to that effect and I said 'yes, I do.' I didn't walk right up and say 'May I go?' But I think everything on my face said that."

Leslie went along with the murderous group that night.

She would join Manson, Tex Watson, Patricia Krenwinkel, Susan Atkins, Linda Kasabian and Steve "Clem" Grogan as they staked out a house in the city of Los Feliz.

The home belonged to Rosemary and Leno LaBianca. They had the misfortune of being neighbors with a Manson friend named Phil Kaufman. Kaufman had been another music executive who had interactions with Manson and did not help him advance his career.

"The thinking was," Orange said. "And this is supported by Susan Atkins' testimony, was that Manson wanted to put the fear of God into Phil Kaufman and every other music executive that rejected him. The LaBianca's happen to live in the wrong place at the wrong time."

Leno LaBianca was a well-to-do owner of a chain of grocery stores while his wife, Rosemary, owned a boutique. Rosemary had been deeply disturbed by the Sharon Tate murders and went to the bedroom to go to sleep. LaBianca stayed awake, laying on his couch but falling asleep as he read the sports page.

Manson entered the home first, calmly assuring LaBianca that they were only there to rob the place. He asked where the money was kept and if there were anyone else in the house.

Leno complied, telling them that his wife was in the bedroom and giving them what little money he had on hand. Manson produced a leather strap and tied up Leno's hands.

Leslie and Patricia Krenwinkel came upon Rosemary in the bedroom while her husband was being assaulted.

"Stop stabbing me!" Leno cried out.

Rosemary awakened, startled to see the two women in her bedroom.

"The minute I walked in the house," Leslie said. "It became clear that this was not what I had imagined. You know, before that it had always been an abstract kind of thing and when it was the real thing, I was absolutely torn in half."

Tex Watson placed a pillowcase around Leno's head then secured it with electrical cords from lamps in the home. He then began stabbing the man to death.

Leslie and Pat would hear the screams of Leno as he was being stabbed to death. They tried to hold Rosemary down as she called out for her husband.

"For a brief moment," Leslie recalled. "I realized that these are people that love each other."

Rosemary struggled to break loose as she heard the screams of her husband who was being stabbed by Watson.

"I tried to hold down Mrs. LaBianca as Pat stabbed her," Leslie said. "And I was confused and torn inside. I wanted to do what Manson had asked us to do. And I was battling in my own sense, I was battling something I was not capable of handling. And I didn't hold her down well. And she (Rosemary LaBianca) picked the lamp up and I don't even know if she even knew she had the lamp. She was struggling for her life."

Rosemary broke free, grabbed the lamp at swung it at Leslie.

Leslie fought with the woman and knocked the lamp away. She then held Rosemary down while Krenwinkel stabbed her in the chest.

The knife bent on Rosemary's clavicle and Leslie called for help.

"I don't remember if Pat said to me 'go get Tex' or if I just did," Leslie said. "I ran to Tex and told him that we were not capable or we were not able to kill her. At that point, Tex ran into the bedroom. I stood in the hallway and I looked into a blank room that was like a den."

Watson arrived and began stabbing Rosemary. He then handed Leslie the knife and ordered her to "do something."

"And I took one of the knives," Leslie said. "And Patricia had one knife, and we started stabbing and cutting up the lady."

"I promise I won't call the police," Rosemary said, her life ebbing away. "I won't call the police."

But her use of the word 'police' only egged Leslie on.

"And it seemed like the more she said 'police,'" Leslie said. "The more panicked I got."

Leslie then plunged the knife into the woman's back and buttocks anywhere between fourteen to sixteen times (LaBianca's body would later reveal that she had been stabbed over forty-seven times).

Watson then went into the LaBianca bathroom and took a shower. He then raided the refrigerator, getting cheese and chocolate milk for Leslie and Pat.

Krenwinkel then took a fork and stabbed the corpse of Leno Labianca repeatedly before writing different slogans around the walls in his blood. Words like "Helter Skelter," "Rise," and "Death to Pigs."

All because Manson wanted them to do something "witchy" after the job was down.

The word "War" was carved into Leno LaBianca's stomach.

Tex Watson then ordered Leslie to clean the house for fingerprints.

"I was very uncomfortable and I wanted out of the house," Leslie said. "Manson had told him (Tex) that everyone was going to change their clothes. I didn't have a change of clothes with me and I didn't have anything on my clothes. I asked Tex could I not change my clothes because I didn't need to and he said no, that Manson had wanted everyone to and for me to get clothes out of Mrs. LaBianca's closet and so I went and I found her clothes and I wore them."

Tex stole Leno's wallet which had a credit card inside. Manson ordered him to "leave it where a black person could find it" and then take the blame.

Leslie then hid in the bushes wearing Rosemary's clothes until morning. When sunrise came, all three hitchhiked back to the ranch.

THE AFTERMATH

Leslie did not watch the news broadcasts the next day.

"I went back to the back farmhouse," Leslie said. "It was a movie set and the back farmhouse was where many of us were staying. I went back to the back farm house and I burned the clothes. Tex had taken some money from the house and I was counting the money with Diane Lake. I don't know why he took it (the money) it wasn't a robbery."

Manson then sent Leslie and Krenwinkle to a place called "Fountain of the World." He was adamant on keeping the young women removed from the others at the commune as he didn't want them talking about the murders.

A motorcycle gang then snitched on the Manson followers and Leslie would be arrested in December of 1969. She was much more forthcoming on the crimes of the Family then the other followers, informing the police on who were the perpetrators of the Tate and LaBianca murders. She still tried to play cute during interrogations but ultimately ended up incriminating herself.

"What did you hear about the Tate murders up there?" the detective asked.

"I'm deaf," Linda said, laughing. "I didn't hear nothing."

"Five people were killed up there, on the hill. And I know three for sure that went up there. I think I know the fourth. And I don't know the fifth. But I suspect you do. Why are you holding back? You know what happened."

"I have a pretty good idea."

"I want to know who was involved. How it went down. The little details."

"I told Mr. Patchett. I'll tell him if I changed my mind. I haven't changed my mind yet."

"You're going to have to talk about it someday."

"Not today," Linda said. "How did you ever trace it back to Spahn?"

"Who did you see leave the night of the eight of August?"

"Oh, I went to bed early that night," Linda laughed again. "Really, I don't want to talk about it."

"Who went?"

"That's what I don't want to talk about."

"Tell me about the family," the detective said.

"You couldn't meet a nicer group of people," Leslie said. "I liked Clem the best. He's fun to be with. Sadie was really nice but she tends to be on the rough side. Bruce doesn't do anything but talk. I mean he won't do anything. He is always talking about blowing someone up but he won't do it. The Family is great."

"The family is no more Leslie. Charlie is in jail. Clem is in Jail. Zero killed himself."

"Zero!" Linda said in shock. "What happened?"

"They were playing Russian Roulette. Blew his brains out. Bruce Davis was with him.

"Was Bruce playing it too?"

"No."

"Zero was playing Russian roulette all by himself," Linda said, her voice dripping with sarcasm.

"Kind of odd, isn't it?"

"Yeah, it's odd."

"I know five people had gone to the Tate residence. There were three girls and two men. One of the men was Charles Manson."

"I don't think Charles was in on any of them," Leslie said defensively. "Only four people went to Tate.

TRIALS AND TRIBULATIONS

Tex Watson would not be tried at the main Charles Manson trial. Manson had been accused of being the mastermind of the murders but the only followers on trial along with him for causing were Leslie and Pat Krenwinkel.

During the trial, Leslie appeared to have been on an acid trip. She laughed inappropriately during testimony about the murders. She would take the stand and confess to committing the murders but denied that Manson had taken part.

Manson then carved an X on his forehead and Leslie copied him, which bespoke to the control he had over her. Leslie would fire three defense lawyers in a row as they wanted to blame her actions on Manson's control over her. Her defense lawyer had called an expert witness to the stand to talk about the effects of LSD on personal judgment, Leslie became livid.

"This is all such a big lie," Leslie screamed. "I was influenced by the war in Vietnam and TV."

On March 29th, 1971, Leslie was convicted of murder. She continued to try and defend Manson, testifying that he was not involved in the killing.

During her psychiatric evaluations, Leslie revealed that she had routinely beat her Korean adopted sister. Her psychiatrist called her a "psychologically loaded gun" and he did not believe the fact that Manson had control over her behavior nor had he brainwashed her as so many people believed.

Leslie showed no remorse for what she did to Rosemary LaBianca.

"Sorry is only a five letter word," Leslie said. "You can't undo something that is done."

Leslie would also concede that she could have stabbed Rosemary in the neck which would suggest that she inflicted wounds while the victim was still alive (Leslie remained vague in her testimony on whether or not Rosemary was still alive as she attacked her.)

SENTENCING

Leslie was then sentenced to death and would become the youngest woman ever executed in California. A special unit was built for her as no death row for women prisoners was in existence. But her death sentence was commuted after the California Supreme Court struck it down.

She would then eligible for parole after she had served seven years.

Prosecutor Vincent Bugliosi predicted that all three women followers would be released within fifteen to twenty years.

"All of the Manson followers, in particular, the women, thought they would get off light," Orange said. "Leslie herself thought that she would be out within seven years."

During her trial, Leslie reconnected with her family. She described them as angry and resentful but were reaching out nonetheless.

"I remember telling my mother that she would probably be better off just leaving me alone," Leslie said. "Because I had so easily left her life. She just said that she wasn't made of that kind of stuff."

Despite Leslie's initial attempts to cover for Manson, he did not have the same loyalty to her.

"I didn't know Leslie very well," Manson said. "She was a daddy's girl."

"Part of my job at the ranch was to read to him (Manson) from the Bible. And it's been a very difficult thing for me to find forgiveness. Spiritually. I guess I felt that I had gotten into this mess on my own and AA (Alcoholics Anonymous) talks a lot about God as we understand him and turning our will over to Him, removing defects of character. The more I studied the more I realized I needed to find some kind of peace with what had happened. Not just with the crime but life at the ranch and Manson in general and what he had done and the effect he had over me."

Seven years after the crime, Leslie was interviewed by Barbara Walters on national television.

"Is it something that you think of (as having) happened to somebody else?" Walters asked.

"No, it's very real to me," Leslie said. "It's very real to me at night when I'm alone in my cell with my thoughts. It's at that point that I-I don't try to block it out. That's part of the hell that I'll have to live with forever."

RETRIAL

Leslie was given a retrial in 1977. Her new defense had argued that she should have been given a mistrial when her first lawyer died (some believed that he was murdered by the Manson family.) Leslie's new attorneys argued vigorously for the fact that her mental faculties had been compromised due to her LSD use and Manson's psychological control over her. At trial's end, the jury remained deadlocked as they could not decide on whether Leslie's actions constituted a first-degree murder or a manslaughter.

PAROLE REQUESTS

The male followers of Manson have had moderate success at their parole hearings. Clem Grogan who helped Manson with the torture killing of Donald Shea, was paroled in 1985. An accomplice named Bruce Davis was given a parole board recommendation for release in 2010 but Governor Jerry Brown overruled the decision.

Leslie would be rejected by the parole board thirteen times. She would try seven more times and fail. During these hearings, she had disowned any ties to Manson and had articulated her remorse for the murders.

"Mr. and Mrs. La Bianca died the worst possible deaths a human being can," Leslie said at her last parole hearing. "It affected their families. It affected the community of Los Angeles, which lived in fear. And it destroyed the peace movement going on at the time, and tainted everything from 1969 on."

During her time in jail, Leslie wrote numerous short stories, edited the prison newspaper as well as doing secretarial duties.

"I feel that sometimes when I talk about it (the murders)," Leslie said. "I sound distant and removed. I don't make light of my crimes. I accept responsibility for what I did. I have spent years learning to live with it. As I sobered and grew away from Manson, living with my conscience with what I have done as been a very difficult thing for me...I understand the horrendousness of what I did. It is something that I live with every day."

"She knew what she was doing," Manson said in response. "She was a papa's girl and wanted to do her own thing. Now she blames me for helping her be herself."

On April 14th, 2016, Governor Jerry Brown approved Leslie's eligibility for parole.

PATRICIA KRENWINKEL

"It is countless how many lives were shattered by the path of destruction that I was a part of, and it all comes from such a simple thing as just wanting to be loved."

This is a statement made by Patricia Krenwinkel in her first interview in over 20 years. Her path of destruction that consumed not just her, but all the people she touched, arguably began in 1967 when her life crossed paths with Charles Manson.

Born in 1947 to an insurance-salesman father and a homemaker mother, Krenwinkel grew up in Los Angeles, California. Bullied at school and feeling rejected at home, she developed low self-esteem and often felt isolated and unloved. Her teen years happened to coincide with the 1960s. It was a strange time, with new movements and social upheaval that captivated American and left no home untouched. The Krenwinkel household was no exception. As the relationship between her parents began to deteriorate, her relationship with them did as well. During this time she became increasingly attached to her older half-sister who, while struggling to find her own identity, indulged in underage drinking and drug use. Searching for a place to belong Krenwinkel moved away to attend Spring Hill College, in Mobile, Alabama but quickly became disillusioned with college life. She failed to complete a full semester before dropping out and moving back to California. Here she lived with her half-sister in Manhattan Beach and supported herself with a job as a processing clerk.

In 1967 she happened to make acquaintances with Lynette Fromme and Mary Brunner. At this time they were already known as "Charlie's Girls" and wasted no time in introducing the emotionally venerable Krenwinkel to their charismatic leader. Starved for affection and a sense of belonging, 19-year-old Krenwinkel was no match for Charles Manson's charm and charisma. She would later recount how he was the first person to ever call her beautiful, and how he had seduced her on the first night they meeting. The encounter proved to be so emotionally fulfilling for her that she had been unable to stop herself from crying. In just a few days she had become so completely captivated by Manson that she readily agreed to join Fromme and Brunner in following him to San Francisco. Abiding by this decision meant that she left behind her car, apartment, last pay check, and severed all contact with her family.

Now known as Katie, one of the many names she would later go by, she traveled with the ever growing Mason Family across the American west. Her first 18-months with the group was shrouded in a haze of sex, drugs, and a sense of unconditional love. Even now her memories are tarnished with wistful idealism.

"We were just like wood nymphs and wood creatures," she explained in an interview. "We would run through the woods with flowers in our hair, and Charles would have a small flute."

Manson helped promote this delusion of an enchanted life, by exploiting any opportunity to connect himself to people of fame or influence. One such opportunity presented itself in the summer of 1968. While hitchhiking around Los Angeles with fellow Family member, Ella Bailey, Krenwinkel was offered a lift from Dennis Wilson, a drummer and founding member of the Beach Boys. Since he was needed at a recording session, Wilson invited the women to stay at his home in the meantime. It was an offer that would readily be made in the 60s and he thought nothing of it. When he returned later that evening, however, he was startled to find the entire Manson Family on the premises. Without hesitation, they had moved into his home, ate his food, and slept in his bedrooms. Perhaps the most startling moment for Wilson was his first meeting with Manson himself. According to Wilson, Mason greeted him in his driveway and, in a surreal gesture, invited Wilson into his own home. It is a testament to Mason's skills of manipulation that the Family was not immediately removed. Wilson admits that he had at first been fascinated by Manson, his philosophies, and his music. He allowed the family to stay with him until their presence began to create financial problems, and even then it was Wilson's manager that forced them out.

But as they 60's came to an end, people began to lose interest in the hippie movement. 'Free-love' and liberal drug use were no longer as readily acceptable as they once were and people were beginning to return to a more mainstream way of life. Perceiving the threat this posed to the structure and longevity of his Family, Manson resolved that they should now live in isolated from the rest of the world. He found the perfect location Spahn's Ranch. It was nestled in the hills above the San Fernando Valley and, while it was occasionally used by ranch hands, had only one owner. A blind and eighty-year-old man named George Spahn. Manson convinced Spahn to allow his Family, by then consisting of approximately thirteen women, five men, and a number of illegitimate children, to set up residence. In return, the Family, more specifically the Manson women, would care for the property and Spahn's more personal needs. In 1969 they moved into the now infamous ranch and life in the Manson Family took a disturbing turn.

Devoted Lynette "Squeaky" Fromme took on the task of being Spahn's "eyes", but perhaps more accurately, was his de facto wife. Meanwhile, Krenwinkel, while not being the biological mother to any of the children, had been entrusted to be a motherly figure for all Family members. As she attests, it was common practice for anyone uncomfortable with Manson's increasingly disturbing demands, to be sent to her. She would alleviate their concerns and convince them to stay.

At first, the family drew little attention, perhaps because they weren't the first cult to have made the ranch their home. The Fountain of the World, led by Krishna Venta, had resided there from the 1940s to 1950s. It has never been substantiated, but it is believed that Manson had spent time with this cult and that he may have been involved with ex-members who, in 1958, killed Venta and several others in an explosion.

Without prying eyes, Manson tightened his hold on his Family. Aside from mandatory orgies, his favored technique was to initiate numerous acid trips. As Leslie Van Houten, who was convicted alongside Krenwinkel, once explained, "I became saturated in acid and had no sense of where those who were not part of the psychedelic reality came from. I had no perception or sense that I was no longer in control of my mind." During these times Manson would take a far smaller dose, or abstain altogether, to ensure he was the only person to maintain their mental faculties. He used these unguarded moments to gather personal information from Krenwinkel and his other followers, information that he would then use to manipulate them when sober. He also abused their acid trips to push his standing from leader to god. To secure their loyalty and devotion, Manson would re-enact scenes from the crucifixion with himself as Christ. Krenwinkel has described these portrayals as so detailed and bloody that they were "hard to watch". His efforts paid off, however, and his followers no longer saw him as just a talented and wise man, but as the second coming of the messiah.

Around this time Mason began to repeat long, hypnotic, sermons about what he called "Helter Skelter", which he likened to Armageddon. He convinced Krenwinkel and his Family that a race war was inevitable. According to him, the black population would engage the white population in a war that would destroy not just America, but the world as they knew it. The Family would survive because he would lead them to a hole he had found in the desert and keep them safely there until the fighting was over. He asserted that, while the black population would be victorious, they would not be able to govern themselves and would, therefore, look for a white man to lead them. That is when the Family would emerge from their hiding place and race over the desert in their custom-made dune buggies. On this day

Manson, and by extension his followers, would become the rulers of whatever population remained on earth. Today Krenwinkel is quick to point out just how foolish, naive, and insane the notion is. But surrounded by her then beloved family on Spahn Ranch, with acid in her veins and Manson's voice in her ear, it seemed completely and unquestionably real.

Mason's vision of the future once again twisted life within the Family. They began to steal cars and strip them to create their dune buggies, guns were collected in mass numbers, and each member learned how to shoot. After their arrest, Krenwinkel, Susan Akins, and Leslie Van Houten all attested that they had even been given lessons on how best to stab someone to inflict as much damage as possible. While Mason still tries to distance himself from the crimes of the Family, Krenwinkel, and the others insist that nothing happened on Spahn ranch without Manson's knowledge and expressed approval. Later, prosecutor Vincent Bugliosi noted how his total control would not have been possible if it wasn't for the isolation of the ranch. "There were no newspapers at Spahn Ranch, no clocks. Cut off from the rest of society, he created in this timeless land a tight little society of his own, with its own value system. It was holistic, complete, and totally at odds with the world outside".

But as the months passed without a hint of an uprising, Mason maintained that he wasn't wrong about Helter Skelter. He began to preach that the delay was because the black population lacked the intelligence to initiate the war on their own, and so it was, therefore, their duty to antagonize the white population themselves. His plan to do this was to frame black men for the murder of rich white people. On Friday, August 9, 1969, after an uneventful dinner, Mason told Susan Atkins, Linda Kasabian, and Patricia Krenwinkle, to leave with fellow member "Tex" Watson in a car borrowed from a ranch hand. The women were ordered to obey Tex's every instructed and, as they were leaving, Mason stopped the car and gave them one last command. "Leave a sign. You girls know what to write."

On this fateful night, no-one at 10050 Cielo Drive had any notion of the danger that was closing in on them. While her husband, Roman Polanski, was in Europe, Actress Sharon Tate was taking advantage of the few months she had left before the birth of their first child. She had invited friends Steven Parent, Wojtek Frykowski, Abigail Folger, and Jay Sebring over to enjoy a quite night in. Parent, still just a teenager, was the first to die. As Kasabian remained as a lookout, the others got around the locked security gate by scaling an embankment. They then climbed a telephone pole to cut the phone lines and began up the dimly lit driveway. Parent was caught off guard by Tex Watson as he headed to his car. The older man slashed Parent before shooting him four times in the face at close range. They left his body where it fell and entered the home by slicing open one of the fly screens.

Once they were inside they herded the terrified occupants into the living room and Krenwinkel herself dragged Abigail Folger from the bedroom to join the execution line. They momentarily lost control as their victims fought back, and in the resulting chaos, Jay Sebring was shot and the others scattered. Wojciech Frykowski, who managed to get out the front door, was quickly recaptured. His brutal fate included being shot twice, stabbed 51 times, and receiving more than a dozen strikes with the butt of a pistol to his head.

While this was happening Folger, who had already been stabbed, broke away from Krenwinkel and escaped the house. Folger screamed as she ran across the property but Krenwinkel chased her down, pinned her to the ground, and proceeded to stab her repeatedly. The attack was so vicious that, when Folger's body was discovered the next day, her white nightgown was so stained with blood that the police thought it was originally red. According to Krenwinkel, Folger's last words were, "stop, I'm already dead".

After the attack, Krenwinkel returned to the house and got Watson. He followed her to Folger's body and stabbed her himself. "I stabbed her and I kept stabbing her," Krenwinkel later said at her trial. When she was then asked how she felt during the attack she replied, "Nothing, I mean, what is there to describe? It was just there, and it was right."

Meanwhile, the other Family members had shot Jay Sebring in the face and stabbed him several times. Sharon was the last to die. Reportedly, as she had sustained each of the sixteen stab wounds to her back and chest, she had begged that they spare the life of her unborn child. Atkins would later brag that she had told Tate, "I don't care about you or your baby," before delivering the fatal blow. Krenwinkel proceeded to use Tate's blood to fulfill Mason's order to leave a message by writing things such as 'pig' across the walls.

Only one person, caretaker William Garretson, survived the night. He lived in the caretaker's quarters which were separate from the main house. That night, the distance and the loud music he was blaring, ensured that he couldn't hear the attack. Initially, Garretson was a lead suspect and was taken in for questioning. He was late released and police were left baffled by the senseless, brutal crime.

It took a few days for the real horrors to be reviled, but fear gripped Hollywood overnight. Manson didn't wait to send his Family out for another attack. The next night Krenwinkel was once again selected for the task, along with Watson, Atkins, Kasabian, Steve Grogan and Leslie Van Houten. Together with Manson himself, they traveled to the Los Feliz home of grocers Leon and Rosemary LaBianca. However, once he had helped Watson restrain the couple, he once again took measures to distance himself. He directed Krenwinkel, Van Houten, and Watson to kill the LaBianca's while he left with the others.

This direction was all the trio needed. They obediently carried out his order, holding Mrs. LaBianca in the master bedroom while they tortured and murdered Mr. LaBianca in the living room. Reportedly, as she heard her husband's screams, Mrs. LaBianca had struggled violently. Van Houten held her down while Krenwinkel attempted to stab her with a dull kitchen knife. The blade proved unable to properly break the skin and so the women called for Watson. When he entered the room he was carrying a bayonet the Family had brought to the house with them and proceeded to stab her. According to their later confessions, each member present participated in the repeated stabbing of Mrs. LaBianca.

There is some dispute over who carved the word 'war' onto Leon LaBianca's abdomen. In his book, Will You Die for Me? Watson took responsibility for the macabre act. Be this as it may, many still attribute the act to Krenwinkel. Watson further maintains that, as he washing the blood off of himself, Krenwinkel repeatedly stabbed the already dead Mr. LaBianca with a carving fork, which she left in his abdomen. Krenwinkel admits that she did stab LaBianca, but asserts that it was at Watson's insistence since Manson had instructed that everyone present had to partake in each kill.

Krenwinkel once again used their victim's blood to write their messages, including 'death to pigs' on the walls, and 'helter skelter' on the refrigerator. In no hurry to leave the trio ate and showered within the LaBianca home. Additionally, they also spent time playing with the LaBianca's two dogs before hitchhiking back to the Spahn Ranch. When questioned about this night Krenwinkel will later claim that her only thought during the murders was, "Now he won't be sending any of his children off to war." While the trio carried out his bidding, Mason, Atkins, Grogan, and Kasabian prowled Los Angeles in search for another victim. As perhaps the only mercy of this night they were unable to find one.

The murders forever altered Los Angeles. In the words of one long-term resident, "after the second murders, the gates went up all over the city". Even the Family wasn't left untouched by paranoia and fear. As the police chased down each possible lead, some within the

Family had become suspicious of their own. Rumours began to circle Krenwinkel and the others involved and many began to question Manson's teachings.

The breaking point came for many when, a week after the murders, the Los Angeles County Sheriff's Department arrested Manson, Krenwinkel, and a few other Family members. They were not arrested on homicide, however, but due to an unrelated investigation involving stolen cars that were spotted in and around the ranch. In their absence rumors began to circulate through the Family that Donald "Shorty" Shea, a ranch hand that they knew personally, had been murdered by someone within their ranks. Manson and the others were released when a minor error rendered the search warrant invalid. They quickly returned to the ranch but the damage had already been done.

The Family began to rapidly lose once loyal members and their departures made others question Mason and what they had become involved in. Krenwinkel, however, remained completely dedicated to Manson and a devoted follower of his philosophy. But the raid and subsequent departures had unnerved Manson and he decided to relocate the Family in an attempt to regain control and privacy. Krenwinkel followed him to Baker Ranch near Death Valley and helped to continue the work converting stole cars into dune buggies in preparation for Helter Skelter.

This time, it only took a few months for the authorities to become suspicious. On October 10, 1969, while Manson was elsewhere, the Family was once again raided. A few members, including Krenwinkel, were arrested. This time, however, Krenwinkel's estranged father arrived and posted her bail. Unable to understand or compete with Mason's hold, he failed to keep her from returning to the ranch.

When she arrived, Manson, who suspected the police were closing in, instantly sent her away to stay with her mother in Alabama. He told her that she mustn't return until he sent orders for her to do so. He was arrested on Barker Ranch two days later. Despite the best efforts of local law enforcement, the final unraveling of the Mason Family came from an unlikely source. Susan Atkins, proud of her involvement in both the Tate and LaBianca murders and desperate to brag, had thought her cellmate Veronica "Ronnie" Howard would keep her secret. Instead, she instantly told the authorities. Armed with both Akins' confession and Howard's statement, the police arrested Krenwinkel near her aunt's house in Mobile, Alabama on December 1, 1969. The next day Krenwinkel was indicted for seven counts of first-degree murder and one count of conspiracy to commit murder.

Desperate to fight her extradition to California, Krenwinkel's lawyers asserted that she had only fled to Alabama because she believed Manson would attempt to kill her. In February 1970, as Van Houten, Atkins, and Mason were set to stand trial, Krenwinkel received a letter from Manson. He asked her to join him and the others so that they can put together a united defense. Immediately, despite the protests of her lawyers, she contacted the district attorney of Mobile and stated her wish to sign the extradition and return to California as so as possible. She fired her lawyers and voluntarily returned to California and her Family. For his part, Watson didn't follow suit and fought extradition from his home state of Texas until the end. He was unsuccessful, but the legal process took long enough to ensure that he was tried separately.

The trial of the Manson Family captivated the world. Not just because the horror of the crimes, nor the fame of the victims, but because of the obsessional loyalty that they family continued to show Manson and each other. Free members staged sit-ins outside of the courthouse for the months of the trial and preached to anyone who would listen that Mason had only taught them unconditional love and peace.

Paul Fitzgerald, a lawyer from the public defender's office, offered his services to Frenwinkel and the other 'Manson Girls'. Working on a pro-bono basis the case almost ruined him financially and he faced a battle on all fronts. Not only was there insurmountable evidence against them, and the girl's in-court antics ruined any presumption of innocence that the jury might have held, but he was unable to stem the influence that Charles Manson wielded over his clients.

Of all the lawyers that were hired to represent the trio's defense, few besides Fitzgerald had any real trial experience and none had ever worked a murder case before. Every time it was suggested that the women be tried separately, or that Mason could have even been remotely responsible, the lawyer proposing the argument would be fired. Mason would then hire another, more incompetent and ill prepared, lawyer to represent the girls instead. He would order the girls to confess and say that he was in no way involved. He would instruct Krenwinkel, Atkins, and Van Houten to mark their foreheads in the same manner he did, shave their heads in a sign of solidarity, and disrupt the proceedings of their trial by spontaneously chanting insults and nonsense he selected. By all accounts, Fitzgerald believed that Manson cared less about securing his freedom than he did about maintaining his hold on the minds of these three women.

Over the nine-month trial, Krenwinkel, Atkins, and Van Houten often wore multi-coloured mini dresses that the other Family women had stolen for them, came to court barefoot, and constantly changed their appearance to match Manson. Most of the time they seemed disconnected from reality and unaware of the gravity of their situation. They would skip to and from the courtroom, hold hands, and sing songs Manson had written. They would spend their time doodling pictures of demons and satanic symbols. One of the few times they were interested in the trail was when former Family member Linda Kasabian took the witness stand. Having made a deal for leniency, Kasabian became a star witness for the prosecution. Krenwinkel and the others attempted to intimidate her each time she took the stand by copying her looks, such as matching their hairstyles to hers, and unnervingly staring.

Throughout the trial, Krenwinkel's parents made several attempts to connect with their daughter but were rebuffed each time. Her father described her as having a different personality and this is a sentiment that Krenwinkel herself would later echo. In a recent interview, she said that "at the trial, I had given up every little part of me to a man that demanded every little part of me".

With all the hindrances placed upon him, Fitzgerald could barely mount a reasonable defense. He could do little but argue that Krenwinkel's fingerprints, found in the Tate house, might not have been there from the night of the murder. That perhaps, at another time, she had been "an invited guest or friend". The jury did not agree and, on March 29, 1971, Manson, Krenwinkel, Atkins, and Van Houten were all found guilty of first-degree murder. They were subsequently sentenced to death and the women were transferred to the California Institution for Women (CIW) near Corona, California.

Once again the social changes of the time worked in Manson's favor. During the time of their trial the California Supreme Court was hearing the case of People v. Anderson, to determine if the state of California would abolish the death plenty. It struck many as ironic or unjust that since it was determined that the death plenty was "cruel and unusual" punishment, Manson and his followers would receive the mercy they never offered their victims. Their death sentences were automatically commuted to life in prison.

As she began her life sentence, Krenwinkel remained fiercely loyal to Manson and the Family. When now asked to explain this connection she offers that she might have held onto it because the other choice was admitting that "everything I had believed in was now wrong", and that, without this bond, she would have to confront the fact that she was "fully responsible for the damage, the wreckage, and the horror," that she had created.

Time and distance efficiently worked to erode Mason's hold. After the arduous journey of evaluating who she had become, Krenwinkel, by all accounts, confront her actions and accepted responsibility for them. In so doing she has transformed herself into a model inmate. She has maintained a perfect prison record and is active within prison programs such as Alcoholics Anonymous and Narcotics Anonymous. She teaches illiterate prisoners how to read and participates in the prison volleyball and softball teams. Her development has also been of a personal nature. She now writes both poetry and music, plays the guitar, and has earned a Bachelor's degree in Human Services from the University of La Verne.

The accomplishment she is most proud of, however, is that she is now her own person. "I am who I am today because I fought desperately for it," she said in an interview. As she explained, she can now be certain that each belief, notion, and preference she has is truly her own. Instead of blind obedience, she questions, debates, evaluates and comes to her own conclusions. "I learned choice at a horrific cost".

While all of them have been eligible for parole, only Watson, who was convicted after Manson and the women, has been released back into the general public. Mason remains at Corcoran State Prison, just north of Los Angeles, and in 2007 was denied parole for the 11th time. He no longer has the all-consuming hold he once had, but he still manages to wield public interest and insists on his innocence. He maintains that he had never told Krenwinkel nor anyone else to do anything. According to him, ever decision they made was their own, and in no way included him.

Krenwinkel is still incarcerated in the California Institution for Women in Chino, California. At her parole hearing in 2004, she was asked who she would place at the top of the list for people she has harmed. "Myself," was her response. She was denied parole since, according to the panel, she still posed an "unacceptable risk to public safety". In total, she has been denied parole thirteen times, the last time in January 2011. Each time the panel is swayed by the memory of the crimes and, at the last parole hearing, the 80 letters from all over the world urging them to keep her incarcerated.

Diane Sawyer interviewed Krenwinkel in 1994 and found her honestly remorseful. According to the interview, the victim that haunts her the most is Folger. As she stated to Sawyer, "That was just a young women that I killed, who had parents. She was supposed to live a life and her parents were never supposed to see her dead." She also spoke to Sawyer about her feelings of responsibility and guilt. "I wake up every day knowing that I'm a destroyer of the most precious thing, which is life; and I do that because that is what I deserve, to wake up every morning and know that." Also, during the same interview, she demonstrated that the considerable hold Manson had once had on her was truly severed. In an act that would have been inconceivable during the trial, she asserted that Mason was "absolutely lying" about not ordering the murders. And that nothing would have happened without his direct influence.

In 2009, Susan Akin's, who had also had an exemplary prison record and believed that she had experienced a religious awakening, died of brain cancer. She was 61. Krenwinkel still maintains a close relationship with Leslie Van Houten, who has also expressed remorse and responsibility. Having stated that "being a follower does not excuse", Van Houten has earned a degree, writes short stories, and advocates for the homeless. While many raise questions about the girl's ongoing connection, they argue that no one else would ever be able to understand what it was like to be part of the Family, how hard it was to break away, and difficult it is to live with the consequences. Perhaps it is this support that allowed Krenwinkel, in an interview with filmmaker Olivia Klaus for the documentary, My Life After Manson, to admit that she was a "coward". And that it was this cowardice that led her to not just join the Family, but was also the reason she committed the "horrendous" and "abominable" acts.

Very little remains of the Spahn Ranch. Spahn himself has moved on and the structures that were left behind were destroyed in a fire. Numerous owners have attempted to shake off the history of the land and create something new, but each has failed. Now owned by the state, the property has been left for the elements to claim with no attempt at upkeep. Every so often the ranch would receive tourists of the macabre and, with the rise of paranormal-themed television shows, has been visited by ghost hunters. But there is very little proof that the Manson Family had ever been there. By the creek where they had practiced shooting there is a tree with a rusted chain and a hunk of metal that may have once been a sink. One of the most infamous photographs taken of the Manson Family had been within a cave on the property. Now it stands, littered with beer cans, with a small boulder marking the site. Etched into that stone is a simple sentence that, at one time, would have been benign and forgettable, but now brings to mind madness, murder, and the dozens of innocent lives that were destroyed by one man's pursuit of control and the promise of love.